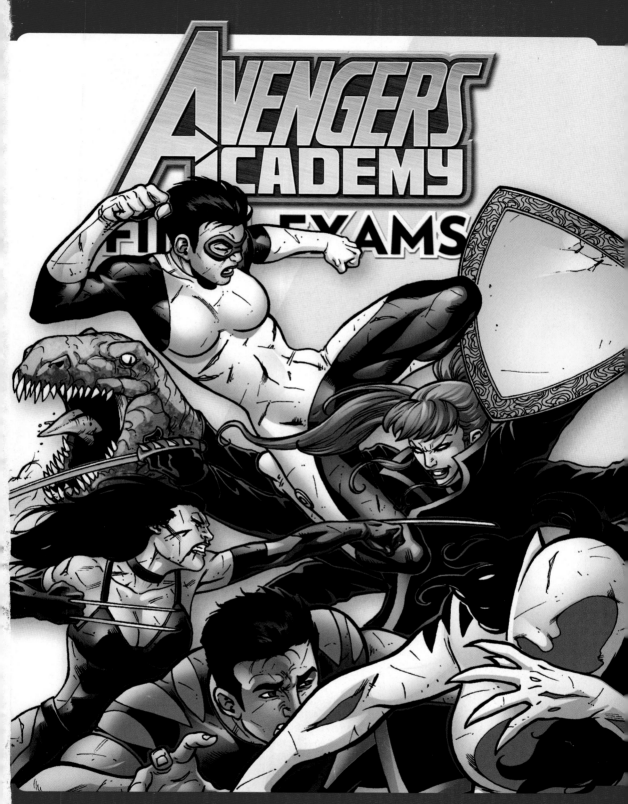

AVENGERS ACADEMY: FINAL EXAMS. Contains material originally published in magazine form as AVENGERS ACADEMY #34-39. First printing 2013. Hardcover ISBN# 978-0-7851-6031-1. Softcover ISBN# 978-0-7851-6032-8. Published by MARVEL WORLDWIDE, INC., a subsidiary of MARVEL ENTERTAINMENT, LLC. OFFICE OF PUBLICATION: 135 West 50th Street, New York, NY 10020. Copyright © 2012 and 2013 Marvel Characters, Inc. All rights reserved. All characters featured in this issue and the distinctive names and likenesses thereof, and all related indicia are trademarks of Marvel Characters, Inc. No similarity between any of the names, characters, persons, and/or institutions in this magazine with those of any living or dead person or institution is intended, and any such similarity which may exist is purely coincidental. **Printed in the U.S.A.** ALAN FINE, EVP - Office of the President, Marvel Worldwide, Inc. and EVP & CMO Marvel Characters B.V.; DAN BUCKLEY, Publisher & President - Print, Animation & Digital Divisions; JOE QUESADA, Chief Creative Officer; TOM BREVOORT, SVP of Publishing; DAVID BOGART, SVP of Operations & Procurement, Publishing; RUWAN JAYATILLEKE, SVP & Associate Publisher, Publishing; C.B. CEBULSKI, SVP of Creator & Content Development; DAVID GABRIEL, SVP of Publishing Sales & Circulation; MICHAEL PASCIULLO, SVP of Brand Planning & Communications; JIM O'KEEFE, VP of Operations & Logistics; DAN CARR, Executive Director of Publishing Technology; SUSAN CRESPI, Editorial Operations Manager; ALEX MORALES, Publishing Operations Manager; STAN LEE, Chairman Emeritus. For information regarding advertising in Marvel Comics or on Marvel.com, please contact Niza Disla, Director of Marvel Partnerships, at ndisla@marvel.com. For Marvel subscription inquiries, please call 800-217-9158. **Manufactured between 11/12/2012 and 12/31/2012 (hardcover), and 11/12/2012 and 7/1/2013 (softcover), by R.R. DONNELLEY, INC., SALEM, VA, USA.**

10 9 8 7 6 5 4 3 2 1

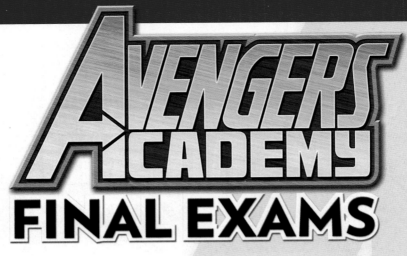

AVENGERS ACADEMY
FINAL EXAMS

Writer
CHRISTOS GAGE

Pencilers
TOM GRUMMETT (Issues #34 & #37-39)
& ANDREA DI VITO (Issues #35-36)

Inkers
CORY HAMSCHER (Issues #34 & #37-39), **ANDREA DI VITO** (Issues #35-36)
& RICK KETCHAM (Issue #38)

Colorist
CHRIS SOTOMAYOR

Letterer
VC'S JOE CARAMAGNA

Cover Artists
GIUSEPPE CAMUNCOLI with **JIM CHARALAMPIDIS**

Assistant Editor
JON MOISAN

Editor
BILL ROSEMANN

Collection Editor **CORY LEVINE**
Assistant Editors **ALEX STARBUCK** & **NELSON RIBEIRO**
Editors, Special Projects **JENNIFER GRÜNWALD** & **MARK D. BEAZLEY**
Senior Editor, Special Projects **JEFF YOUNGQUIST**
Senior Vice President of Sales **DAVID GABRIEL**
SVP of Brand Planning & Communications **MICHAEL PASCIULLO**
Book Design **ARLENE SO**

Editor in Chief **AXEL ALONSO**
Chief Creative Officer **JOE QUESADA**
Publisher **DAN BUCKLEY**
Executive Producer **ALAN FINE**

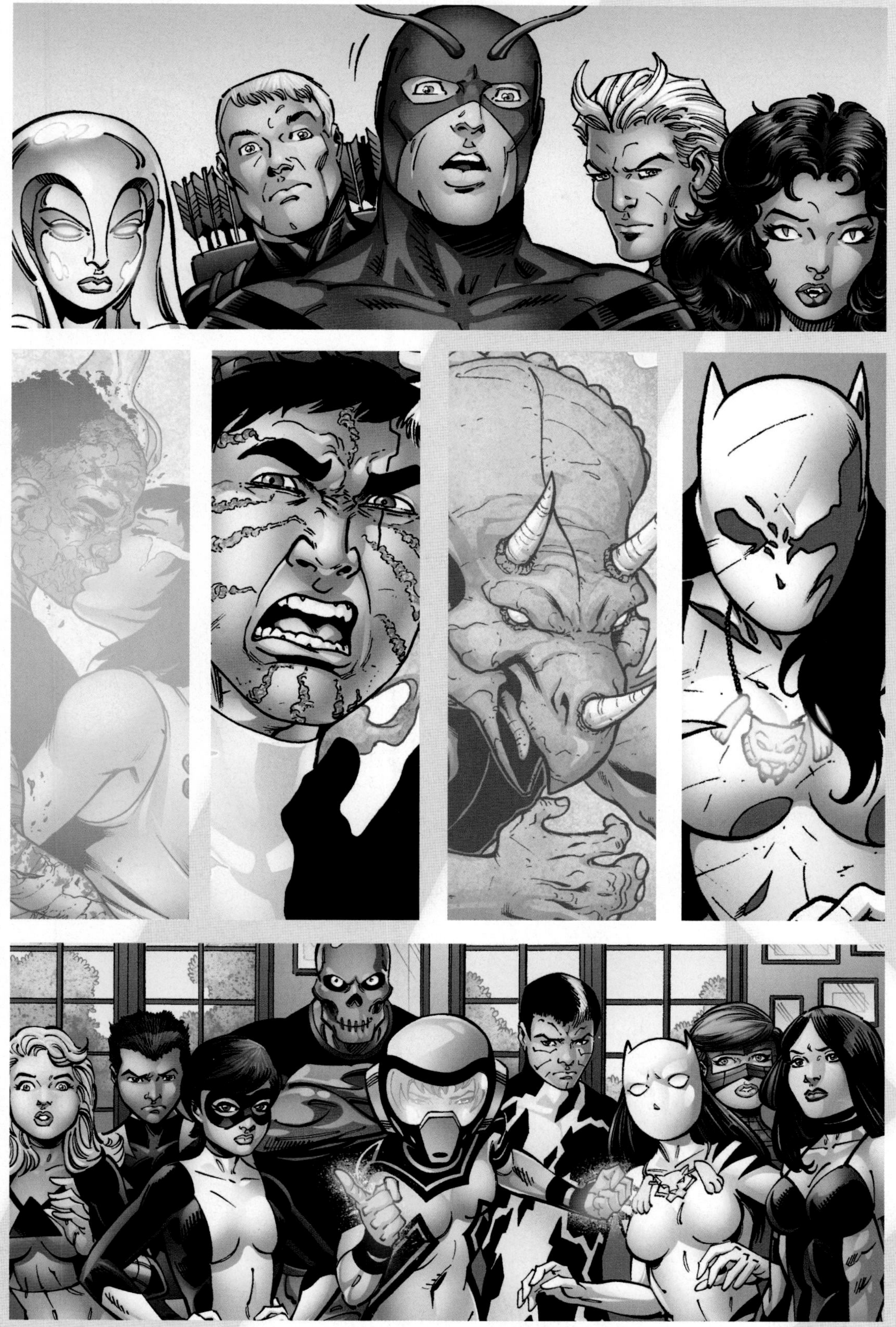

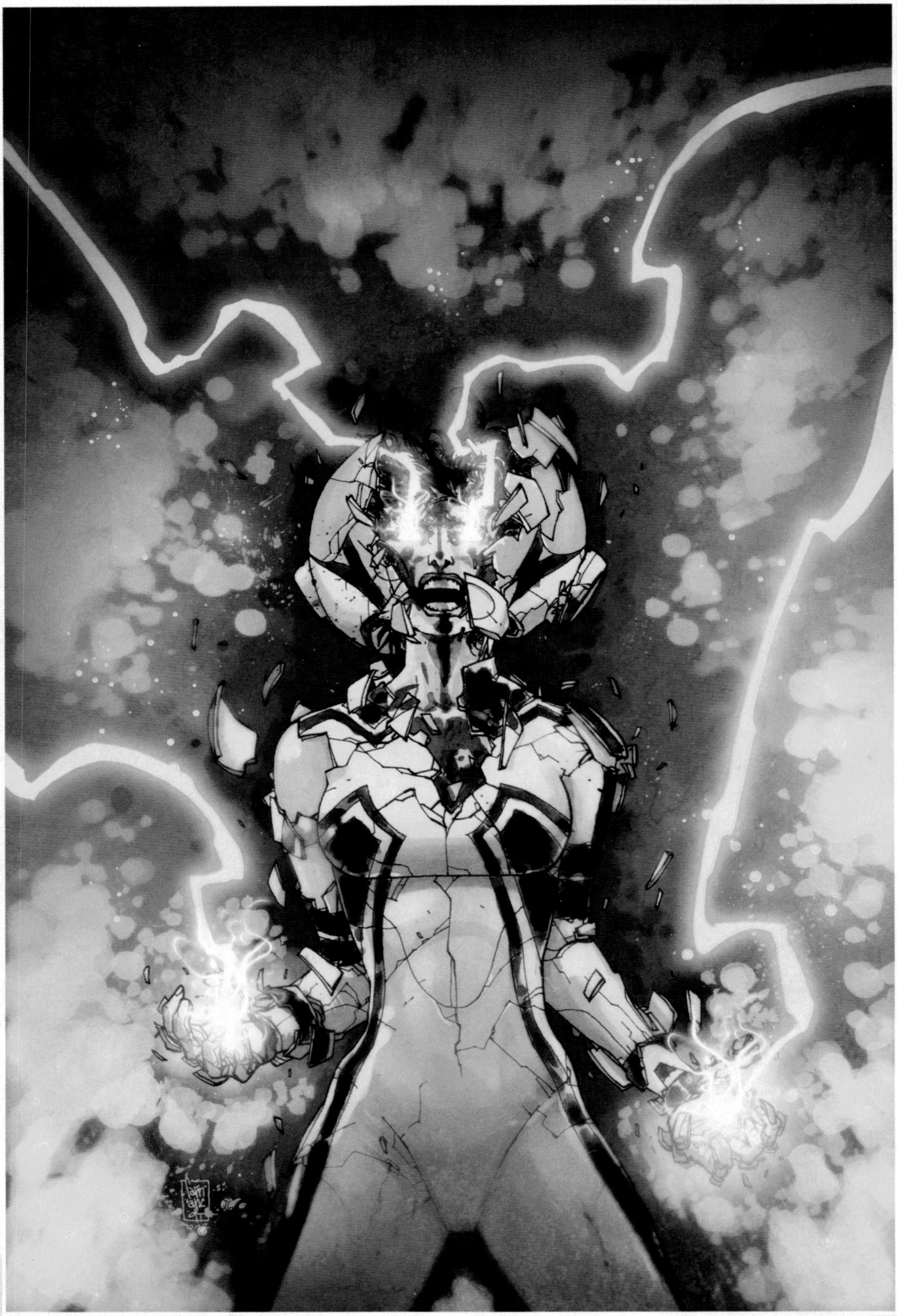

Avengers Academy #34

AND THERE CAME A DAY, A DAY UNLIKE ANY OTHER, WHEN EARTH'S MIGHTIEST HEROES OPENED THEIR DOORS TO TEACH THE NEXT GENERATION! ON THAT DAY, THE AVENGERS ACADEMY WAS BORN, TO TRAIN YOUNG ADULTS TO FIGHT THE FOES NO SINGLE SUPER HERO COULD WITHSTAND!

AVENGERS ACADEMY

GIANT-MAN RECENTLY RELOCATED THE ACADEMY TO THE NEWLY REFURBISHED AND REINFORCED WEST COAST AVENGERS COMPOUND AND OPENED ITS DOORS TO ANY SUPER-POWERED TEEN IN SEARCH OF TRAINING.

DUE TO THE DANGER OF THE ESCALATING AVENGERS/X-MEN WAR, GIANT-MAN AND **TIGRA** DECIDED THAT THE SCHOOL WAS NOT SAFE ANYMORE, AND CLOSED THE AVENGERS ACADEMY, EFFECTIVE IMMEDIATELY.

BILLIONAIRE SUPERHUMAN YOUTH **JEREMY BRIGGS,** A.K.A. THE **ALCHEMIST**, HAS SET UP AN ORGANIZATION DEDICATED TO FINDING ALTERNATIVES TO WHAT HE CONSIDERS THE HARMFUL HERO/VILLAIN PARADIGM PERPETUATED BY THE AVENGERS. HE HAS PERSUADED SOME AVENGERS ACADEMY PERSONNEL, INCLUDING INAUGURAL STUDENT **VEIL** AND FORMER TEACHER **JOCASTA**, TO JOIN HIS CAUSE.

STUDENTS

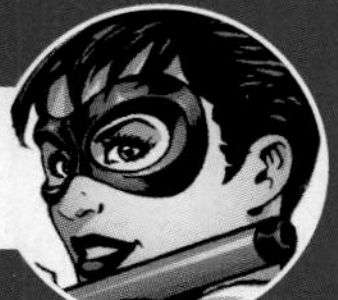

FINESSE

PHOTOGRAPHIC FIGHTER. ALL HEAD, NO HEART.

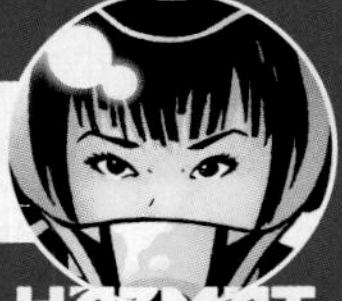

HAZMAT

HUMAN TOXIC SPILL. CAUSTIC PERSONALITY.

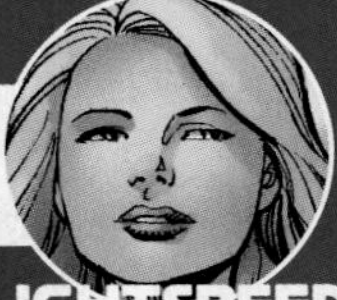

LIGHTSPEED

ABLE TO FLY, LOOKING TO BE MORE GROUNDED.

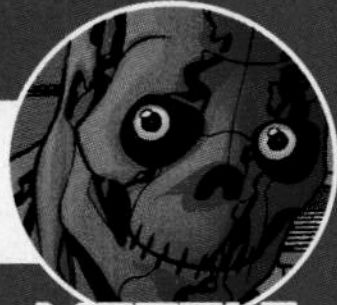

METTLE

STEEL-SKINNED POWERHOUSE. ARMORED SHELL PROTECTING INNER FEELINGS.

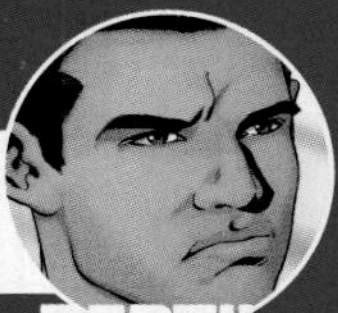

REPTIL

DINOSAUR MORPHER. FUTURE HERO OR NAIVE OPTIMIST?

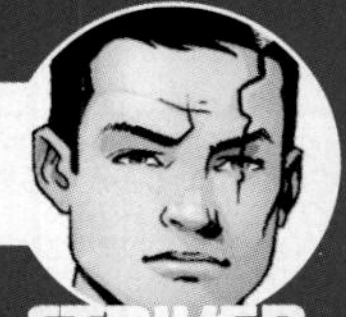

STRIKER

ELECTRIC DYNAMO. SELF-PROMOTES THROUGH SHOCK TACTICS.

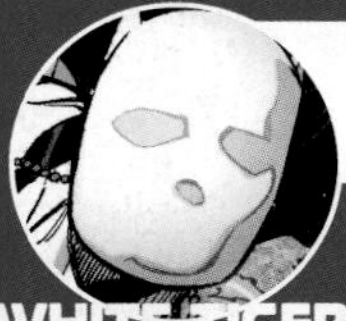

WHITE TIGER

POWERED BY MYSTICAL AMULET, FUELED BY FAMILY PRIDE.

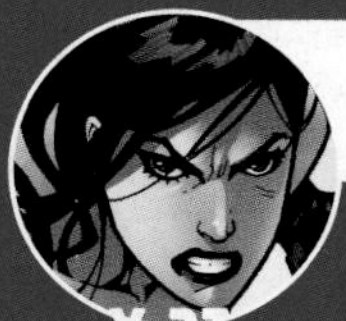

X-23

FEMALE CLONE OF WOLVERINE SEARCHING FOR HER SOUL.

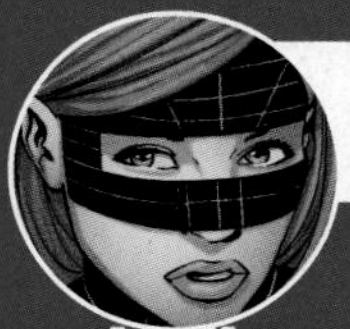

VEIL

VARIABLE GAS GENERATOR. UNSEEN POTENTIAL... UNTIL SHE DISCORPORATES.

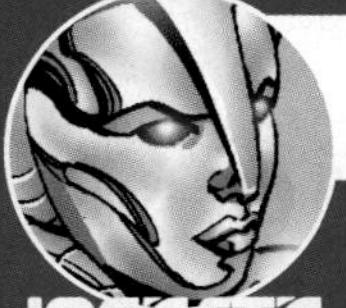

JOCASTA

SYNTHETIC BEING. LOYAL TO GIANT-MAN... OR ULTRON?

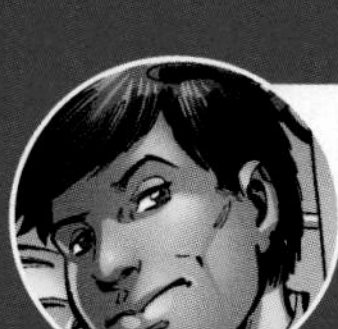

JEREMY BRIGGS

ABLE TO ALTER MATTER ON A MOLECULAR LEVEL. UNABLE TO BE TRUSTED.

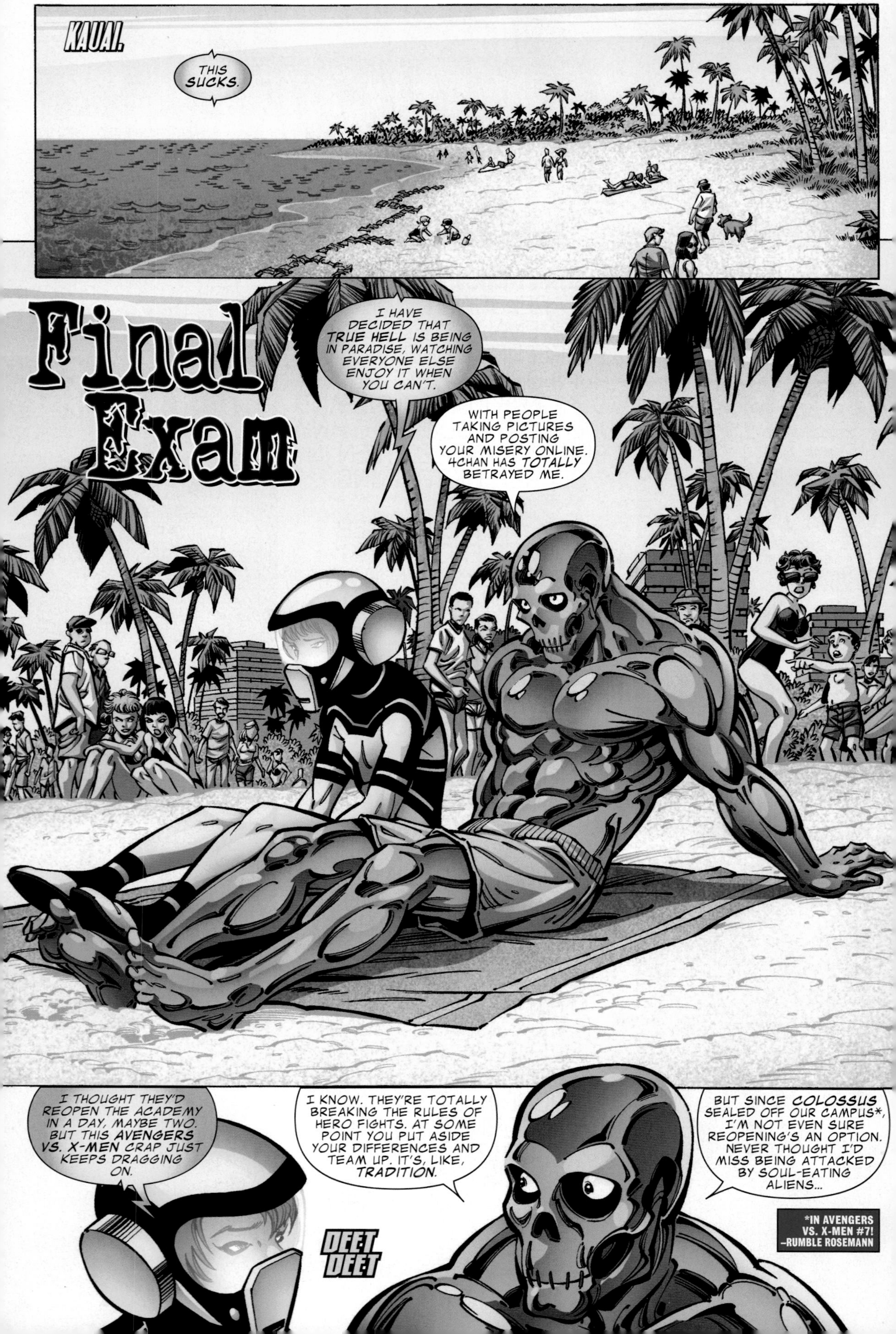
KAUAI.
THIS SUCKS.
Final Exam
I HAVE DECIDED THAT TRUE HELL IS BEING IN PARADISE, WATCHING EVERYONE ELSE ENJOY IT WHEN YOU CAN'T.
WITH PEOPLE TAKING PICTURES AND POSTING YOUR MISERY ONLINE. 4CHAN HAS TOTALLY BETRAYED ME.
I THOUGHT THEY'D REOPEN THE ACADEMY IN A DAY, MAYBE TWO. BUT THIS AVENGERS VS. X-MEN CRAP JUST KEEPS DRAGGING ON.
I KNOW. THEY'RE TOTALLY BREAKING THE RULES OF HERO FIGHTS. AT SOME POINT YOU PUT ASIDE YOUR DIFFERENCES AND TEAM UP. IT'S, LIKE, TRADITION.
BUT SINCE COLOSSUS SEALED OFF OUR CAMPUS*, I'M NOT EVEN SURE REOPENING'S AN OPTION. NEVER THOUGHT I'D MISS BEING ATTACKED BY SOUL-EATING ALIENS...
*IN AVENGERS VS. X-MEN #7! –RUMBLE ROSEMANN
DEET DEET

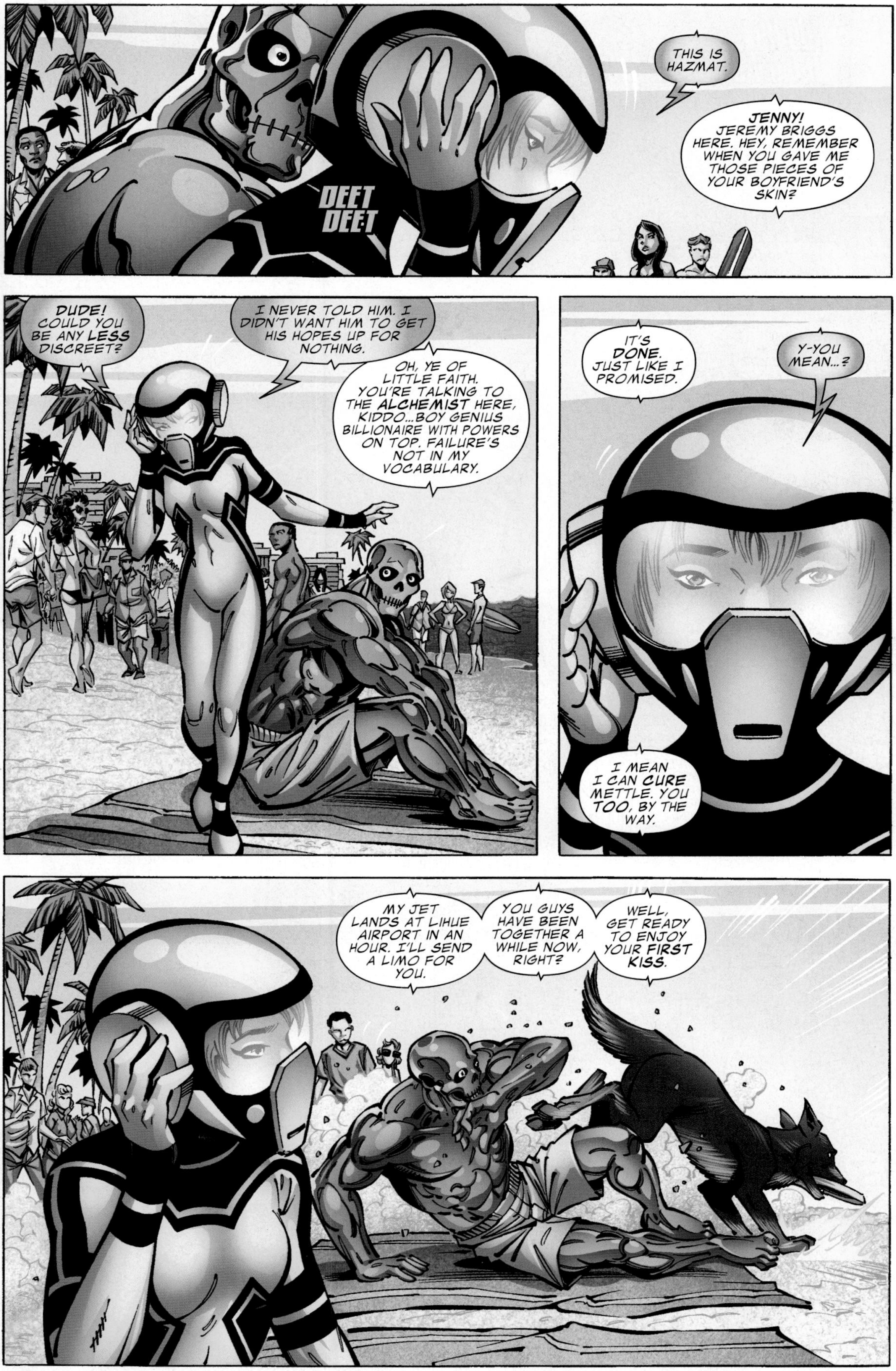
DEET DEET
THIS IS HAZMAT.
JENNY! JEREMY BRIGGS HERE. HEY, REMEMBER WHEN YOU GAVE ME THOSE PIECES OF YOUR BOYFRIEND'S SKIN?
DUDE! COULD YOU BE ANY LESS DISCREET?
I NEVER TOLD HIM. I DIDN'T WANT HIM TO GET HIS HOPES UP FOR NOTHING.
OH, YE OF LITTLE FAITH. YOU'RE TALKING TO THE ALCHEMIST HERE, KIDDO...BOY GENIUS BILLIONAIRE WITH POWERS ON TOP. FAILURE'S NOT IN MY VOCABULARY.
IT'S DONE. JUST LIKE I PROMISED.
Y-YOU MEAN...?
I MEAN I CAN CURE METTLE. YOU TOO, BY THE WAY.
MY JET LANDS AT LIHUE AIRPORT IN AN HOUR. I'LL SEND A LIMO FOR YOU.
YOU GUYS HAVE BEEN TOGETHER A WHILE NOW, RIGHT?
WELL, GET READY TO ENJOY YOUR FIRST KISS.

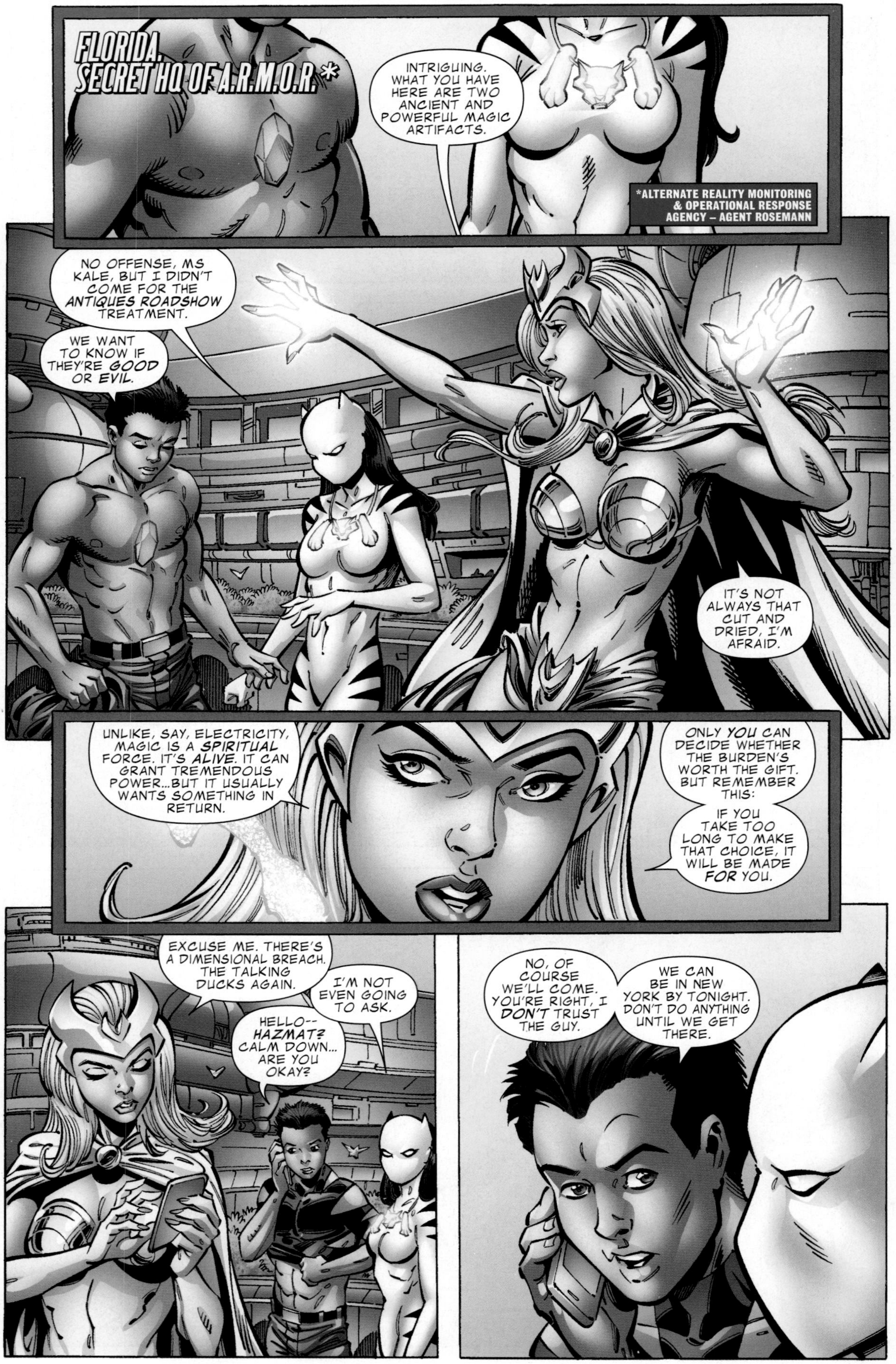
FLORIDA. SECRET HQ OF A.R.M.O.R.*
INTRIGUING. WHAT YOU HAVE HERE ARE TWO ANCIENT AND POWERFUL MAGIC ARTIFACTS.
*ALTERNATE REALITY MONITORING & OPERATIONAL RESPONSE AGENCY – AGENT ROSEMANN
NO OFFENSE, MS KALE, BUT I DIDN'T COME FOR THE ANTIQUES ROADSHOW TREATMENT.
WE WANT TO KNOW IF THEY'RE GOOD OR EVIL.
IT'S NOT ALWAYS THAT CUT AND DRIED, I'M AFRAID.
UNLIKE, SAY, ELECTRICITY, MAGIC IS A SPIRITUAL FORCE. IT'S ALIVE. IT CAN GRANT TREMENDOUS POWER...BUT IT USUALLY WANTS SOMETHING IN RETURN.
ONLY YOU CAN DECIDE WHETHER THE BURDEN'S WORTH THE GIFT. BUT REMEMBER THIS:
IF YOU TAKE TOO LONG TO MAKE THAT CHOICE, IT WILL BE MADE FOR YOU.
EXCUSE ME. THERE'S A DIMENSIONAL BREACH. THE TALKING DUCKS AGAIN.
I'M NOT EVEN GOING TO ASK.
HELLO-- HAZMAT? CALM DOWN... ARE YOU OKAY?
NO, OF COURSE WE'LL COME. YOU'RE RIGHT, I DON'T TRUST THE GUY.
WE CAN BE IN NEW YORK BY TONIGHT. DON'T DO ANYTHING UNTIL WE GET THERE.

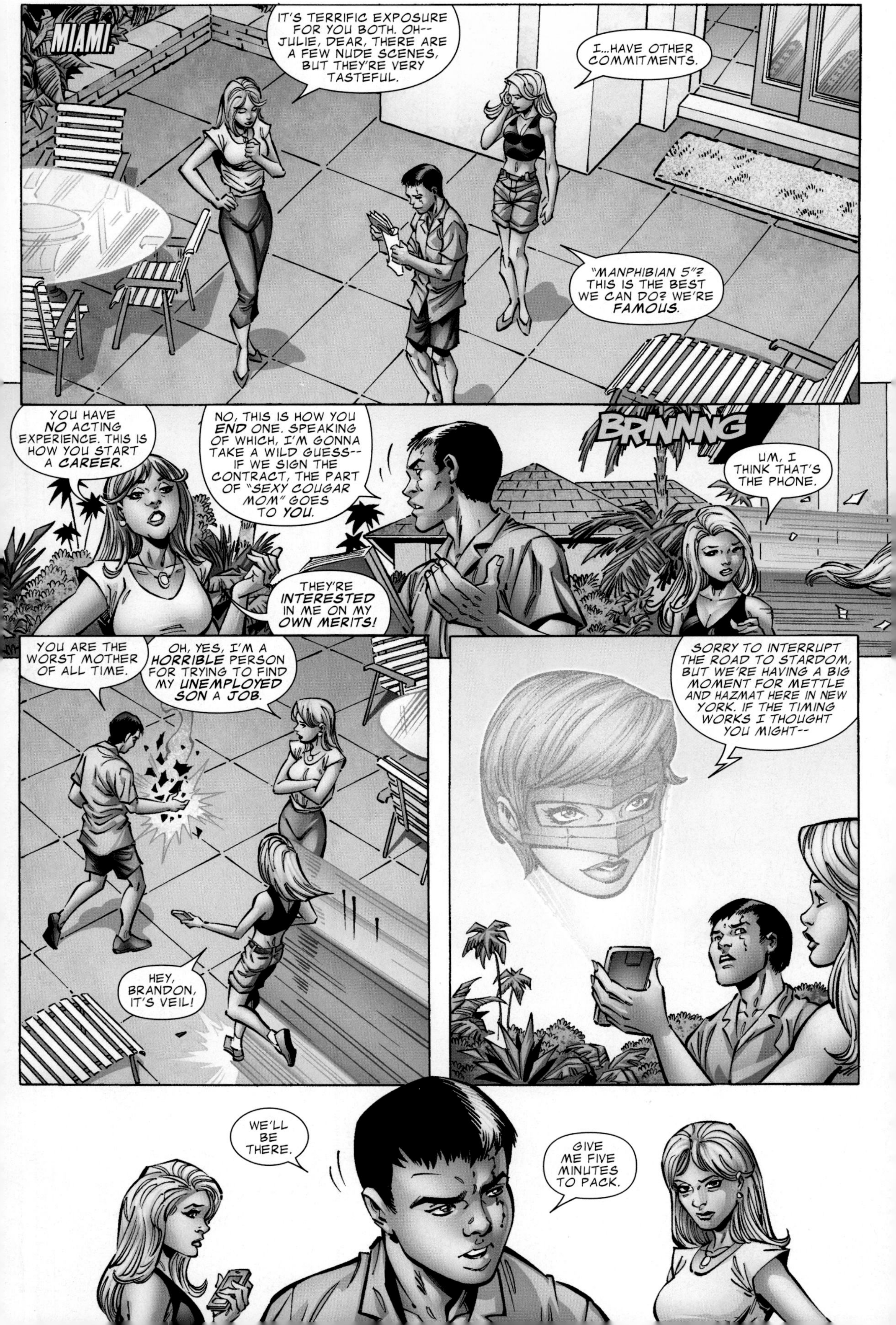
MIAMI.
IT'S TERRIFIC EXPOSURE FOR YOU BOTH. OH-- JULIE, DEAR, THERE ARE A FEW NUDE SCENES, BUT THEY'RE VERY TASTEFUL.
I...HAVE OTHER COMMITMENTS.
"MANPHIBIAN 5"? THIS IS THE BEST WE CAN DO? WE'RE FAMOUS.
YOU HAVE NO ACTING EXPERIENCE. THIS IS HOW YOU START A CAREER.
NO, THIS IS HOW YOU END ONE. SPEAKING OF WHICH, I'M GONNA TAKE A WILD GUESS-- IF WE SIGN THE CONTRACT, THE PART OF "SEXY COUGAR MOM" GOES TO YOU.
THEY'RE INTERESTED IN ME ON MY OWN MERITS!
BRINNNG
UM, I THINK THAT'S THE PHONE.
YOU ARE THE WORST MOTHER OF ALL TIME.
OH, YES, I'M A HORRIBLE PERSON FOR TRYING TO FIND MY UNEMPLOYED SON A JOB.
HEY, BRANDON, IT'S VEIL!
SORRY TO INTERRUPT THE ROAD TO STARDOM, BUT WE'RE HAVING A BIG MOMENT FOR METTLE AND HAZMAT HERE IN NEW YORK. IF THE TIMING WORKS I THOUGHT YOU MIGHT--
WE'LL BE THERE.
GIVE ME FIVE MINUTES TO PACK.

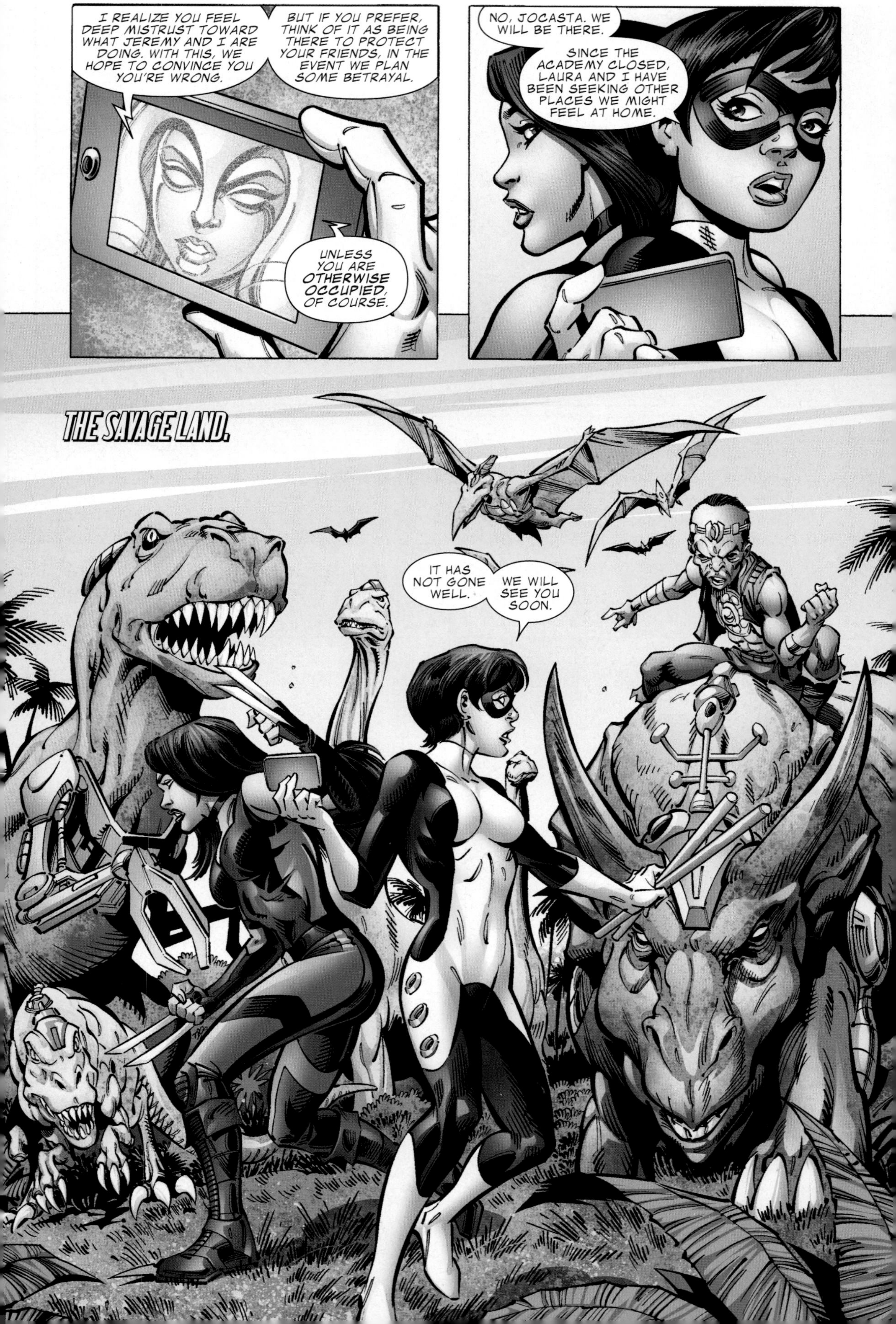
I REALIZE YOU FEEL DEEP MISTRUST TOWARD WHAT JEREMY AND I ARE DOING. WITH THIS, WE HOPE TO CONVINCE YOU YOU'RE WRONG.
BUT IF YOU PREFER, THINK OF IT AS BEING THERE TO PROTECT YOUR FRIENDS, IN THE EVENT WE PLAN SOME BETRAYAL.
UNLESS YOU ARE OTHERWISE OCCUPIED, OF COURSE.
NO, JOCASTA. WE WILL BE THERE.
SINCE THE ACADEMY CLOSED, LAURA AND I HAVE BEEN SEEKING OTHER PLACES WE MIGHT FEEL AT HOME.
THE SAVAGE LAND.
IT HAS NOT GONE WELL.
WE WILL SEE YOU SOON.

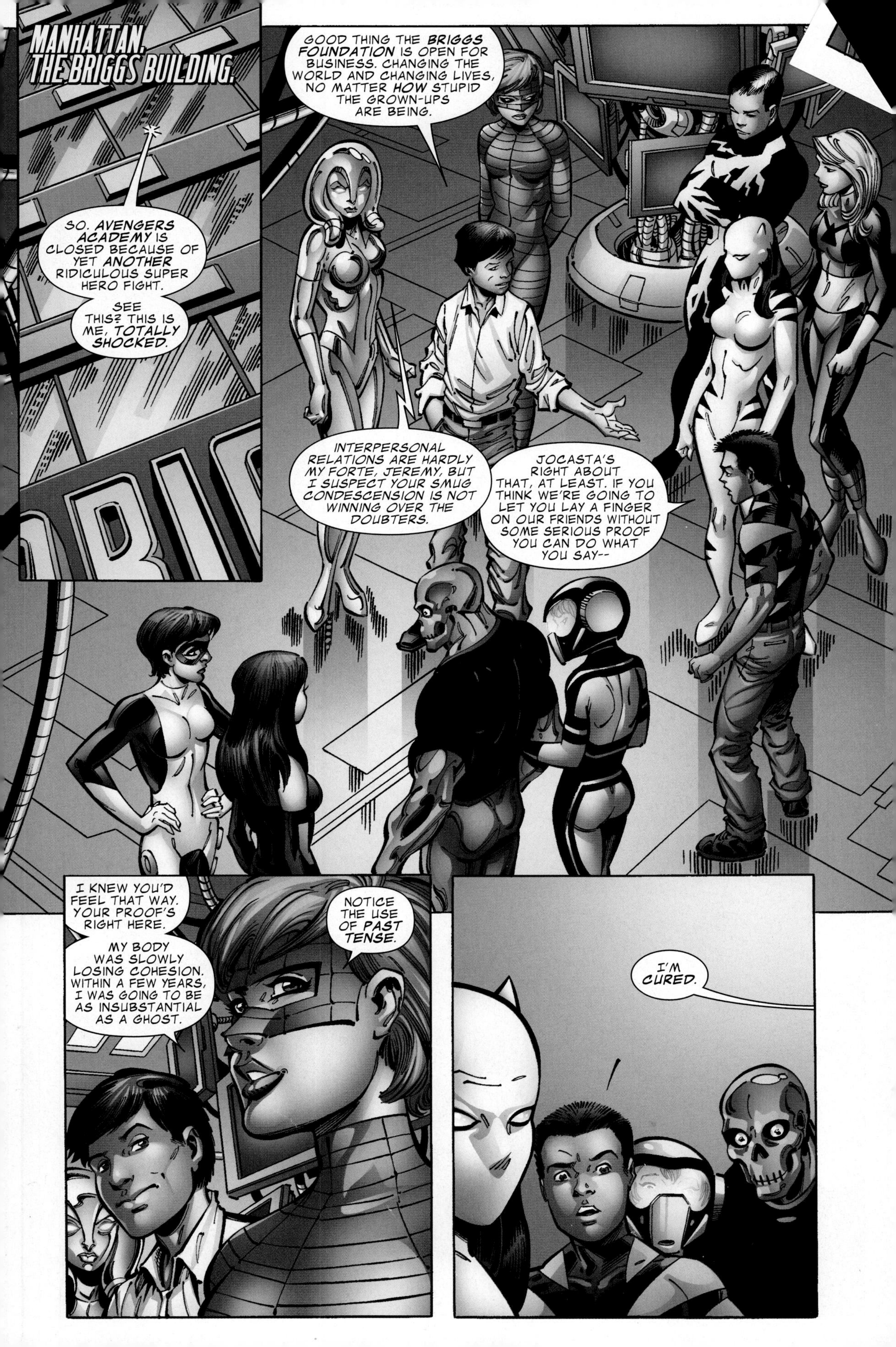

MANHATTAN. THE BRIGGS BUILDING.
SO. AVENGERS ACADEMY IS CLOSED BECAUSE OF YET ANOTHER RIDICULOUS SUPER HERO FIGHT.
SEE THIS? THIS IS ME, TOTALLY SHOCKED.
GOOD THING THE BRIGGS FOUNDATION IS OPEN FOR BUSINESS. CHANGING THE WORLD AND CHANGING LIVES, NO MATTER HOW STUPID THE GROWN-UPS ARE BEING.
INTERPERSONAL RELATIONS ARE HARDLY MY FORTE, JEREMY, BUT I SUSPECT YOUR SMUG CONDESCENSION IS NOT WINNING OVER THE DOUBTERS.
JOCASTA'S RIGHT ABOUT THAT, AT LEAST. IF YOU THINK WE'RE GOING TO LET YOU LAY A FINGER ON OUR FRIENDS WITHOUT SOME SERIOUS PROOF YOU CAN DO WHAT YOU SAY--
I KNEW YOU'D FEEL THAT WAY. YOUR PROOF'S RIGHT HERE.
MY BODY WAS SLOWLY LOSING COHESION. WITHIN A FEW YEARS, I WAS GOING TO BE AS INSUBSTANTIAL AS A GHOST.
NOTICE THE USE OF PAST TENSE.
I'M CURED.

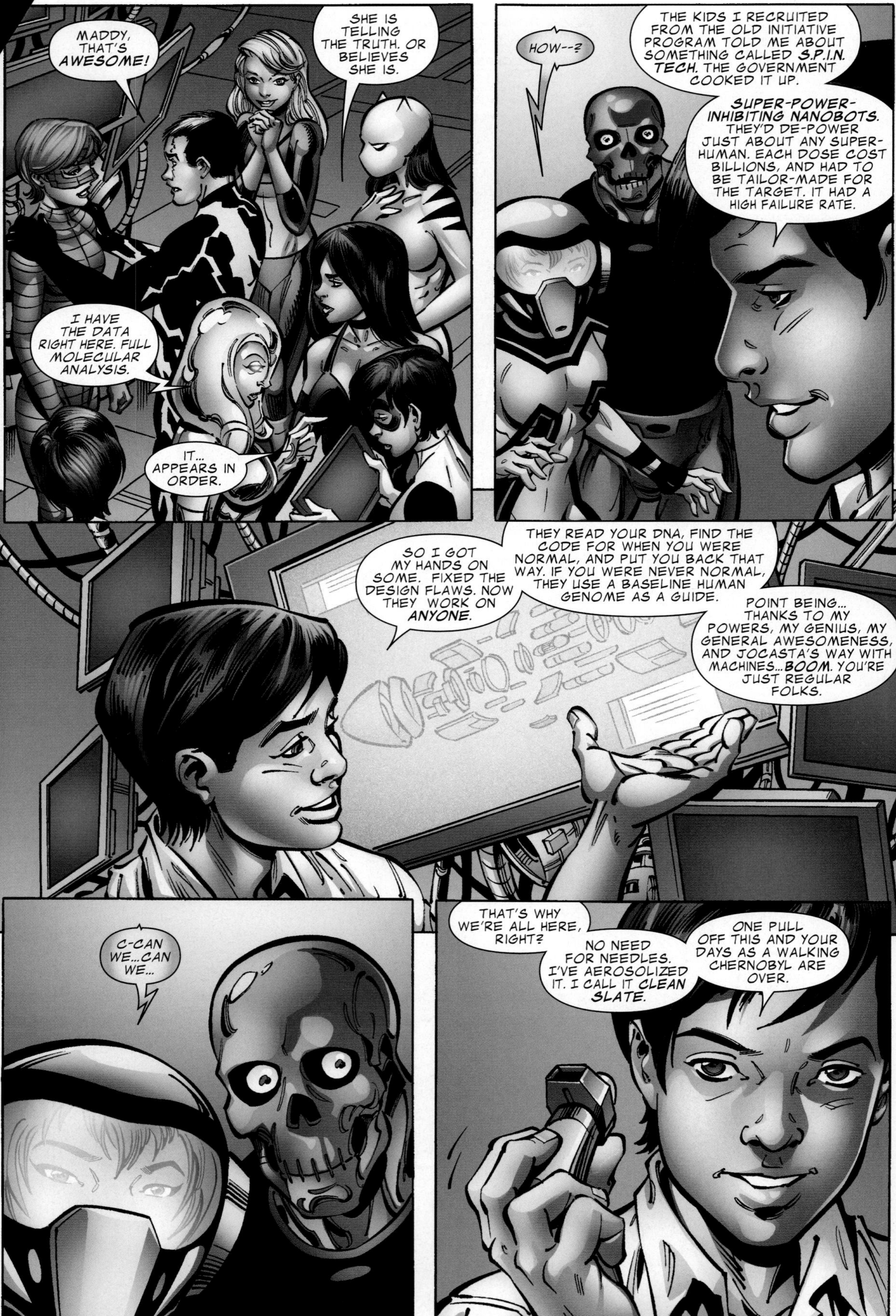
MADDY, THAT'S *AWESOME!*
SHE IS TELLING THE TRUTH. OR BELIEVES SHE IS.
I HAVE THE DATA RIGHT HERE. FULL MOLECULAR ANALYSIS.
IT... APPEARS IN ORDER.
HOW--?
THE KIDS I RECRUITED FROM THE OLD INITIATIVE PROGRAM TOLD ME ABOUT SOMETHING CALLED *S.P.I.N. TECH.* THE GOVERNMENT COOKED IT UP.
SUPER-POWER-INHIBITING NANOBOTS. THEY'D DE-POWER JUST ABOUT ANY SUPER-HUMAN. EACH DOSE COST BILLIONS, AND HAD TO BE TAILOR-MADE FOR THE TARGET. IT HAD A HIGH FAILURE RATE.
SO I GOT MY HANDS ON SOME. FIXED THE DESIGN FLAWS. NOW THEY WORK ON *ANYONE*.
THEY READ YOUR DNA, FIND THE CODE FOR WHEN YOU WERE NORMAL, AND PUT YOU BACK THAT WAY. IF YOU WERE NEVER NORMAL, THEY USE A BASELINE HUMAN GENOME AS A GUIDE.
POINT BEING... THANKS TO MY POWERS, MY GENIUS, MY GENERAL AWESOMENESS, AND JOCASTA'S WAY WITH MACHINES...*BOOM*. YOU'RE JUST REGULAR FOLKS.
C-CAN WE...CAN WE...
THAT'S WHY WE'RE ALL HERE, RIGHT?
NO NEED FOR NEEDLES. I'VE AEROSOLIZED IT. I CALL IT *CLEAN SLATE*.
ONE PULL OFF THIS AND YOUR DAYS AS A WALKING CHERNOBYL ARE OVER.

WAIT. THAT COULD BE ANYTHING.

I DON'T GIVE A DAMN. I'M *TRYING* IT.

DR. PYM ALWAYS SAID IF HE NEGATED MY POWERS, I'D *DIE*. BECAUSE ALL MY SKIN HAD TO BE *PEELED OFF* TO MAKE ME LIKE THIS...

YEAH, YOU WERE A TRICKY ONE. BUT I THINK I CAN USE YOUR *STEM CELLS* TO GROW YOU NEW SKIN. WE'RE GONNA HAVE TO GO IN THROUGH YOUR MOUTH...ACCESS YOUR BONE MARROW...

HOLD ON, KEN. YOU ASKED ME TO COME HERE TO MAKE SURE THIS IS ON THE LEVEL. I'M NOT EVEN *CLOSE* TO BEING CONVINCED--

I AM.

CHHSSHH

THERE'S A GEIGER COUNTER BUILT INTO MY SUIT. IT MEASURES TOXICITY. AND GUESS WHAT?

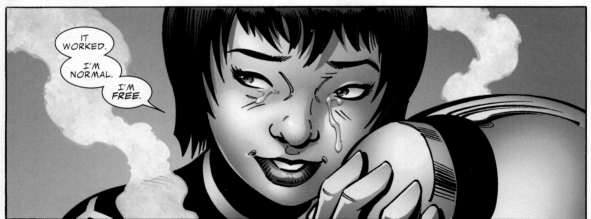

IT WORKED.

I'M NORMAL.

I'M FREE.

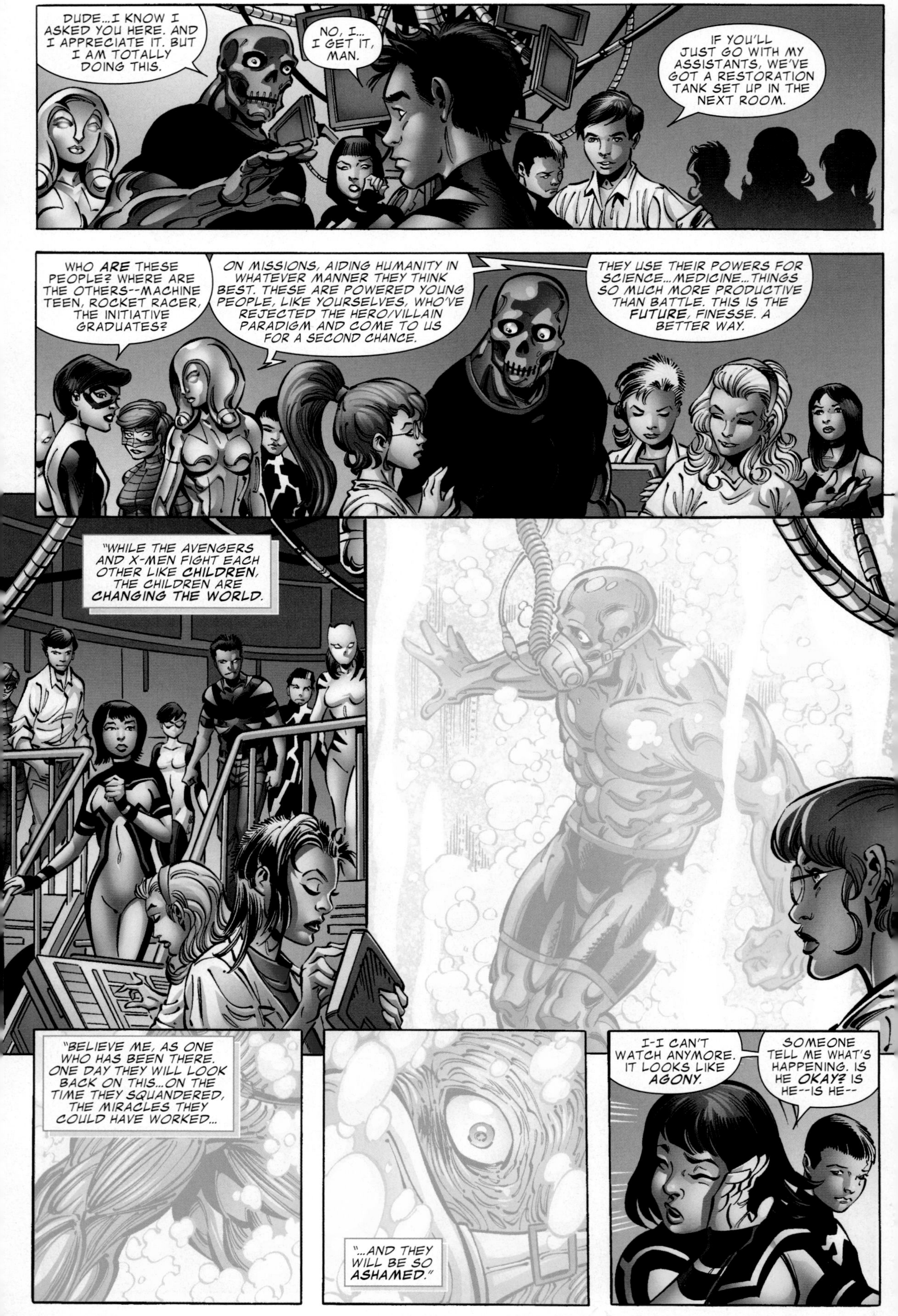
DUDE...I KNOW I ASKED YOU HERE. AND I APPRECIATE IT. BUT I AM TOTALLY DOING THIS.
NO, I... I GET IT, MAN.
IF YOU'LL JUST GO WITH MY ASSISTANTS, WE'VE GOT A RESTORATION TANK SET UP IN THE NEXT ROOM.
WHO ARE THESE PEOPLE? WHERE ARE THE OTHERS--MACHINE TEEN, ROCKET RACER, THE INITIATIVE GRADUATES?
ON MISSIONS, AIDING HUMANITY IN WHATEVER MANNER THEY THINK BEST. THESE ARE POWERED YOUNG PEOPLE, LIKE YOURSELVES, WHO'VE REJECTED THE HERO/VILLAIN PARADIGM AND COME TO US FOR A SECOND CHANCE.
THEY USE THEIR POWERS FOR SCIENCE...MEDICINE...THINGS SO MUCH MORE PRODUCTIVE THAN BATTLE. THIS IS THE FUTURE, FINESSE. A BETTER WAY.
"WHILE THE AVENGERS AND X-MEN FIGHT EACH OTHER LIKE CHILDREN, THE CHILDREN ARE CHANGING THE WORLD.
"BELIEVE ME, AS ONE WHO HAS BEEN THERE. ONE DAY THEY WILL LOOK BACK ON THIS...ON THE TIME THEY SQUANDERED, THE MIRACLES THEY COULD HAVE WORKED...
"...AND THEY WILL BE SO ASHAMED."
I-I CAN'T WATCH ANYMORE. IT LOOKS LIKE AGONY.
SOMEONE TELL ME WHAT'S HAPPENING. IS HE OKAY? IS HE--IS HE--

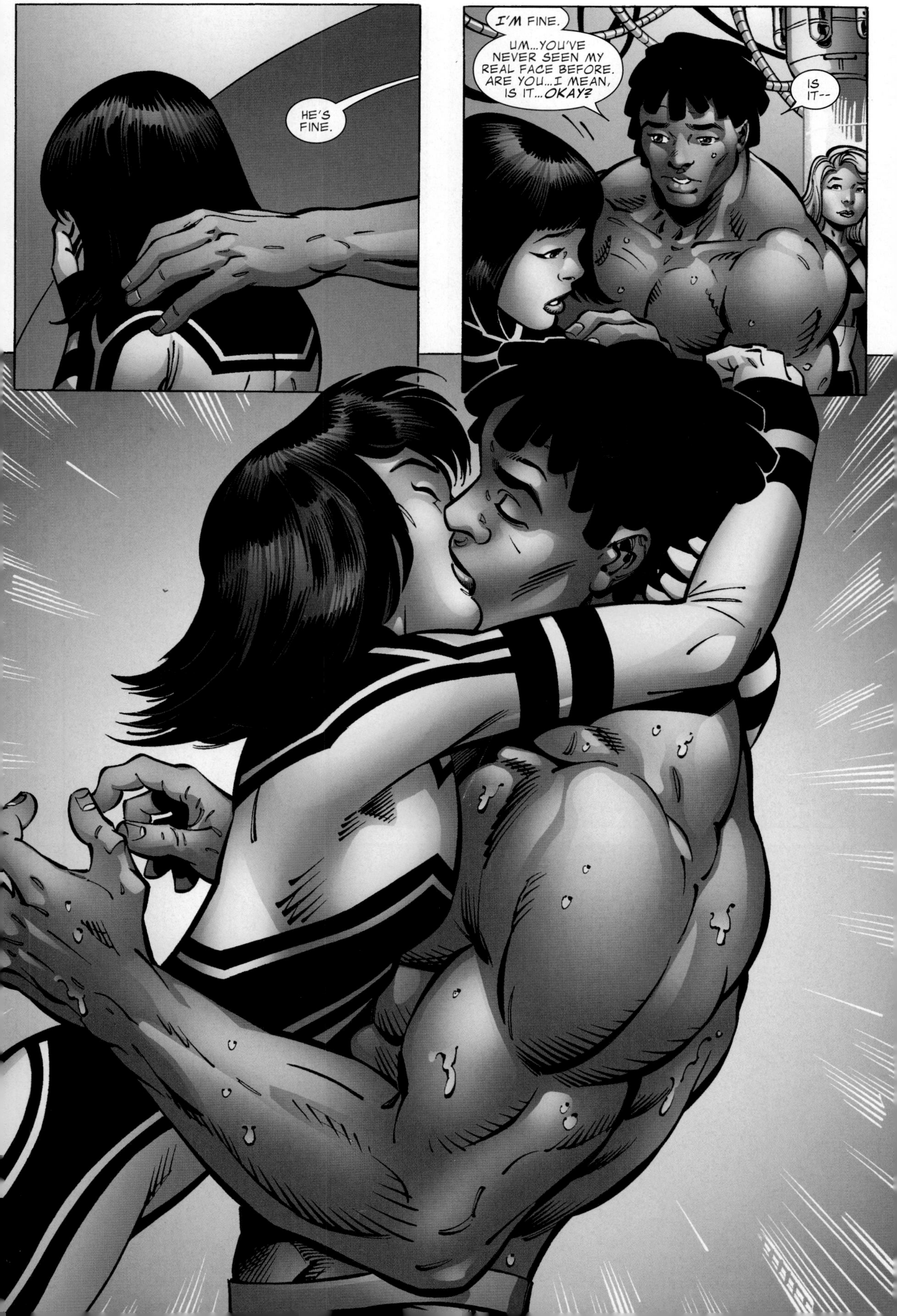
HE'S FINE.
I'M FINE.
UM...YOU'VE NEVER SEEN MY REAL FACE BEFORE. ARE YOU...I MEAN, IS IT...OKAY?
IS IT--

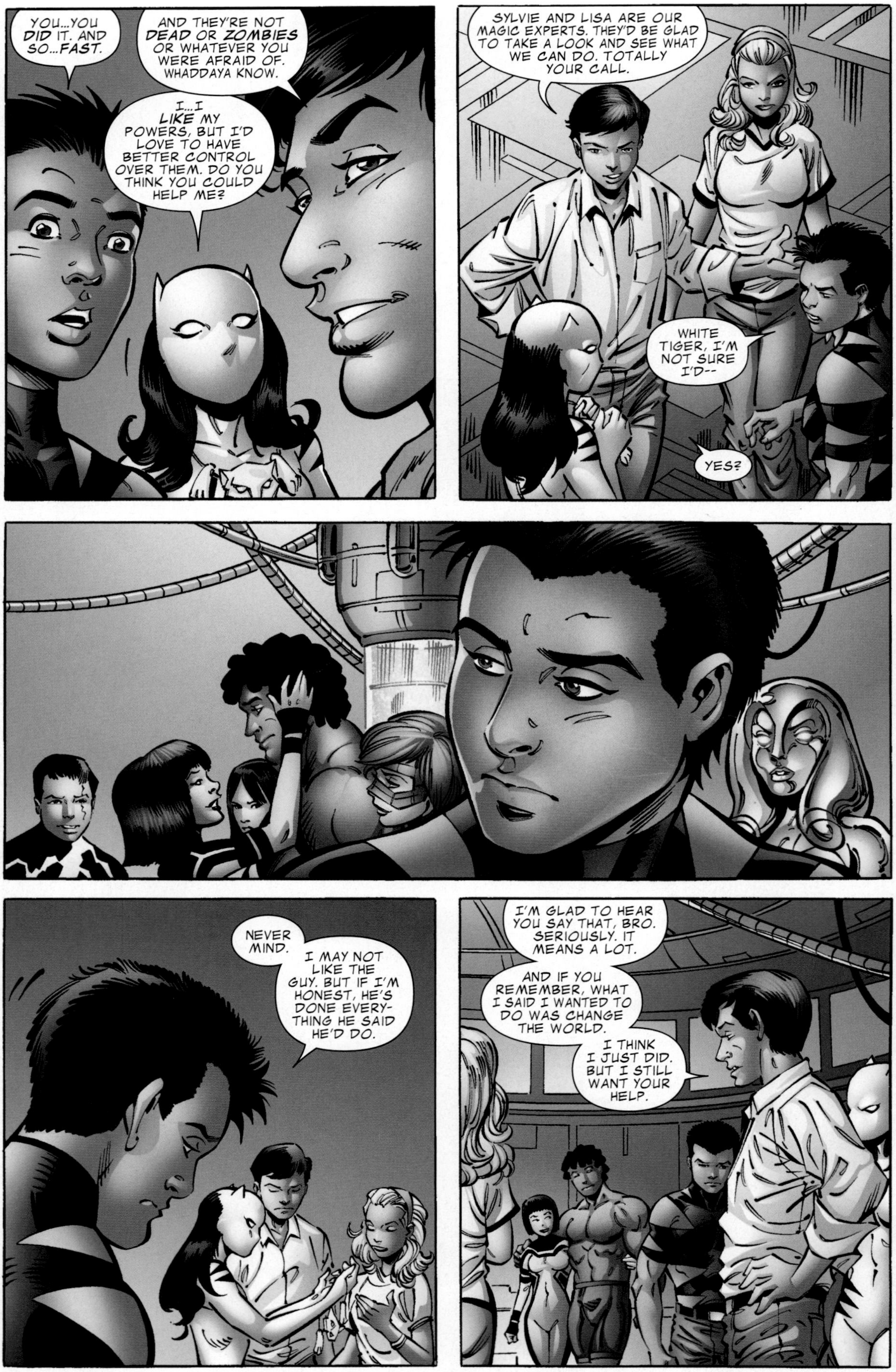
YOU...YOU DID IT. AND SO...FAST.
AND THEY'RE NOT DEAD OR ZOMBIES OR WHATEVER YOU WERE AFRAID OF. WHADDAYA KNOW.
I...I LIKE MY POWERS, BUT I'D LOVE TO HAVE BETTER CONTROL OVER THEM. DO YOU THINK YOU COULD HELP ME?
SYLVIE AND LISA ARE OUR MAGIC EXPERTS. THEY'D BE GLAD TO TAKE A LOOK AND SEE WHAT WE CAN DO. TOTALLY YOUR CALL.
WHITE TIGER, I'M NOT SURE I'D--
YES?
NEVER MIND.
I MAY NOT LIKE THE GUY. BUT IF I'M HONEST, HE'S DONE EVERY-THING HE SAID HE'D DO.
I'M GLAD TO HEAR YOU SAY THAT, BRO. SERIOUSLY. IT MEANS A LOT.
AND IF YOU REMEMBER, WHAT I SAID I WANTED TO DO WAS CHANGE THE WORLD.
I THINK I JUST DID. BUT I STILL WANT YOUR HELP.

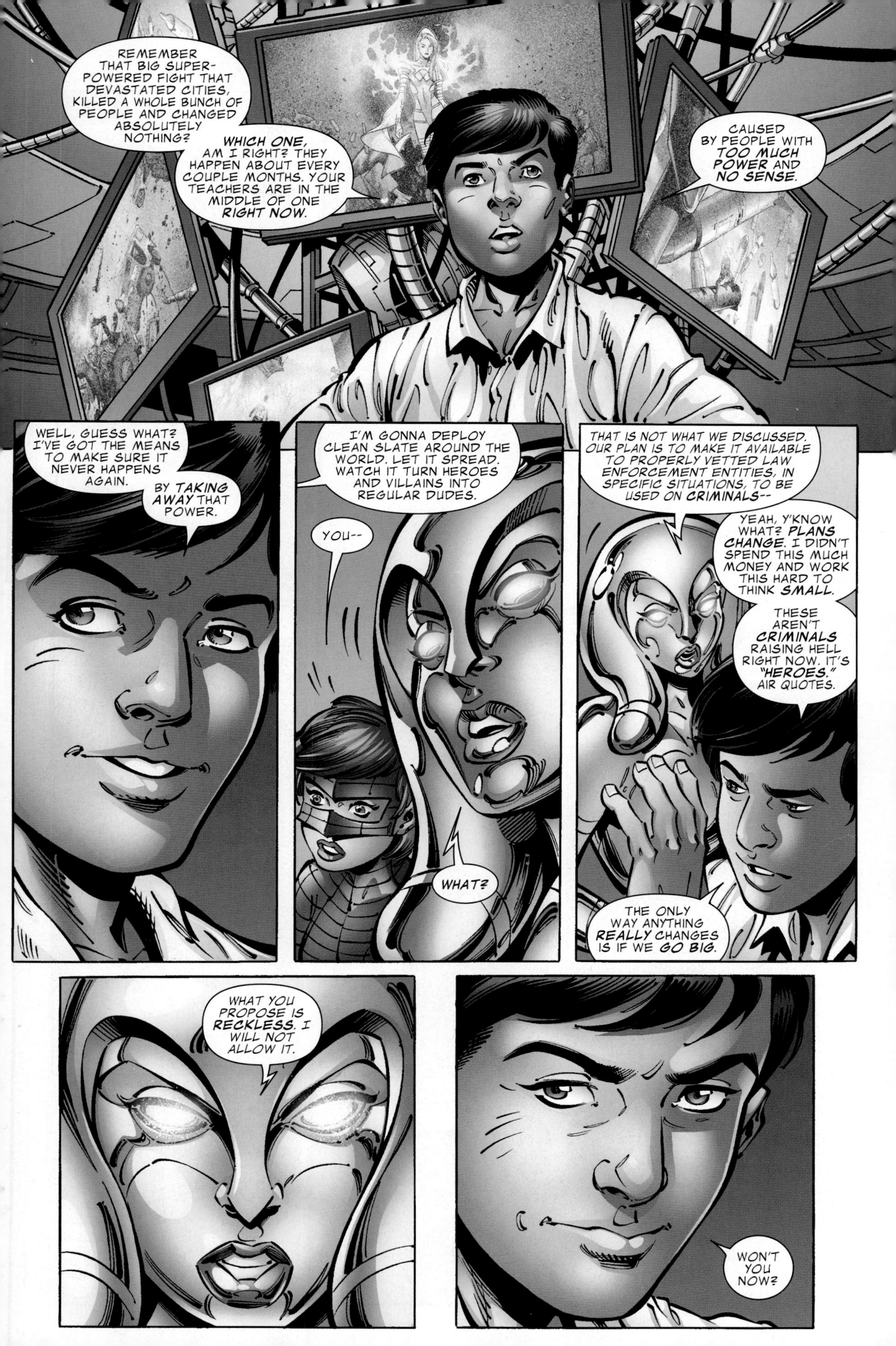
REMEMBER THAT BIG SUPER-POWERED FIGHT THAT DEVASTATED CITIES, KILLED A WHOLE BUNCH OF PEOPLE AND CHANGED ABSOLUTELY NOTHING?
WHICH ONE, AM I RIGHT? THEY HAPPEN ABOUT EVERY COUPLE MONTHS. YOUR TEACHERS ARE IN THE MIDDLE OF ONE RIGHT NOW.
CAUSED BY PEOPLE WITH TOO MUCH POWER AND NO SENSE.
WELL, GUESS WHAT? I'VE GOT THE MEANS TO MAKE SURE IT NEVER HAPPENS AGAIN.
BY TAKING AWAY THAT POWER.
I'M GONNA DEPLOY CLEAN SLATE AROUND THE WORLD. LET IT SPREAD. WATCH IT TURN HEROES AND VILLAINS INTO REGULAR DUDES.
YOU--
WHAT?
THAT IS NOT WHAT WE DISCUSSED. OUR PLAN IS TO MAKE IT AVAILABLE TO PROPERLY VETTED LAW ENFORCEMENT ENTITIES, IN SPECIFIC SITUATIONS, TO BE USED ON CRIMINALS--
YEAH, Y'KNOW WHAT? PLANS CHANGE. I DIDN'T SPEND THIS MUCH MONEY AND WORK THIS HARD TO THINK SMALL.
THESE AREN'T CRIMINALS RAISING HELL RIGHT NOW. IT'S "HEROES." AIR QUOTES.
THE ONLY WAY ANYTHING REALLY CHANGES IS IF WE GO BIG.
WHAT YOU PROPOSE IS RECKLESS. I WILL NOT ALLOW IT.
WON'T YOU NOW?

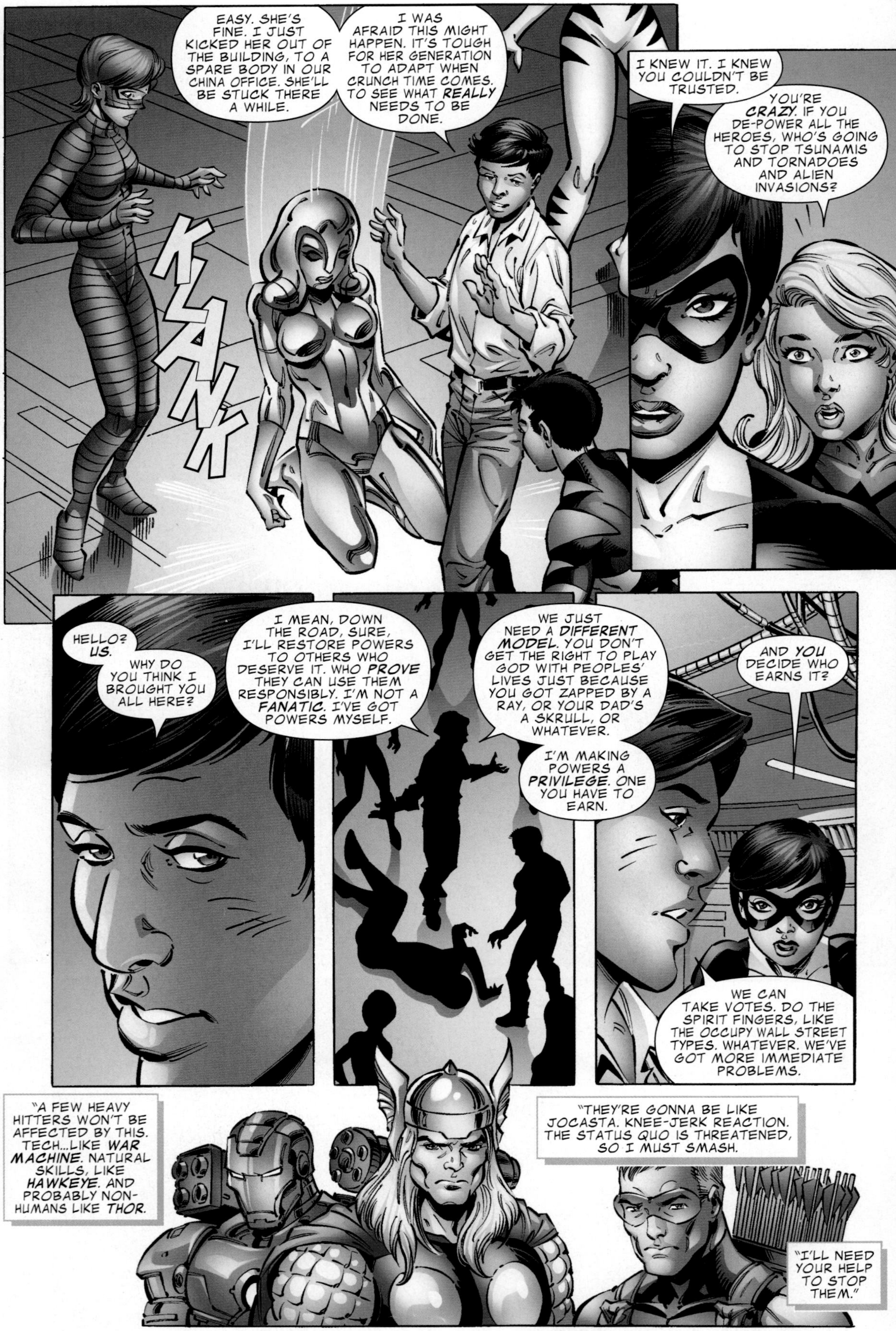
EASY. SHE'S FINE. I JUST KICKED HER OUT OF THE BUILDING, TO A SPARE BODY IN OUR CHINA OFFICE. SHE'LL BE STUCK THERE A WHILE.
I WAS AFRAID THIS MIGHT HAPPEN. IT'S TOUGH FOR HER GENERATION TO ADAPT WHEN CRUNCH TIME COMES. TO SEE WHAT REALLY NEEDS TO BE DONE.
KLANK
I KNEW IT. I KNEW YOU COULDN'T BE TRUSTED.
YOU'RE CRAZY. IF YOU DE-POWER ALL THE HEROES, WHO'S GOING TO STOP TSUNAMIS AND TORNADOES AND ALIEN INVASIONS?
HELLO? US.
WHY DO YOU THINK I BROUGHT YOU ALL HERE?
I MEAN, DOWN THE ROAD, SURE, I'LL RESTORE POWERS TO OTHERS WHO DESERVE IT. WHO PROVE THEY CAN USE THEM RESPONSIBLY. I'M NOT A FANATIC. I'VE GOT POWERS MYSELF.
WE JUST NEED A DIFFERENT MODEL. YOU DON'T GET THE RIGHT TO PLAY GOD WITH PEOPLES' LIVES JUST BECAUSE YOU GOT ZAPPED BY A RAY, OR YOUR DAD'S A SKRULL, OR WHATEVER.
I'M MAKING POWERS A PRIVILEGE. ONE YOU HAVE TO EARN.
AND YOU DECIDE WHO EARNS IT?
WE CAN TAKE VOTES. DO THE SPIRIT FINGERS, LIKE THE OCCUPY WALL STREET TYPES. WHATEVER. WE'VE GOT MORE IMMEDIATE PROBLEMS.
"A FEW HEAVY HITTERS WON'T BE AFFECTED BY THIS. TECH...LIKE WAR MACHINE. NATURAL SKILLS, LIKE HAWKEYE. AND PROBABLY NON-HUMANS LIKE THOR.
"THEY'RE GONNA BE LIKE JOCASTA. KNEE-JERK REACTION. THE STATUS QUO IS THREATENED, SO I MUST SMASH.
"I'LL NEED YOUR HELP TO STOP THEM."

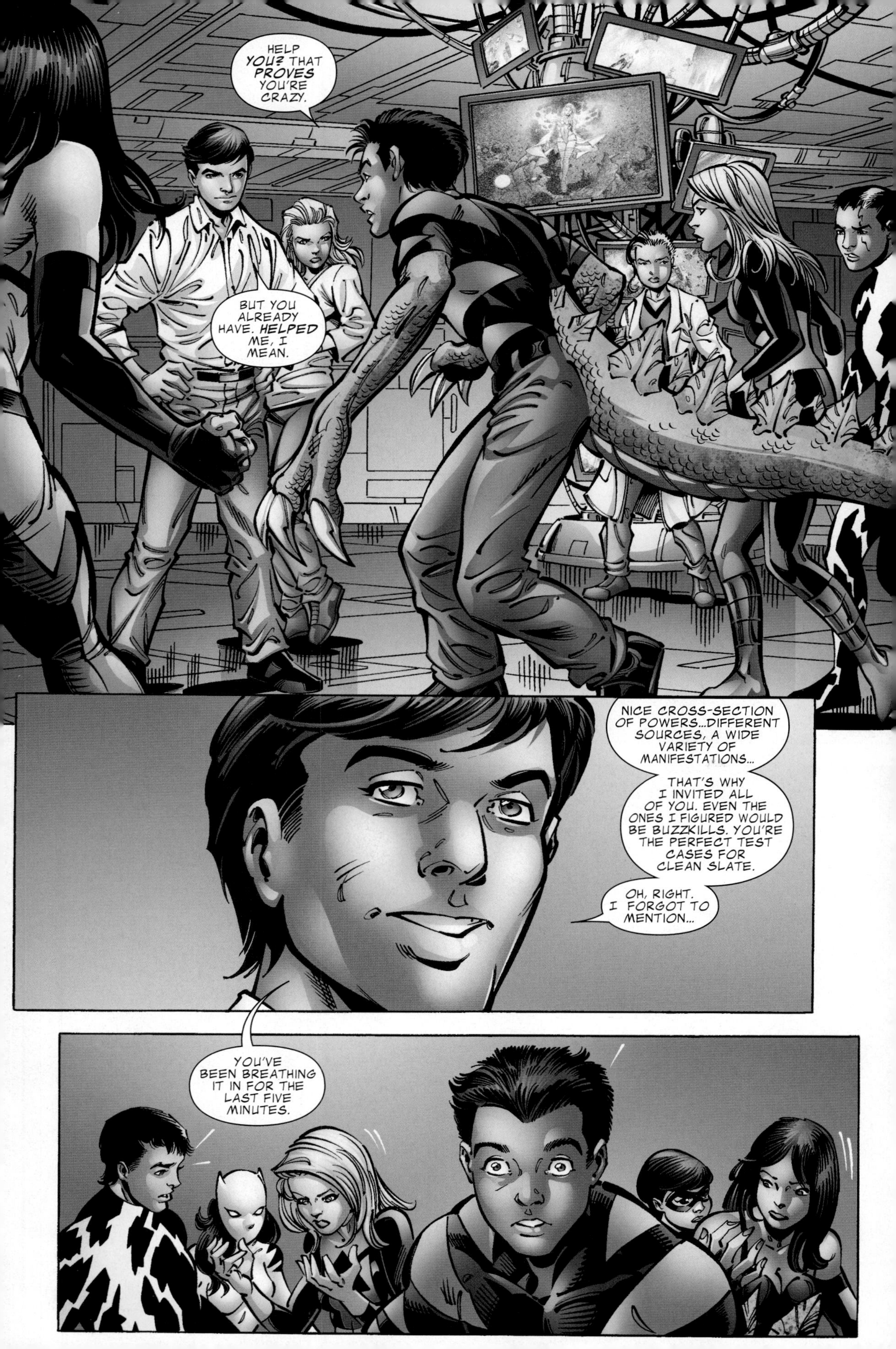
HELP YOU? THAT PROVES YOU'RE CRAZY.
BUT YOU ALREADY HAVE. HELPED ME, I MEAN.
NICE CROSS-SECTION OF POWERS...DIFFERENT SOURCES, A WIDE VARIETY OF MANIFESTATIONS...
THAT'S WHY I INVITED ALL OF YOU. EVEN THE ONES I FIGURED WOULD BE BUZZKILLS. YOU'RE THE PERFECT TEST CASES FOR CLEAN SLATE.
OH, RIGHT. I FORGOT TO MENTION...
YOU'VE BEEN BREATHING IT IN FOR THE LAST FIVE MINUTES.

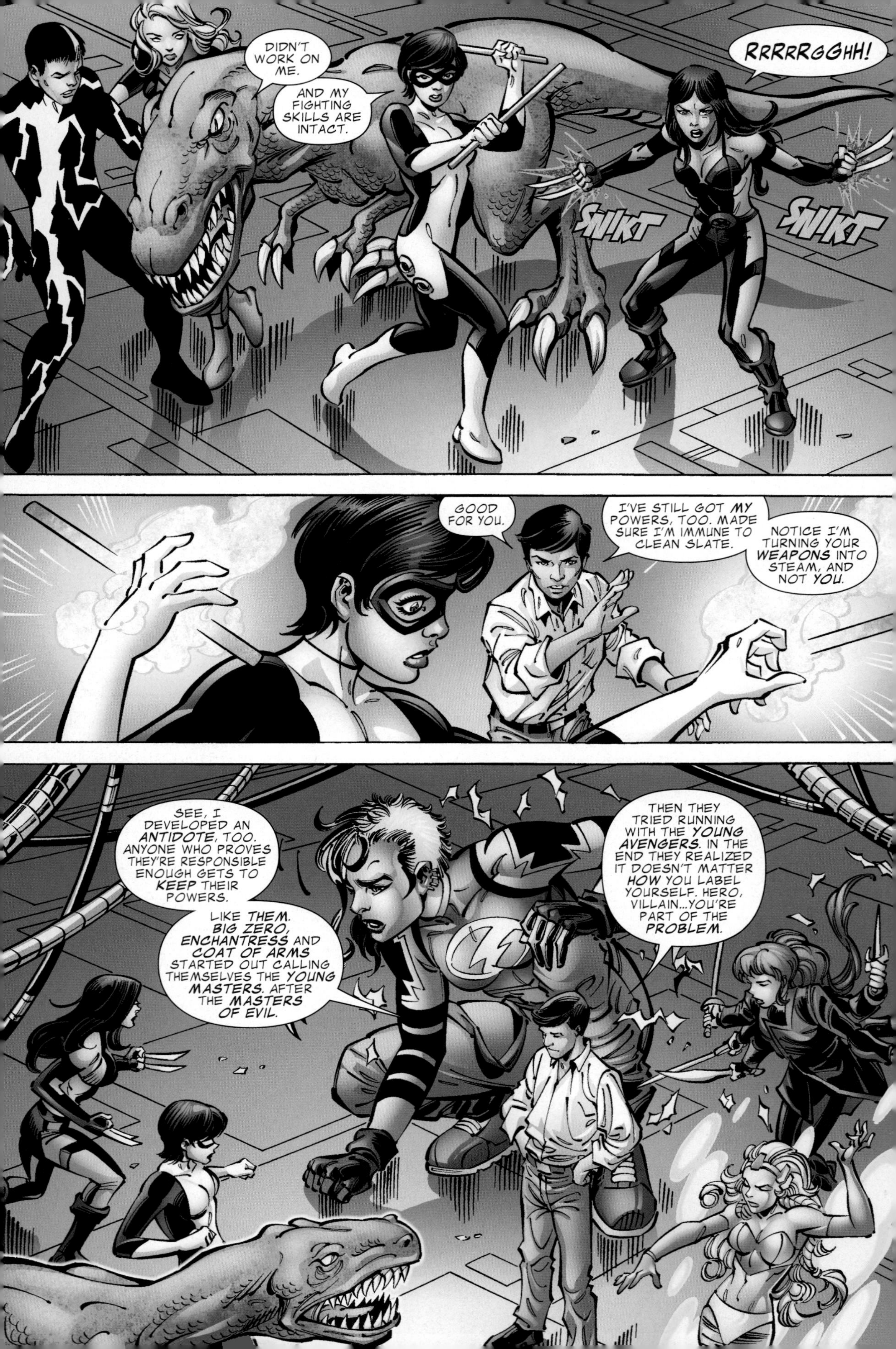

DIDN'T WORK ON ME.
AND MY FIGHTING SKILLS ARE INTACT.
RRRRRGGHH!
SNIKT
SNIKT
GOOD FOR YOU.
I'VE STILL GOT MY POWERS, TOO. MADE SURE I'M IMMUNE TO CLEAN SLATE.
NOTICE I'M TURNING YOUR WEAPONS INTO STEAM, AND NOT YOU.
SEE, I DEVELOPED AN ANTIDOTE, TOO. ANYONE WHO PROVES THEY'RE RESPONSIBLE ENOUGH GETS TO KEEP THEIR POWERS.
LIKE THEM. BIG ZERO, ENCHANTRESS AND COAT OF ARMS STARTED OUT CALLING THEMSELVES THE YOUNG MASTERS. AFTER THE MASTERS OF EVIL.
THEN THEY TRIED RUNNING WITH THE YOUNG AVENGERS. IN THE END THEY REALIZED IT DOESN'T MATTER HOW YOU LABEL YOURSELF. HERO, VILLAIN...YOU'RE PART OF THE PROBLEM.

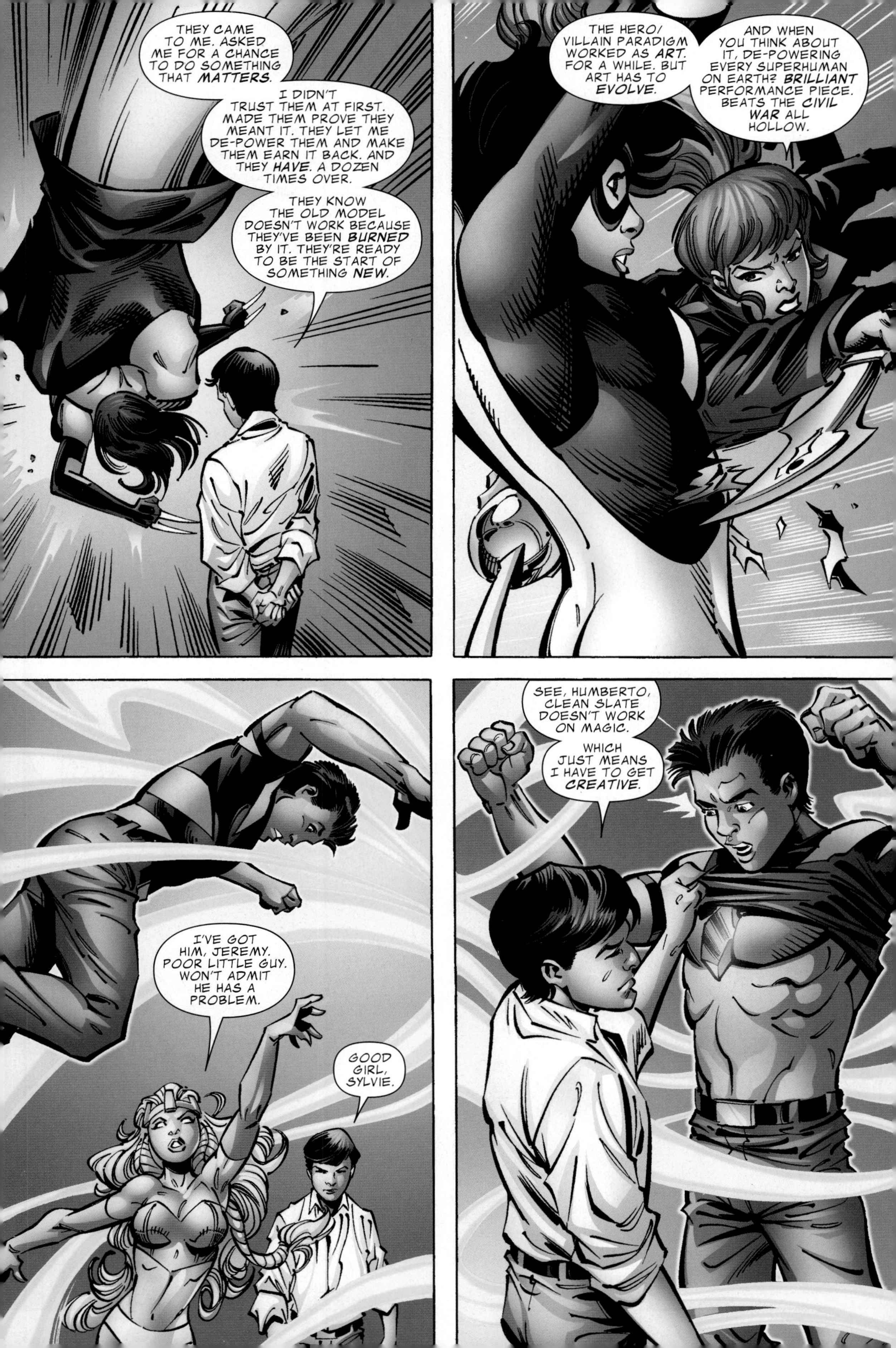
THEY CAME TO ME. ASKED ME FOR A CHANCE TO DO SOMETHING THAT MATTERS.
I DIDN'T TRUST THEM AT FIRST. MADE THEM PROVE THEY MEANT IT. THEY LET ME DE-POWER THEM AND MAKE THEM EARN IT BACK. AND THEY HAVE. A DOZEN TIMES OVER.
THEY KNOW THE OLD MODEL DOESN'T WORK BECAUSE THEY'VE BEEN BURNED BY IT. THEY'RE READY TO BE THE START OF SOMETHING NEW.
THE HERO/ VILLAIN PARADIGM WORKED AS ART. FOR A WHILE. BUT ART HAS TO EVOLVE.
AND WHEN YOU THINK ABOUT IT, DE-POWERING EVERY SUPERHUMAN ON EARTH? BRILLIANT PERFORMANCE PIECE. BEATS THE CIVIL WAR ALL HOLLOW.
I'VE GOT HIM, JEREMY. POOR LITTLE GUY. WON'T ADMIT HE HAS A PROBLEM.
GOOD GIRL, SYLVIE.
SEE, HUMBERTO, CLEAN SLATE DOESN'T WORK ON MAGIC.
WHICH JUST MEANS I HAVE TO GET CREATIVE.

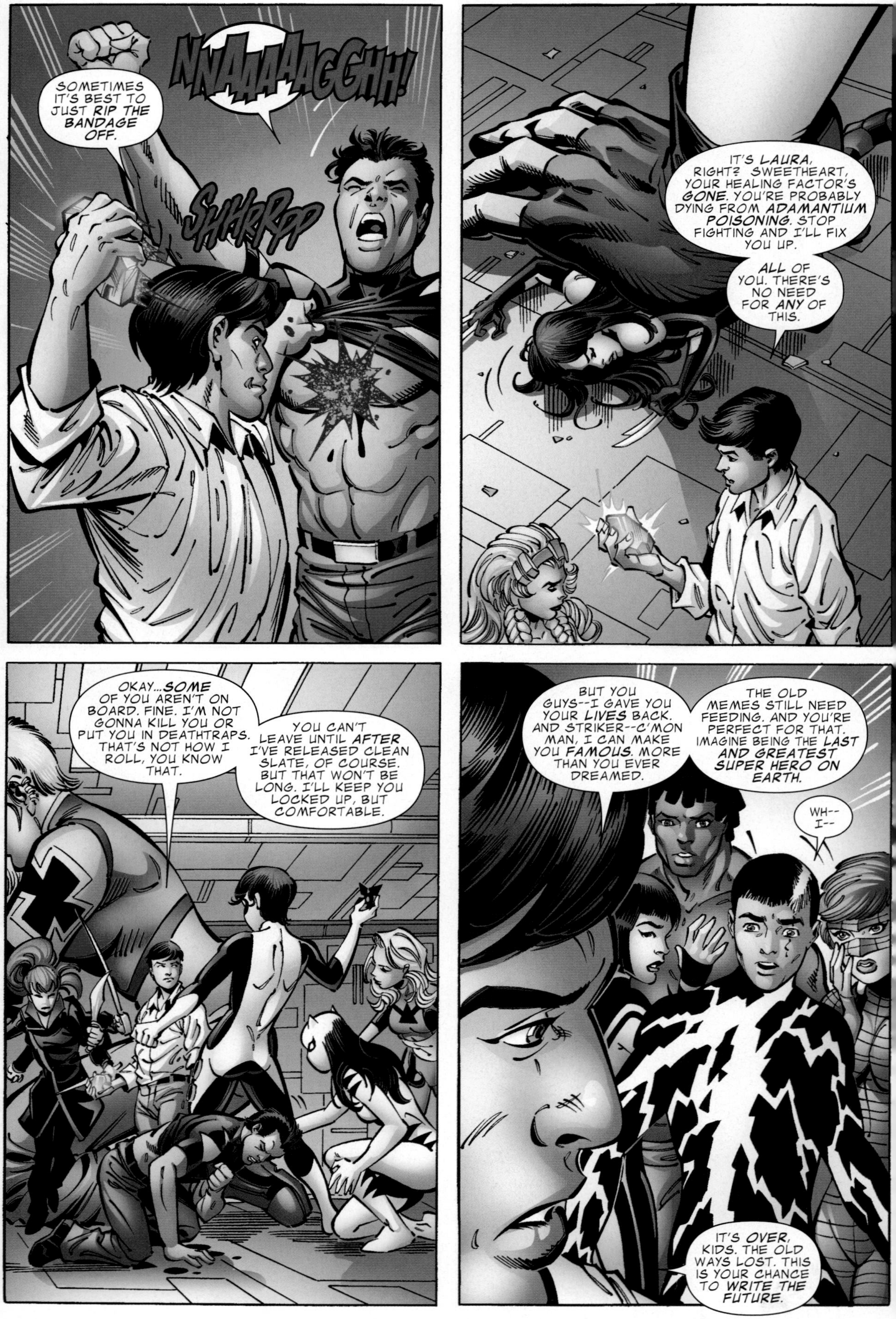
NNAAAAAAGGHH!
SOMETIMES IT'S BEST TO JUST RIP THE BANDAGE OFF.
SHHRRPP
IT'S LAURA, RIGHT? SWEETHEART, YOUR HEALING FACTOR'S GONE. YOU'RE PROBABLY DYING FROM ADAMANTIUM POISONING. STOP FIGHTING AND I'LL FIX YOU UP.
ALL OF YOU. THERE'S NO NEED FOR ANY OF THIS.
OKAY...SOME OF YOU AREN'T ON BOARD. FINE. I'M NOT GONNA KILL YOU OR PUT YOU IN DEATHTRAPS. THAT'S NOT HOW I ROLL, YOU KNOW THAT.
YOU CAN'T LEAVE UNTIL AFTER I'VE RELEASED CLEAN SLATE, OF COURSE. BUT THAT WON'T BE LONG. I'LL KEEP YOU LOCKED UP, BUT COMFORTABLE.
BUT YOU GUYS--I GAVE YOU YOUR LIVES BACK. AND STRIKER--C'MON MAN, I CAN MAKE YOU FAMOUS. MORE THAN YOU EVER DREAMED.
THE OLD MEMES STILL NEED FEEDING. AND YOU'RE PERFECT FOR THAT. IMAGINE BEING THE LAST AND GREATEST SUPER HERO ON EARTH.
WH-- I--
IT'S OVER, KIDS. THE OLD WAYS LOST. THIS IS YOUR CHANCE TO WRITE THE FUTURE.

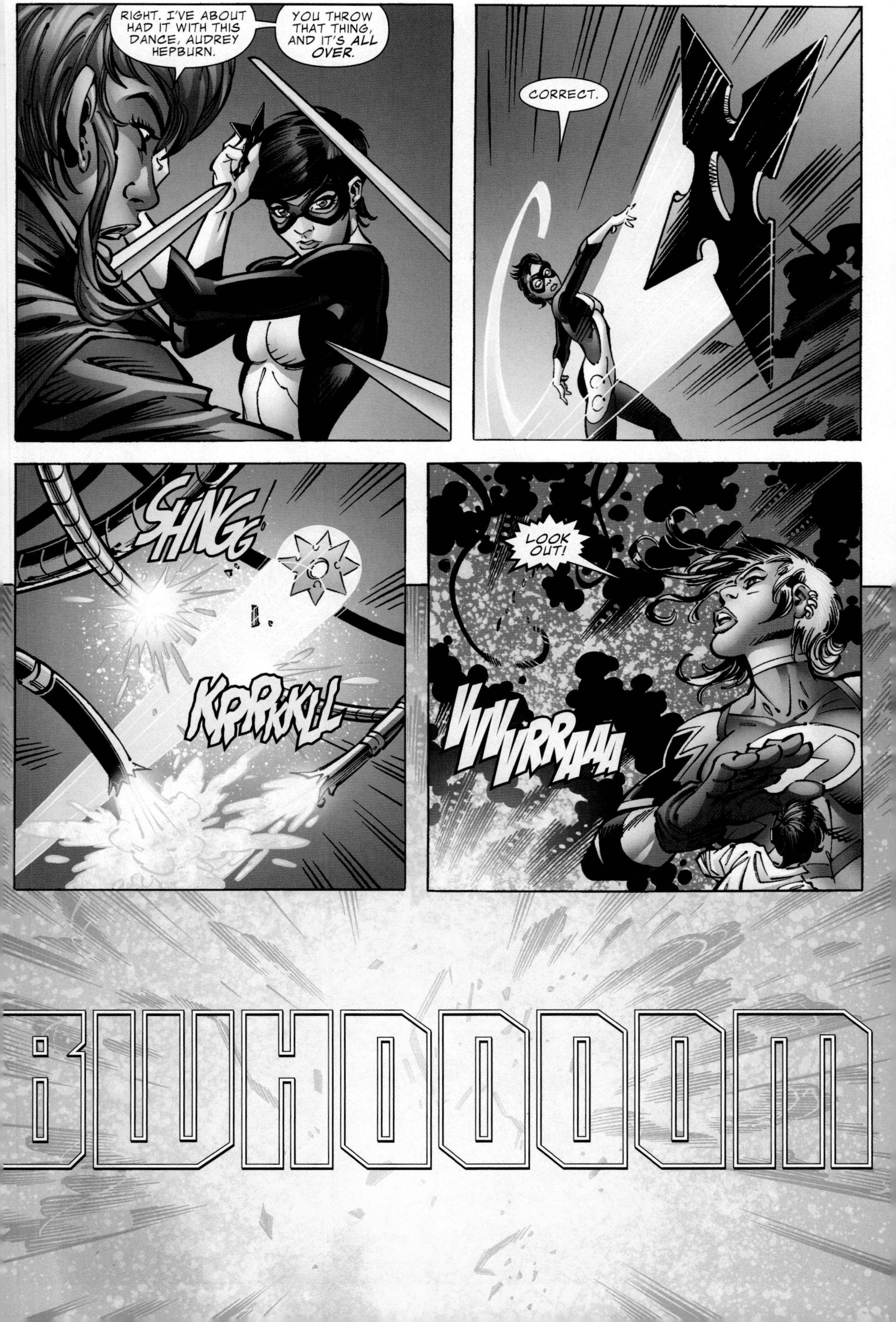
RIGHT. I'VE ABOUT HAD IT WITH THIS DANCE, AUDREY HEPBURN.
YOU THROW THAT THING, AND IT'S ALL OVER.
CORRECT.
SHINGG
KRRKKLL
LOOK OUT!
VVVVRRAAA
BWHOOOOM

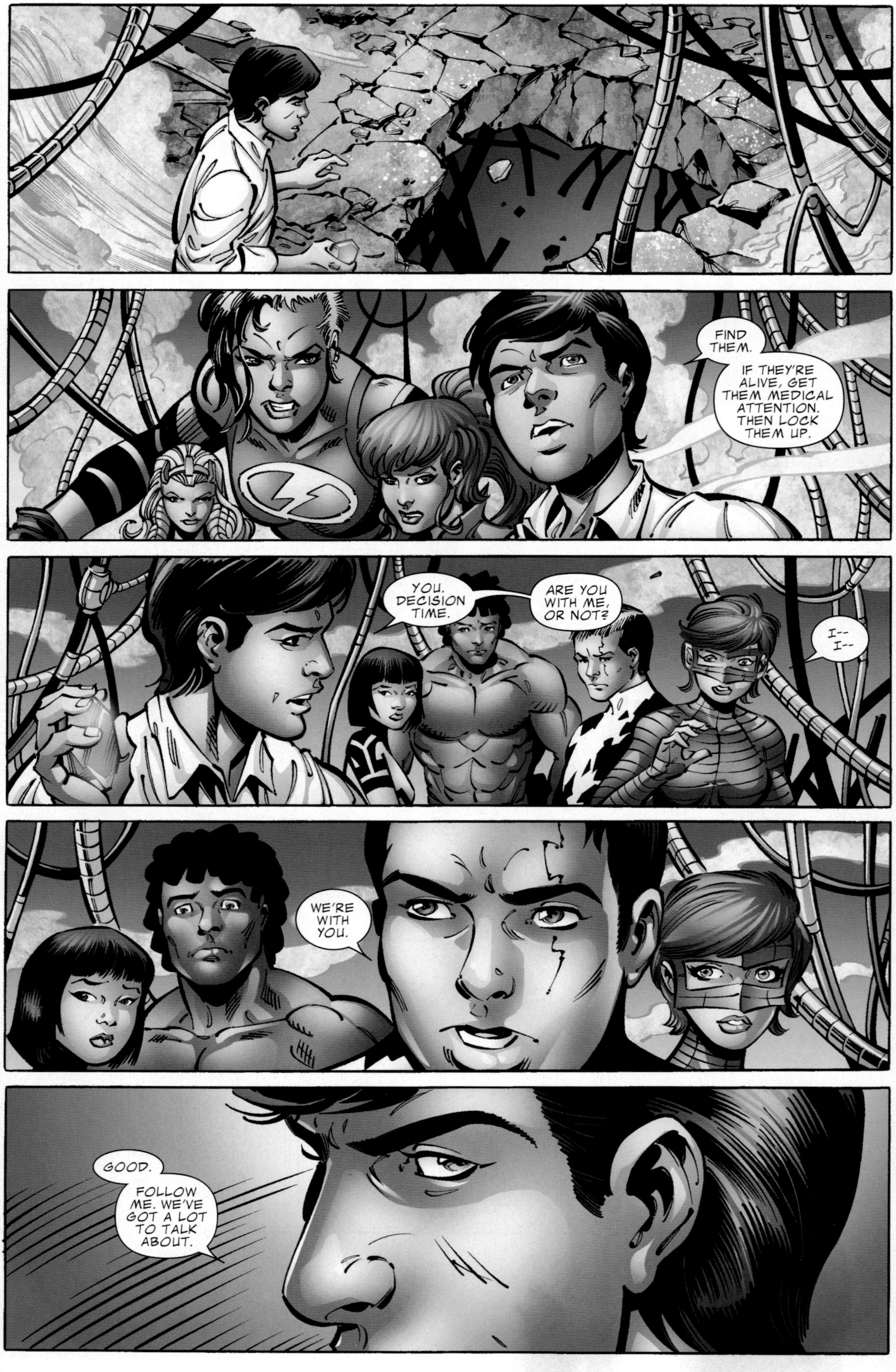
FIND THEM.
IF THEY'RE ALIVE, GET THEM MEDICAL ATTENTION. THEN LOCK THEM UP.
YOU. DECISION TIME.
ARE YOU WITH ME, OR NOT?
I-- I--
WE'RE WITH YOU.
GOOD.
FOLLOW ME. WE'VE GOT A LOT TO TALK ABOUT.

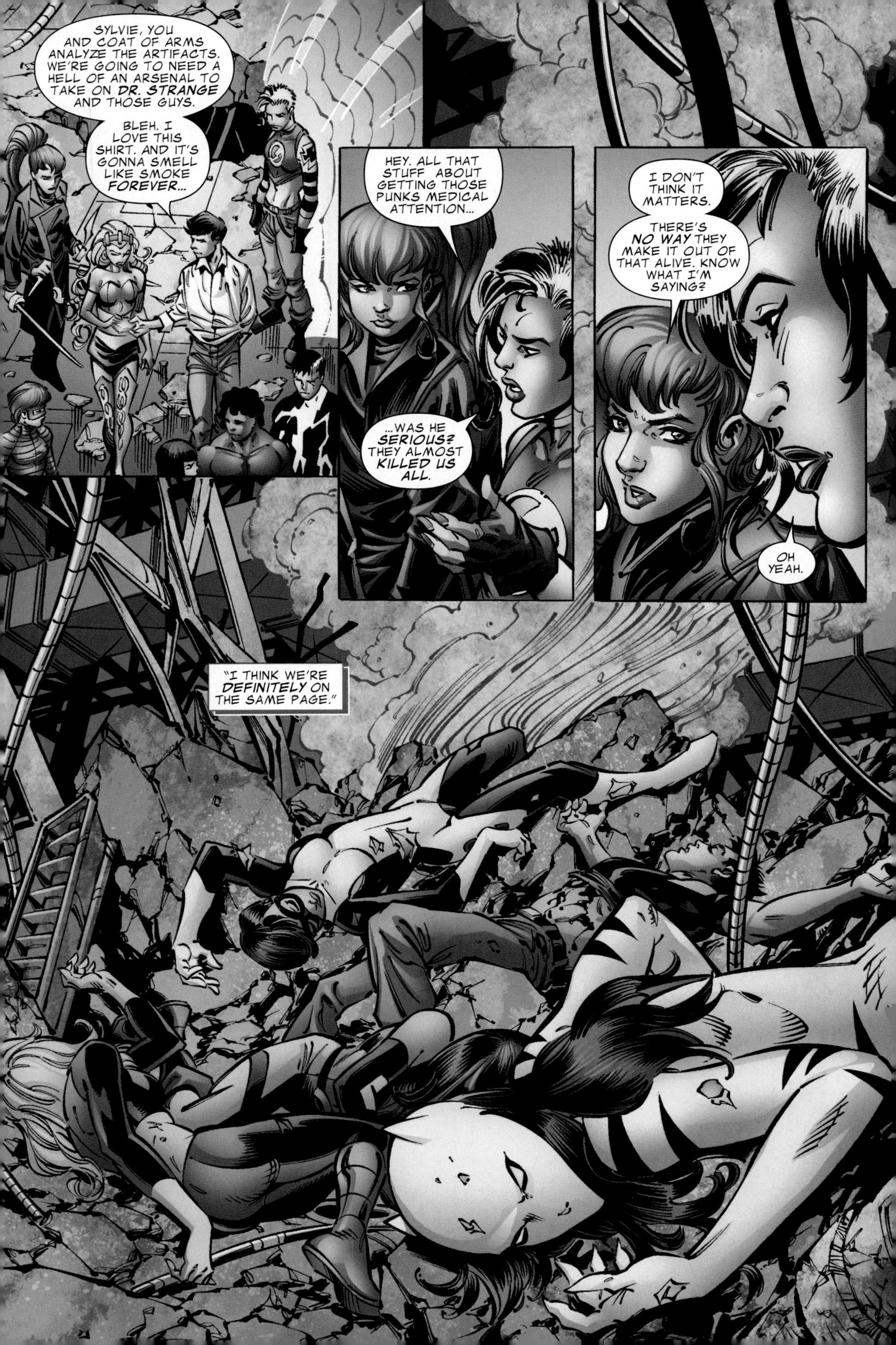
SYLVIE, YOU AND COAT OF ARMS ANALYZE THE ARTIFACTS. WE'RE GOING TO NEED A HELL OF AN ARSENAL TO TAKE ON DR. STRANGE AND THOSE GUYS.
BLEH. I LOVE THIS SHIRT. AND IT'S GONNA SMELL LIKE SMOKE FOREVER...
HEY. ALL THAT STUFF ABOUT GETTING THOSE PUNKS MEDICAL ATTENTION...
...WAS HE SERIOUS? THEY ALMOST KILLED US ALL.
I DON'T THINK IT MATTERS.
THERE'S NO WAY THEY MAKE IT OUT OF THAT ALIVE. KNOW WHAT I'M SAYING?
OH YEAH.
"I THINK WE'RE DEFINITELY ON THE SAME PAGE."

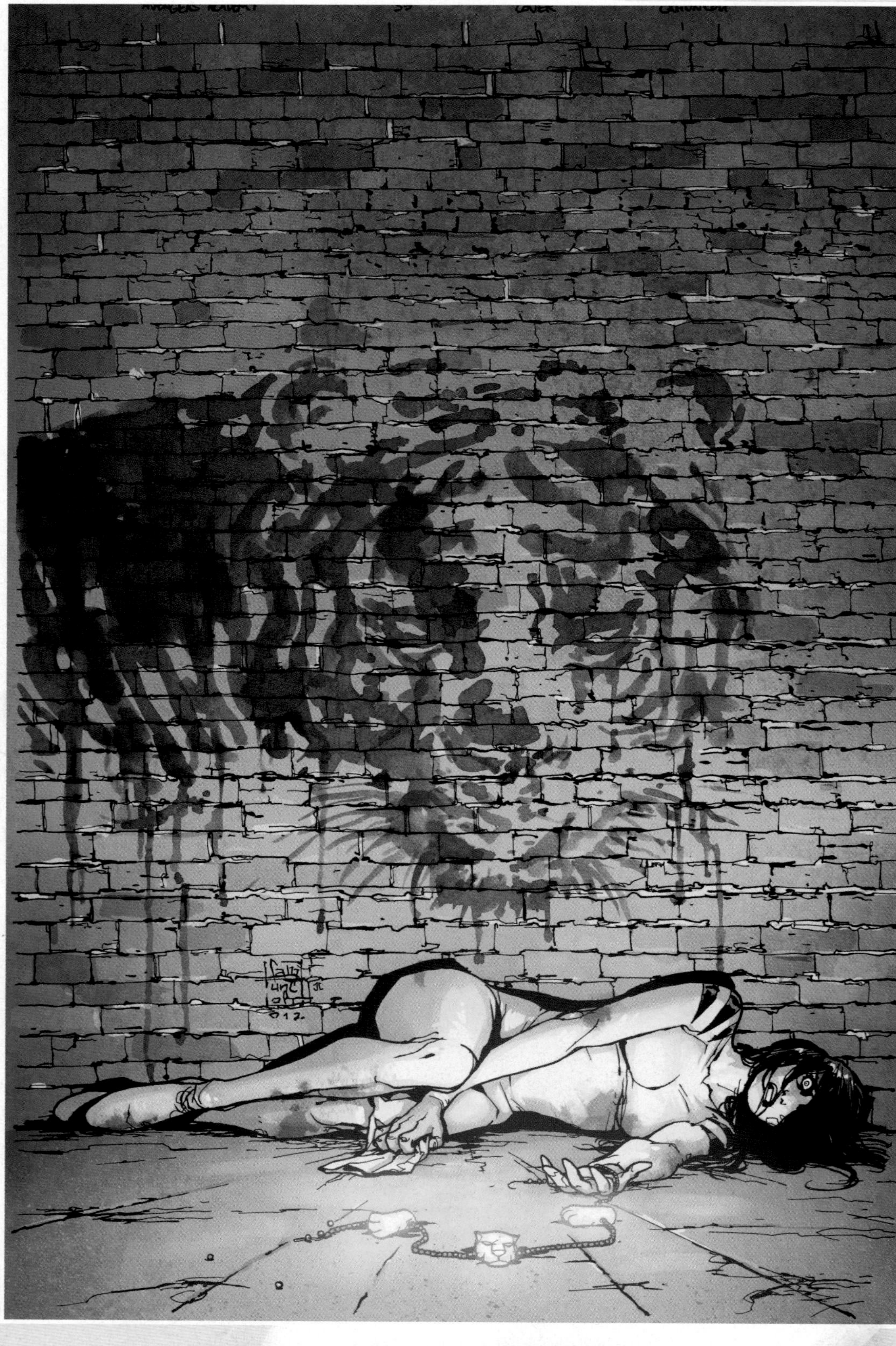

Avengers Academy #35

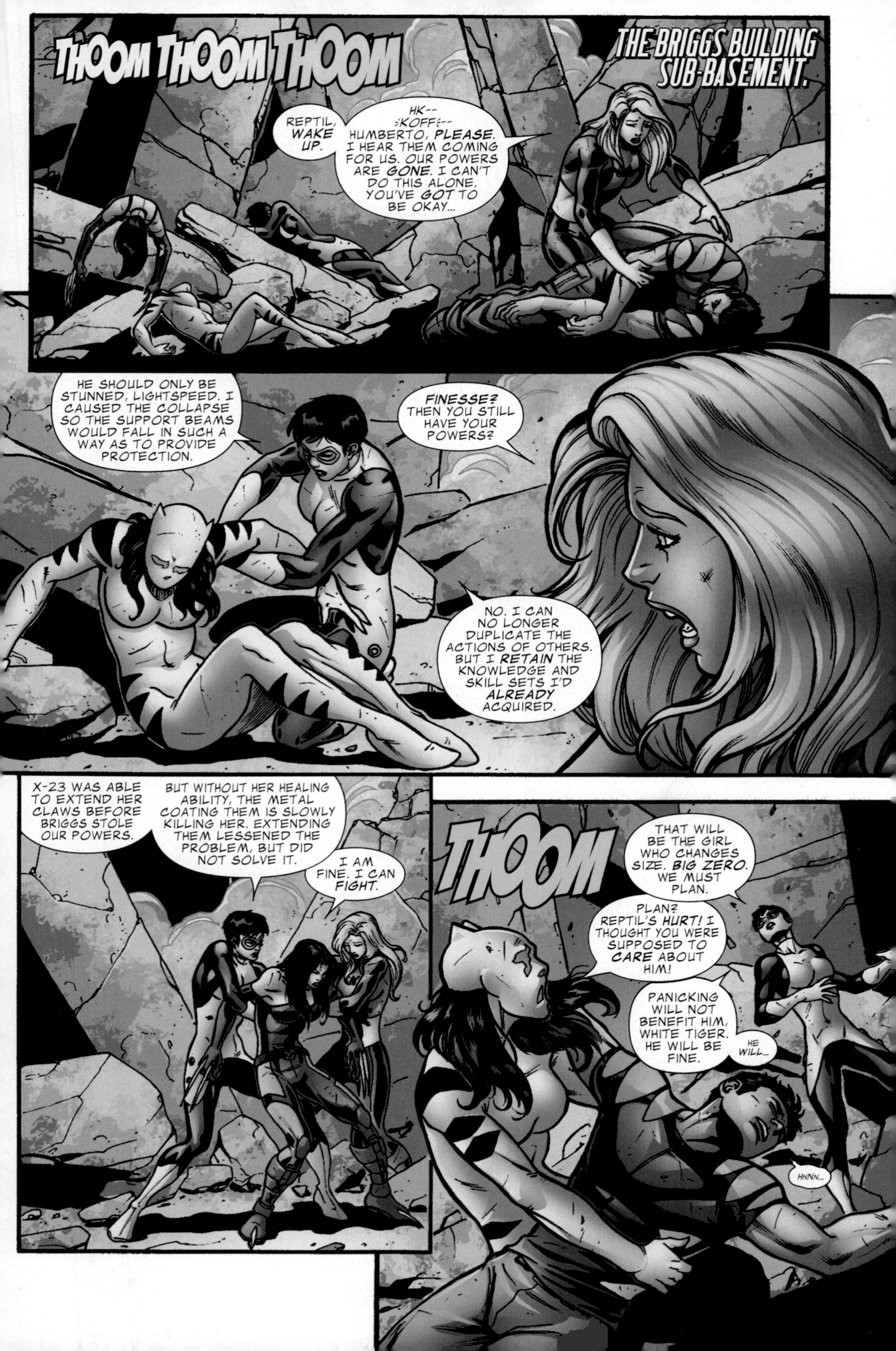
THOOM THOOM THOOM
THE BRIGGS BUILDING SUB-BASEMENT.
REPTIL, WAKE UP.
HK-- *KOFF*-- HUMBERTO, PLEASE. I HEAR THEM COMING FOR US. OUR POWERS ARE GONE. I CAN'T DO THIS ALONE. YOU'VE GOT TO BE OKAY...
HE SHOULD ONLY BE STUNNED, LIGHTSPEED. I CAUSED THE COLLAPSE SO THE SUPPORT BEAMS WOULD FALL IN SUCH A WAY AS TO PROVIDE PROTECTION.
FINESSE? THEN YOU STILL HAVE YOUR POWERS?
NO. I CAN NO LONGER DUPLICATE THE ACTIONS OF OTHERS. BUT I RETAIN THE KNOWLEDGE AND SKILL SETS I'D ALREADY ACQUIRED.
X-23 WAS ABLE TO EXTEND HER CLAWS BEFORE BRIGGS STOLE OUR POWERS.
BUT WITHOUT HER HEALING ABILITY, THE METAL COATING THEM IS SLOWLY KILLING HER. EXTENDING THEM LESSENED THE PROBLEM, BUT DID NOT SOLVE IT.
I AM FINE. I CAN FIGHT.
THOOM
THAT WILL BE THE GIRL WHO CHANGES SIZE. BIG ZERO. WE MUST PLAN.
PLAN? REPTIL'S HURT! I THOUGHT YOU WERE SUPPOSED TO CARE ABOUT HIM!
PANICKING WILL NOT BENEFIT HIM, WHITE TIGER. HE WILL BE FINE.
HE WILL...
HNNN...

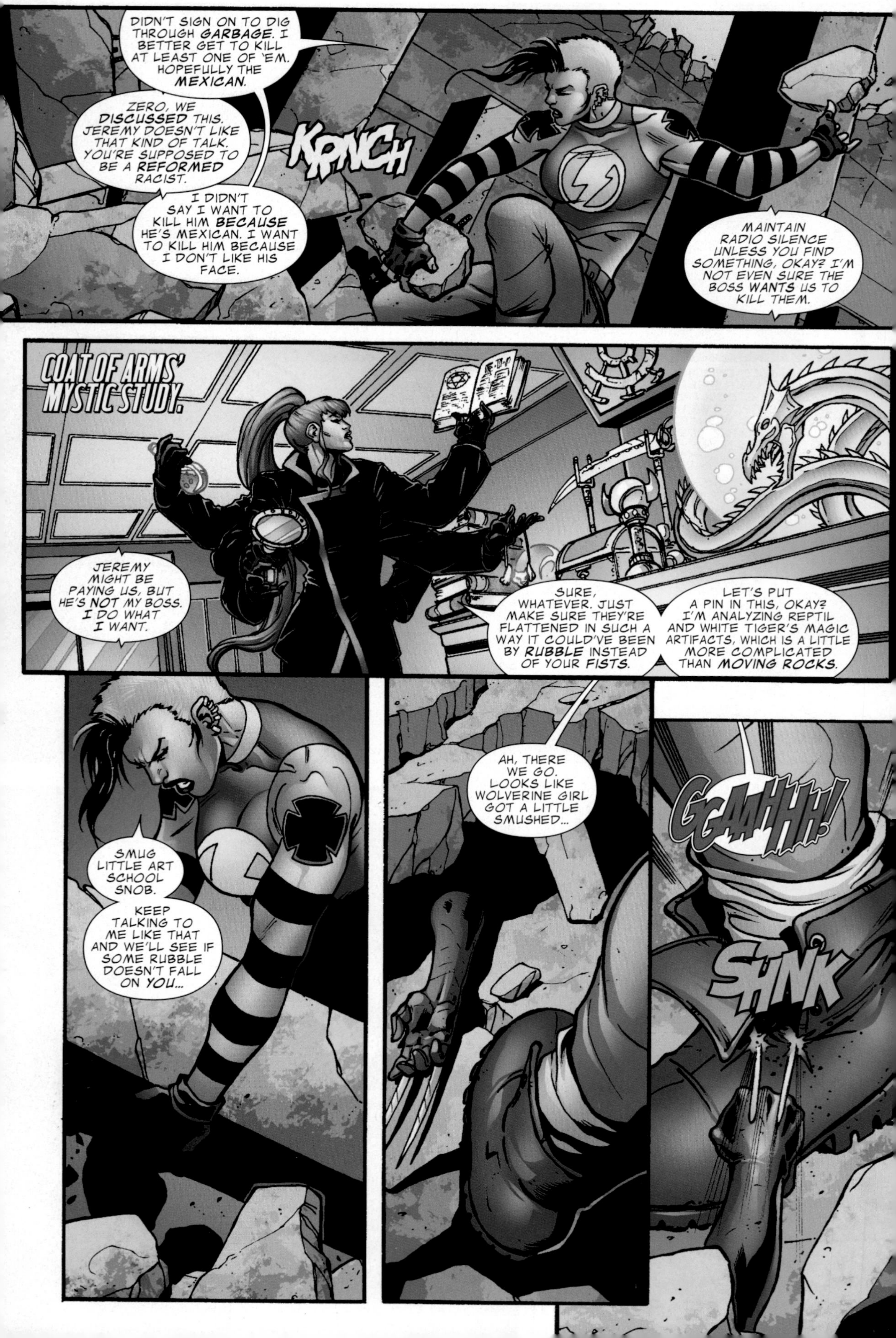

DIDN'T SIGN ON TO DIG THROUGH GARBAGE. I BETTER GET TO KILL AT LEAST ONE OF 'EM. HOPEFULLY THE MEXICAN.
ZERO, WE DISCUSSED THIS. JEREMY DOESN'T LIKE THAT KIND OF TALK. YOU'RE SUPPOSED TO BE A REFORMED RACIST.
KRNCH
I DIDN'T SAY I WANT TO KILL HIM BECAUSE HE'S MEXICAN. I WANT TO KILL HIM BECAUSE I DON'T LIKE HIS FACE.
MAINTAIN RADIO SILENCE UNLESS YOU FIND SOMETHING, OKAY? I'M NOT EVEN SURE THE BOSS WANTS US TO KILL THEM.
COAT OF ARMS' MYSTIC STUDY.
JEREMY MIGHT BE PAYING US, BUT HE'S NOT MY BOSS. I DO WHAT I WANT.
SURE, WHATEVER. JUST MAKE SURE THEY'RE FLATTENED IN SUCH A WAY IT COULD'VE BEEN BY RUBBLE INSTEAD OF YOUR FISTS.
LET'S PUT A PIN IN THIS, OKAY? I'M ANALYZING REPTIL AND WHITE TIGER'S MAGIC ARTIFACTS, WHICH IS A LITTLE MORE COMPLICATED THAN MOVING ROCKS.
SMUG LITTLE ART SCHOOL SNOB.
KEEP TALKING TO ME LIKE THAT AND WE'LL SEE IF SOME RUBBLE DOESN'T FALL ON YOU...
AH, THERE WE GO. LOOKS LIKE WOLVERINE GIRL GOT A LITTLE SMUSHED...
GGAAHHH!
SHNK

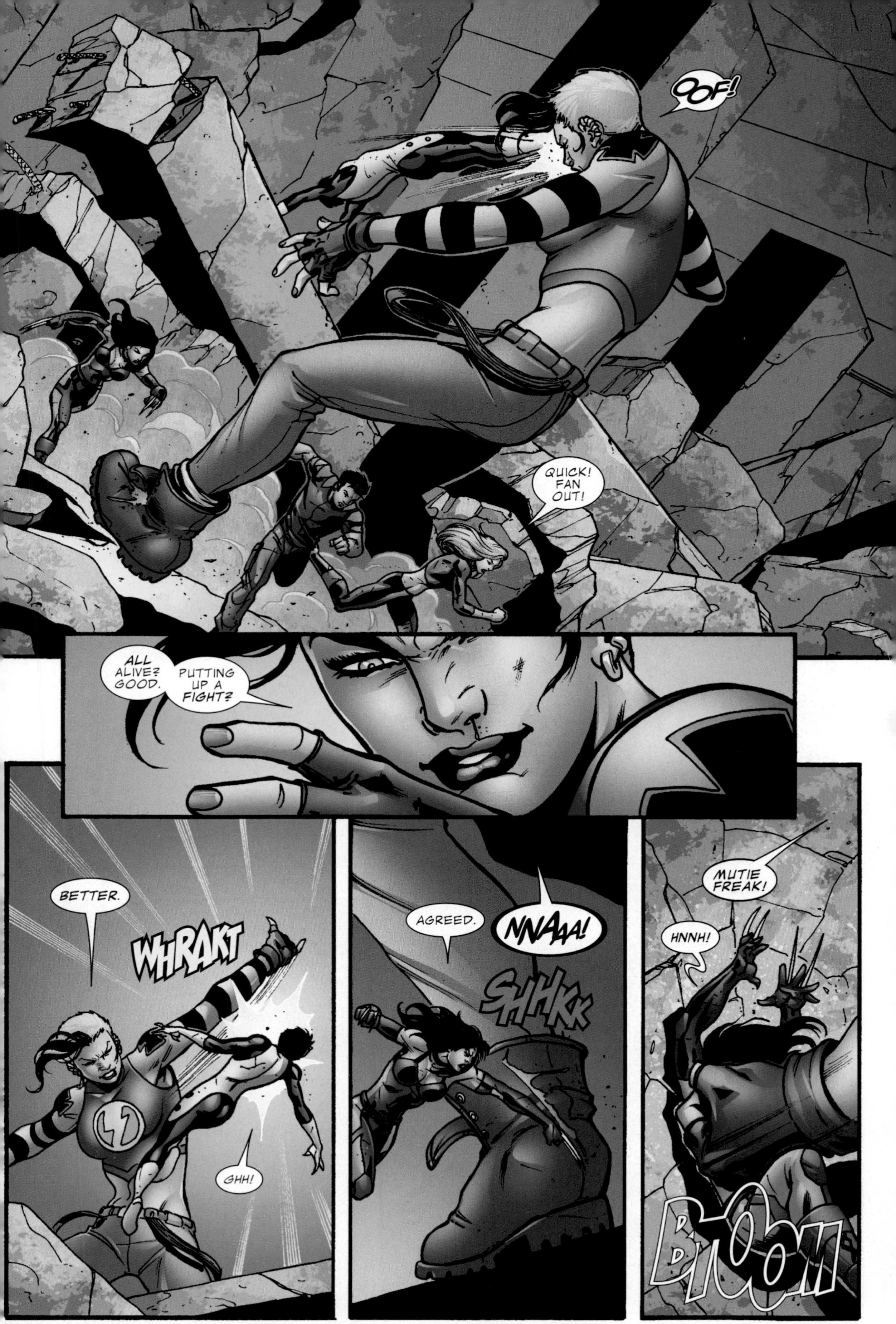

OOF!
QUICK! FAN OUT!
ALL ALIVE? GOOD.
PUTTING UP A FIGHT?
BETTER.
WHRAKT
GHH!
AGREED.
NNAAA!
SHHKK
MUTIE FREAK!
HNNH!
BOOOM

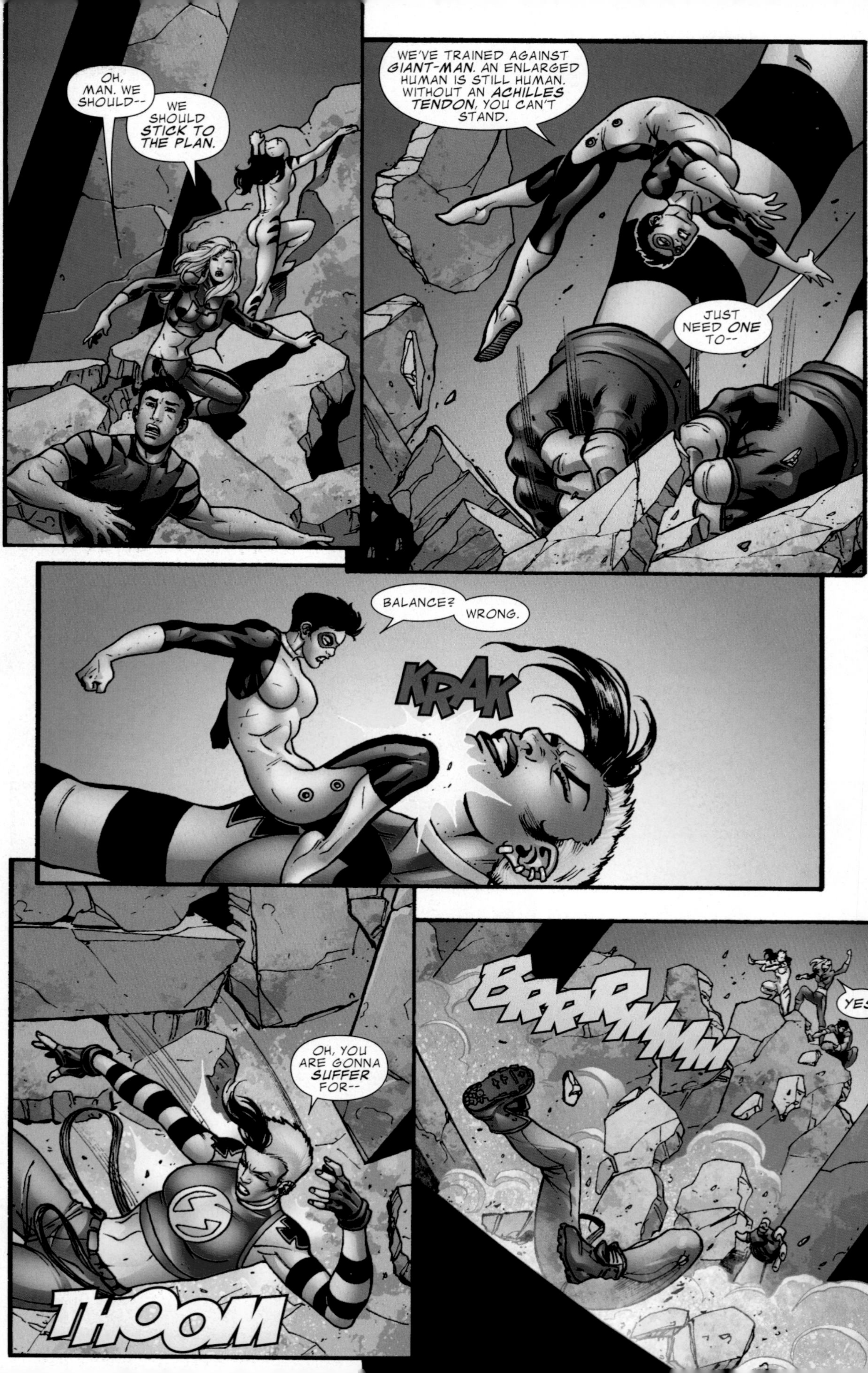
OH, MAN. WE SHOULD--
WE SHOULD STICK TO THE PLAN.
WE'VE TRAINED AGAINST GIANT-MAN. AN ENLARGED HUMAN IS STILL HUMAN. WITHOUT AN ACHILLES TENDON, YOU CAN'T STAND.
JUST NEED ONE TO--
BALANCE?
WRONG.
KRAK
OH, YOU ARE GONNA SUFFER FOR--
THOOM
BRRRMMMM
YES!

IS SHE DEAD?

SHE'S BREATHING.

WHAT IF HER SKULL'S *FRACTURED?*

I AM NOT CONCERNED ABOUT OUR ENEMY JUST NOW. *LAURA!* YOU'RE--

I--÷KFF÷-- WILL BE OKAY.

THIS IS BAD. WE HAVE TO GET *OUT...*

NO. I...I THINK THAT'S WHAT BRIGGS WILL EXPECT. HE'LL HAVE SECURITY MEASURES IN PLACE, AND WHEN HE RELEASES HIS POWER-NEUTRALIZING NANOBOTS, THE WHOLE *WORLD'S* IN TROUBLE.

WE NEED TO GET OUR POWERS *BACK.* STOP HIM.

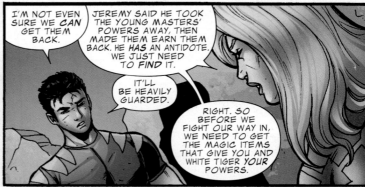

I'M NOT EVEN SURE WE *CAN* GET THEM BACK.

JEREMY SAID HE TOOK THE YOUNG MASTERS' POWERS AWAY, THEN MADE THEM EARN THEM BACK. HE *HAS* AN ANTIDOTE. WE JUST NEED TO *FIND* IT.

IT'LL BE HEAVILY GUARDED.

RIGHT. SO BEFORE WE FIGHT OUR WAY IN, WE NEED TO GET THE MAGIC ITEMS THAT GIVE YOU AND WHITE TIGER *YOUR* POWERS.

THEY THINK WE'RE DEAD. WHEN THEY FIND OUT WE'RE NOT, THEY'LL EXPECT US TO RUN. BUT INSTEAD...

WE'RE GOING *DIE HARD* ON THESE JERKS.

KEN, YOU'RE SO... *SOFT*.

NOT WHAT A GUY WANTS TO HEAR.

SORRY. I JUST MEANT... AFTER ALL THIS TIME, TO ACTUALLY GET TO *TOUCH* YOU...

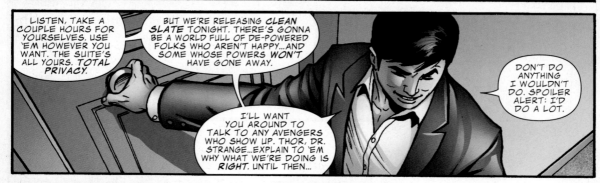

NO NEED TO THANK ME. JUST HELP ME SAVE THE WORLD AND WE'LL CALL IT EVEN.

JEREMY. I ALMOST--

FORGOT I WAS HERE? I'M NOT SURPRISED. THIS HAS BEEN A LONG TIME COMING FOR YOU TWO.

LISTEN, TAKE A COUPLE HOURS FOR YOURSELVES. USE 'EM HOWEVER YOU WANT. THE SUITE'S ALL YOURS. *TOTAL PRIVACY*.

BUT WE'RE RELEASING *CLEAN SLATE* TONIGHT. THERE'S GONNA BE A WORLD FULL OF DE-POWERED FOLKS WHO AREN'T HAPPY...AND SOME WHOSE POWERS *WON'T* HAVE GONE AWAY.

I'LL WANT YOU AROUND TO TALK TO ANY AVENGERS WHO SHOW UP. THOR, DR. STRANGE...EXPLAIN TO 'EM WHY WHAT WE'RE DOING IS *RIGHT*. UNTIL THEN...

DON'T DO ANYTHING I WOULDN'T DO. SPOILER ALERT: I'D DO A LOT.

WAIT. OUR FRIENDS--

NO WORD YET. THEY'LL GET MEDICAL ATTENTION. I'M SURE THEY'LL BE FINE. ALTHOUGH I STILL CAN'T BELIEVE THEY'RE SO *BRAINWASHED* THEY'D RISK THEIR OWN LIVES.

LOOK, JENNY, PUT IT OUT OF YOUR MIND. WHEN I KNOW SOMETHING, YOU'LL KNOW. BUT THIS IS *YOUR* MOMENT. MAKE THE MOST OF IT.

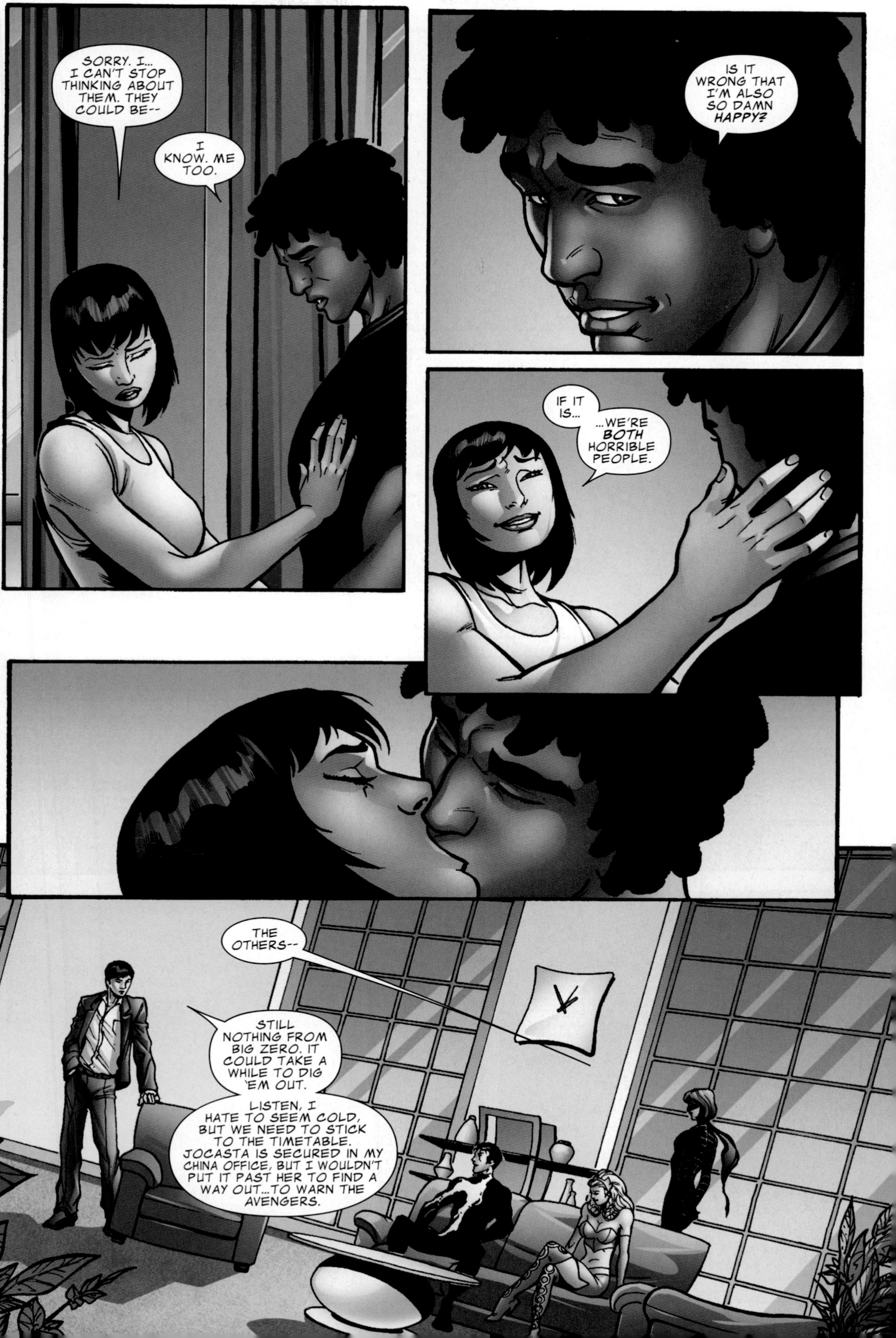
SORRY. I... I CAN'T STOP THINKING ABOUT THEM. THEY COULD BE--
I KNOW. ME TOO.
IS IT WRONG THAT I'M ALSO SO DAMN HAPPY?
IF IT IS...
...WE'RE BOTH HORRIBLE PEOPLE.
THE OTHERS--
STILL NOTHING FROM BIG ZERO. IT COULD TAKE A WHILE TO DIG 'EM OUT.
LISTEN, I HATE TO SEEM COLD, BUT WE NEED TO STICK TO THE TIMETABLE. JOCASTA IS SECURED IN MY CHINA OFFICE, BUT I WOULDN'T PUT IT PAST HER TO FIND A WAY OUT...TO WARN THE AVENGERS.

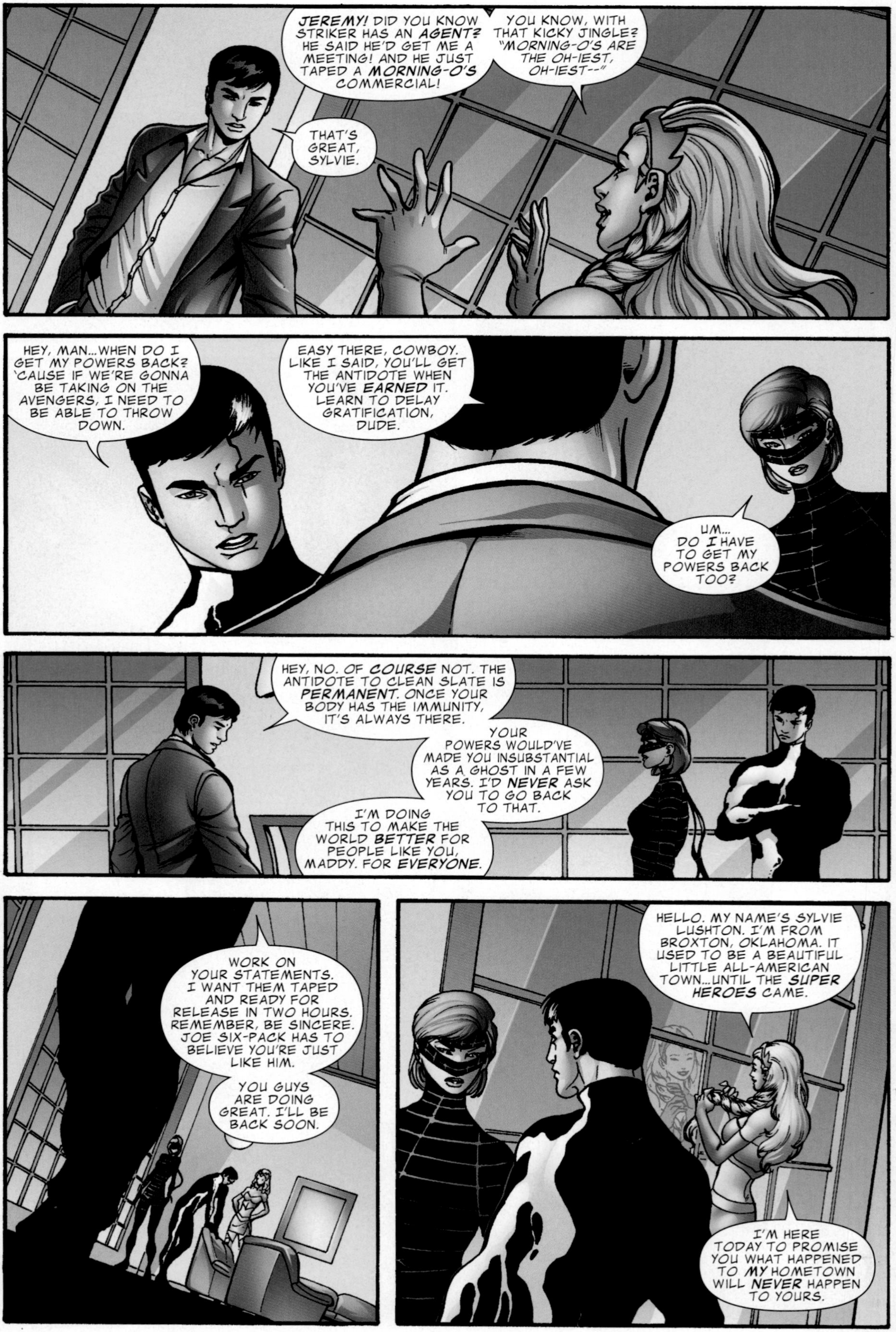
JEREMY! DID YOU KNOW STRIKER HAS AN AGENT? HE SAID HE'D GET ME A MEETING! AND HE JUST TAPED A MORNING-O'S COMMERCIAL!
YOU KNOW, WITH THAT KICKY JINGLE? "MORNING-O'S ARE THE OH-IEST, OH-IEST--"
THAT'S GREAT, SYLVIE.
HEY, MAN...WHEN DO I GET MY POWERS BACK? 'CAUSE IF WE'RE GONNA BE TAKING ON THE AVENGERS, I NEED TO BE ABLE TO THROW DOWN.
EASY THERE, COWBOY. LIKE I SAID, YOU'LL GET THE ANTIDOTE WHEN YOU'VE EARNED IT. LEARN TO DELAY GRATIFICATION, DUDE.
UM... DO I HAVE TO GET MY POWERS BACK TOO?
HEY, NO. OF COURSE NOT. THE ANTIDOTE TO CLEAN SLATE IS PERMANENT. ONCE YOUR BODY HAS THE IMMUNITY, IT'S ALWAYS THERE.
YOUR POWERS WOULD'VE MADE YOU INSUBSTANTIAL AS A GHOST IN A FEW YEARS. I'D NEVER ASK YOU TO GO BACK TO THAT.
I'M DOING THIS TO MAKE THE WORLD BETTER FOR PEOPLE LIKE YOU, MADDY. FOR EVERYONE.
WORK ON YOUR STATEMENTS. I WANT THEM TAPED AND READY FOR RELEASE IN TWO HOURS. REMEMBER, BE SINCERE. JOE SIX-PACK HAS TO BELIEVE YOU'RE JUST LIKE HIM.
YOU GUYS ARE DOING GREAT. I'LL BE BACK SOON.
HELLO. MY NAME'S SYLVIE LUSHTON. I'M FROM BROXTON, OKLAHOMA. IT USED TO BE A BEAUTIFUL LITTLE ALL-AMERICAN TOWN...UNTIL THE SUPER HEROES CAME.
I'M HERE TODAY TO PROMISE YOU WHAT HAPPENED TO MY HOMETOWN WILL NEVER HAPPEN TO YOURS.

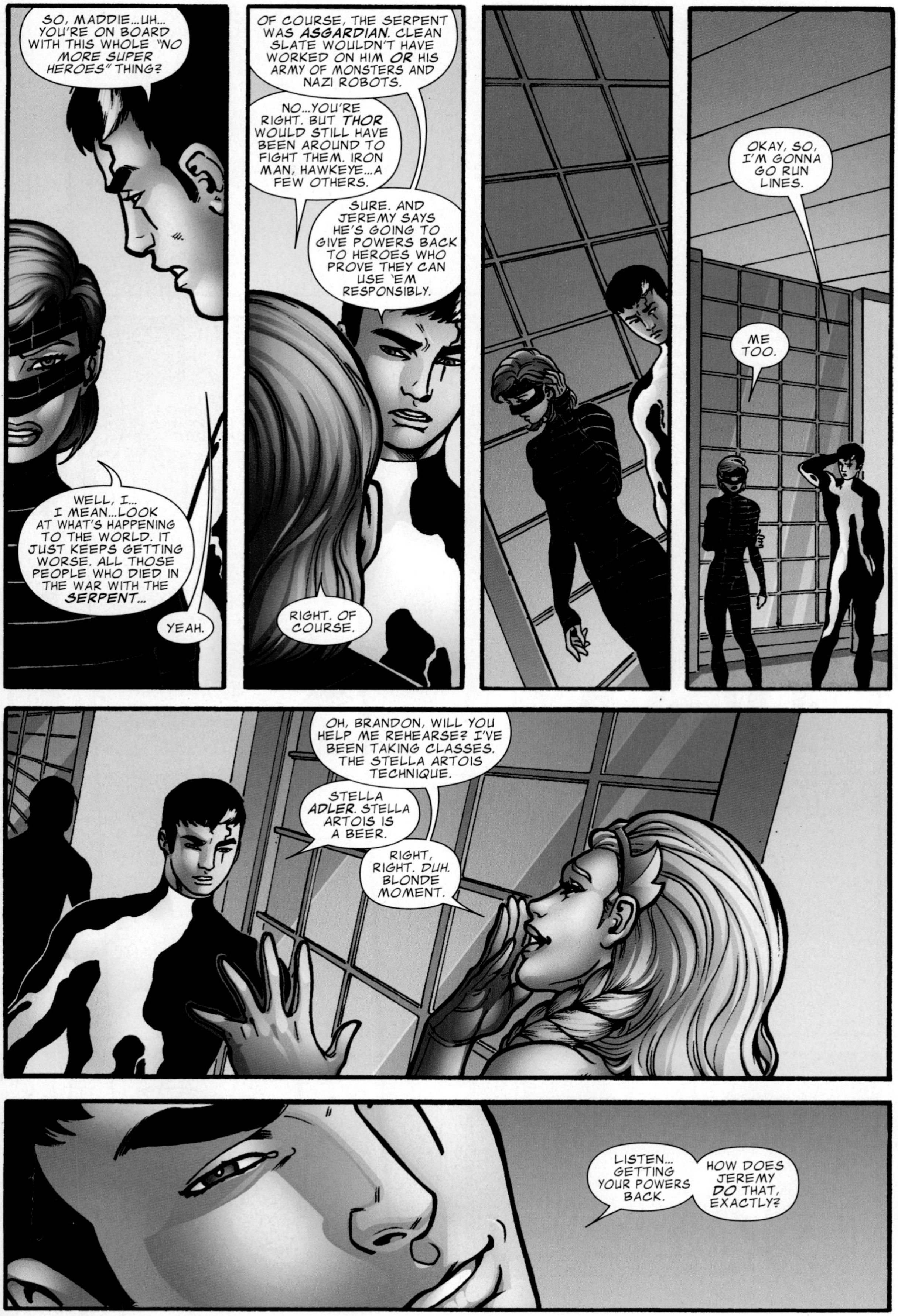
SO, MADDIE...UH... YOU'RE ON BOARD WITH THIS WHOLE "NO MORE SUPER HEROES" THING?
WELL, I... I MEAN...LOOK AT WHAT'S HAPPENING TO THE WORLD. IT JUST KEEPS GETTING WORSE. ALL THOSE PEOPLE WHO DIED IN THE WAR WITH THE SERPENT...
YEAH.
OF COURSE, THE SERPENT WAS ASGARDIAN. CLEAN SLATE WOULDN'T HAVE WORKED ON HIM OR HIS ARMY OF MONSTERS AND NAZI ROBOTS.
NO...YOU'RE RIGHT. BUT THOR WOULD STILL HAVE BEEN AROUND TO FIGHT THEM. IRON MAN, HAWKEYE...A FEW OTHERS.
SURE. AND JEREMY SAYS HE'S GOING TO GIVE POWERS BACK TO HEROES WHO PROVE THEY CAN USE 'EM RESPONSIBLY.
RIGHT. OF COURSE.
OKAY, SO, I'M GONNA GO RUN LINES.
ME TOO.
OH, BRANDON, WILL YOU HELP ME REHEARSE? I'VE BEEN TAKING CLASSES. THE STELLA ARTOIS TECHNIQUE.
STELLA ADLER. STELLA ARTOIS IS A BEER.
RIGHT, RIGHT. DUH. BLONDE MOMENT.
LISTEN... GETTING YOUR POWERS BACK.
HOW DOES JEREMY DO THAT, EXACTLY?

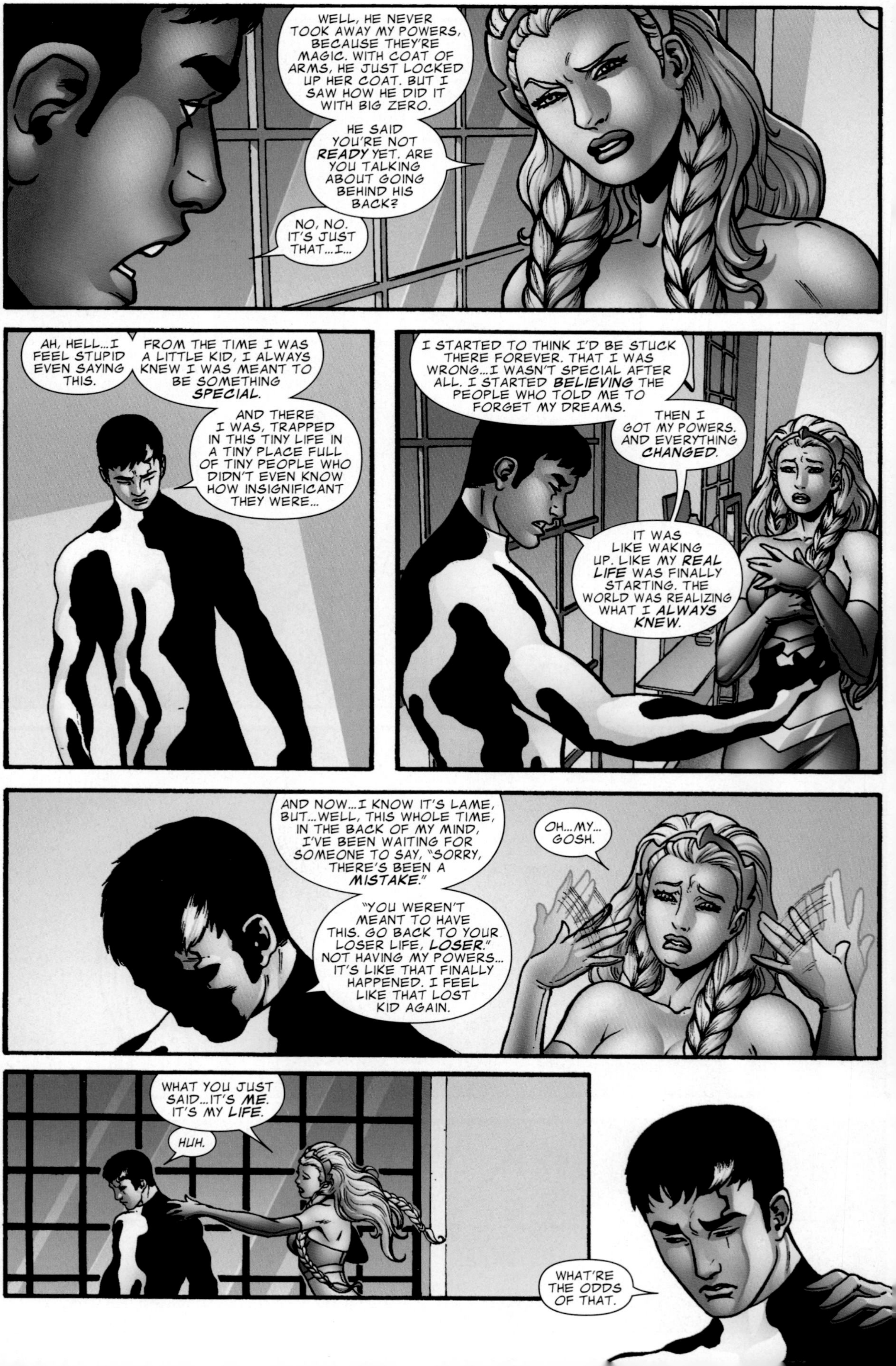
WELL, HE NEVER TOOK AWAY MY POWERS, BECAUSE THEY'RE MAGIC. WITH COAT OF ARMS, HE JUST LOCKED UP HER COAT. BUT I SAW HOW HE DID IT WITH BIG ZERO.
HE SAID YOU'RE NOT READY YET. ARE YOU TALKING ABOUT GOING BEHIND HIS BACK?
NO, NO. IT'S JUST THAT...I...
AH, HELL...I FEEL STUPID EVEN SAYING THIS.
FROM THE TIME I WAS A LITTLE KID, I ALWAYS KNEW I WAS MEANT TO BE SOMETHING SPECIAL.
AND THERE I WAS, TRAPPED IN THIS TINY LIFE IN A TINY PLACE FULL OF TINY PEOPLE WHO DIDN'T EVEN KNOW HOW INSIGNIFICANT THEY WERE...
I STARTED TO THINK I'D BE STUCK THERE FOREVER. THAT I WAS WRONG...I WASN'T SPECIAL AFTER ALL. I STARTED BELIEVING THE PEOPLE WHO TOLD ME TO FORGET MY DREAMS.
THEN I GOT MY POWERS. AND EVERYTHING CHANGED.
IT WAS LIKE WAKING UP. LIKE MY REAL LIFE WAS FINALLY STARTING. THE WORLD WAS REALIZING WHAT I ALWAYS KNEW.
AND NOW...I KNOW IT'S LAME, BUT...WELL, THIS WHOLE TIME, IN THE BACK OF MY MIND, I'VE BEEN WAITING FOR SOMEONE TO SAY, "SORRY, THERE'S BEEN A MISTAKE."
"YOU WEREN'T MEANT TO HAVE THIS. GO BACK TO YOUR LOSER LIFE, LOSER." NOT HAVING MY POWERS... IT'S LIKE THAT FINALLY HAPPENED. I FEEL LIKE THAT LOST KID AGAIN.
OH...MY... GOSH.
WHAT YOU JUST SAID...IT'S ME. IT'S MY LIFE.
HUH.
WHAT'RE THE ODDS OF THAT.

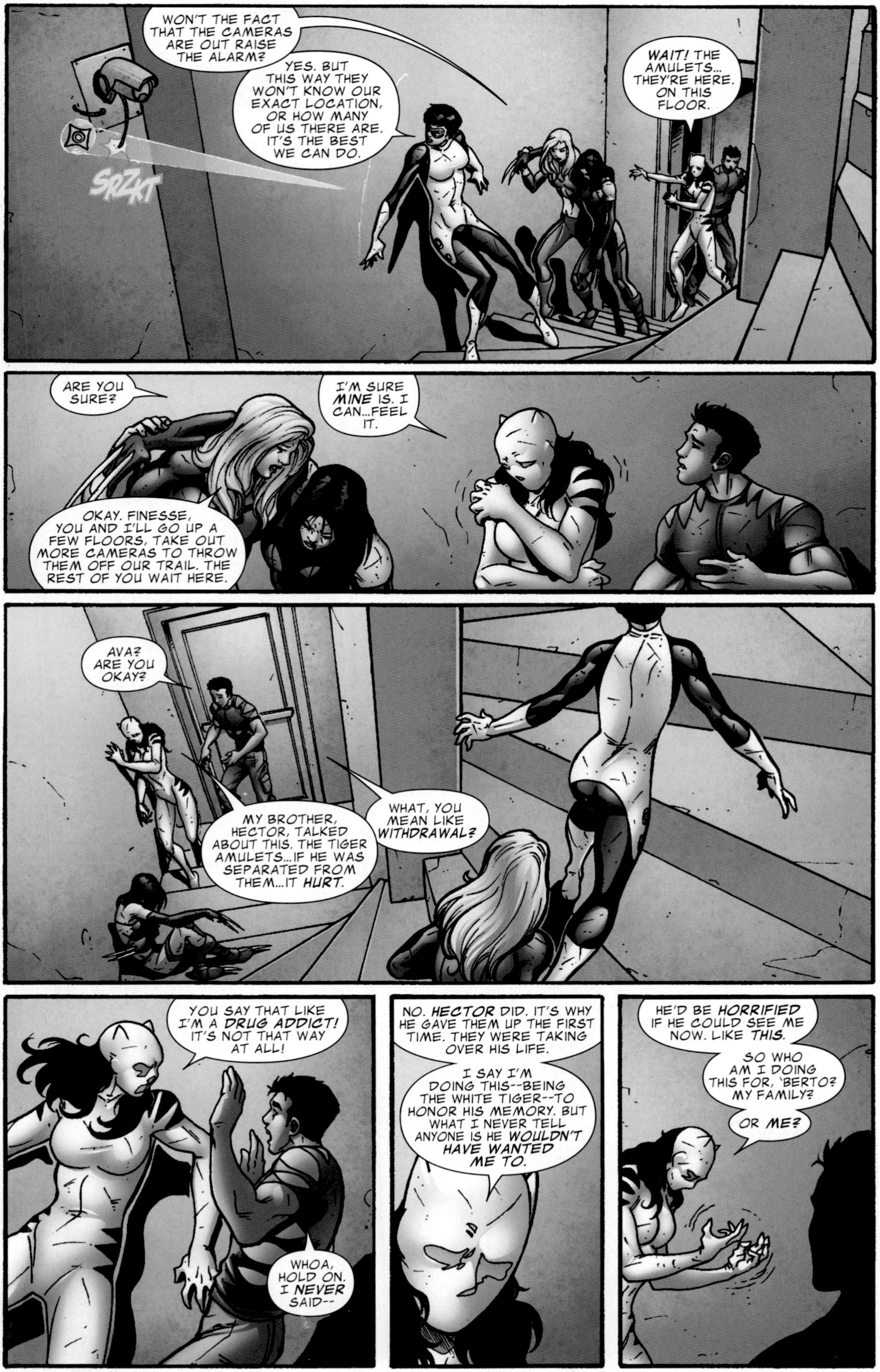
WON'T THE FACT THAT THE CAMERAS ARE OUT RAISE THE ALARM?
YES. BUT THIS WAY THEY WON'T KNOW OUR EXACT LOCATION, OR HOW MANY OF US THERE ARE. IT'S THE BEST WE CAN DO.
SRZKT
WAIT! THE AMULETS... THEY'RE HERE. ON THIS FLOOR.
ARE YOU SURE?
I'M SURE MINE IS. I CAN...FEEL IT.
OKAY. FINESSE, YOU AND I'LL GO UP A FEW FLOORS, TAKE OUT MORE CAMERAS TO THROW THEM OFF OUR TRAIL. THE REST OF YOU WAIT HERE.
AVA? ARE YOU OKAY?
MY BROTHER, HECTOR, TALKED ABOUT THIS. THE TIGER AMULETS...IF HE WAS SEPARATED FROM THEM...IT HURT.
WHAT, YOU MEAN LIKE WITHDRAWAL?
YOU SAY THAT LIKE I'M A DRUG ADDICT! IT'S NOT THAT WAY AT ALL!
WHOA, HOLD ON. I NEVER SAID--
NO. HECTOR DID. IT'S WHY HE GAVE THEM UP THE FIRST TIME. THEY WERE TAKING OVER HIS LIFE.
I SAY I'M DOING THIS--BEING THE WHITE TIGER--TO HONOR HIS MEMORY. BUT WHAT I NEVER TELL ANYONE IS HE WOULDN'T HAVE WANTED ME TO.
HE'D BE HORRIFIED IF HE COULD SEE ME NOW. LIKE THIS.
SO WHO AM I DOING THIS FOR, 'BERTO? MY FAMILY?
OR ME?

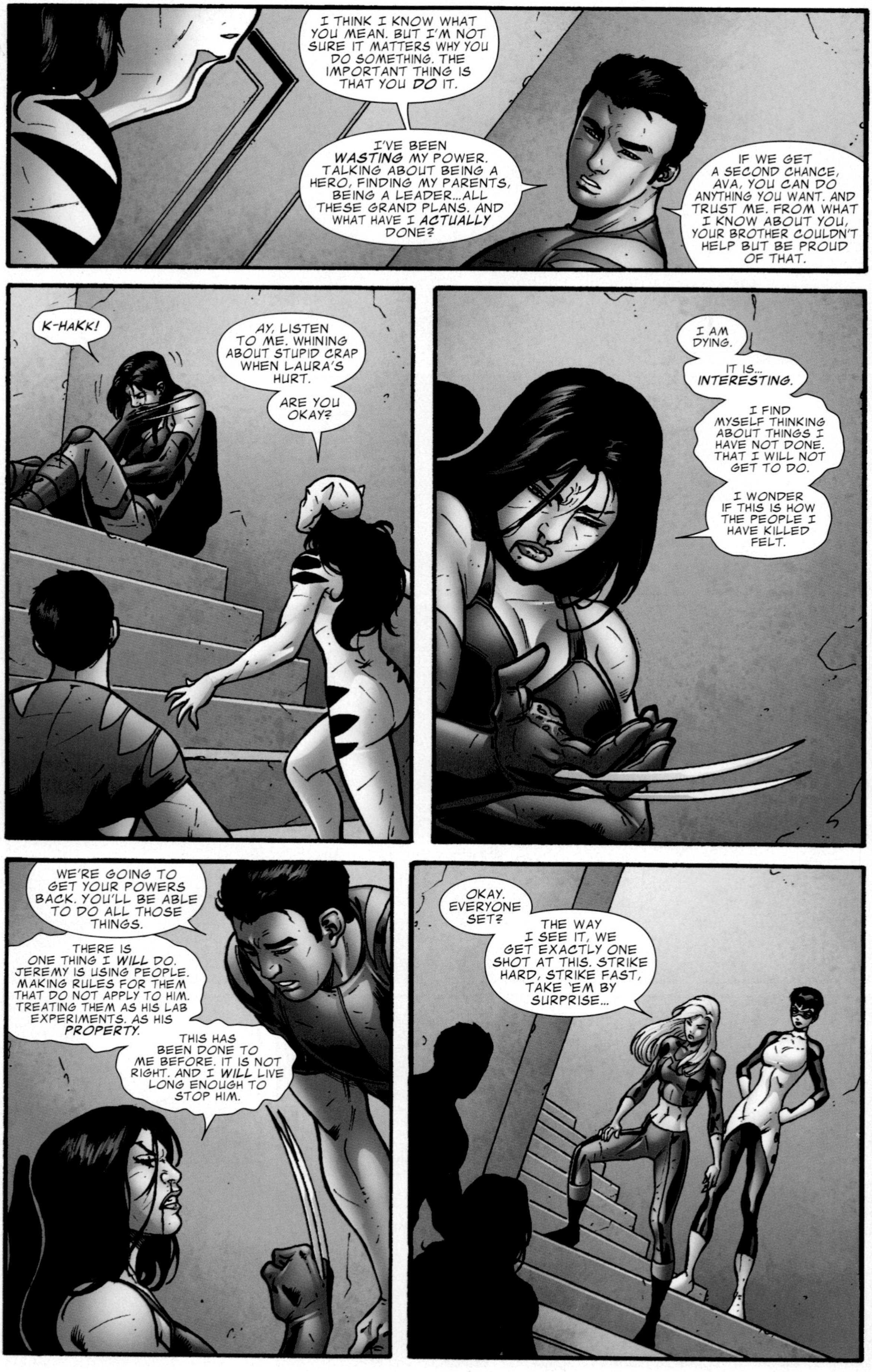

I THINK I KNOW WHAT YOU MEAN. BUT I'M NOT SURE IT MATTERS WHY YOU DO SOMETHING. THE IMPORTANT THING IS THAT YOU DO IT.
I'VE BEEN WASTING MY POWER. TALKING ABOUT BEING A HERO, FINDING MY PARENTS, BEING A LEADER...ALL THESE GRAND PLANS. AND WHAT HAVE I ACTUALLY DONE?
IF WE GET A SECOND CHANCE, AVA, YOU CAN DO ANYTHING YOU WANT. AND TRUST ME. FROM WHAT I KNOW ABOUT YOU, YOUR BROTHER COULDN'T HELP BUT BE PROUD OF THAT.
K-HAKK!
AY, LISTEN TO ME. WHINING ABOUT STUPID CRAP WHEN LAURA'S HURT.
ARE YOU OKAY?
I AM DYING.
IT IS... INTERESTING.
I FIND MYSELF THINKING ABOUT THINGS I HAVE NOT DONE. THAT I WILL NOT GET TO DO.
I WONDER IF THIS IS HOW THE PEOPLE I HAVE KILLED FELT.
WE'RE GOING TO GET YOUR POWERS BACK. YOU'LL BE ABLE TO DO ALL THOSE THINGS.
THERE IS ONE THING I WILL DO. JEREMY IS USING PEOPLE. MAKING RULES FOR THEM THAT DO NOT APPLY TO HIM. TREATING THEM AS HIS LAB EXPERIMENTS. AS HIS PROPERTY.
THIS HAS BEEN DONE TO ME BEFORE. IT IS NOT RIGHT. AND I WILL LIVE LONG ENOUGH TO STOP HIM.
OKAY. EVERYONE SET?
THE WAY I SEE IT, WE GET EXACTLY ONE SHOT AT THIS. STRIKE HARD, STRIKE FAST, TAKE 'EM BY SURPRISE...

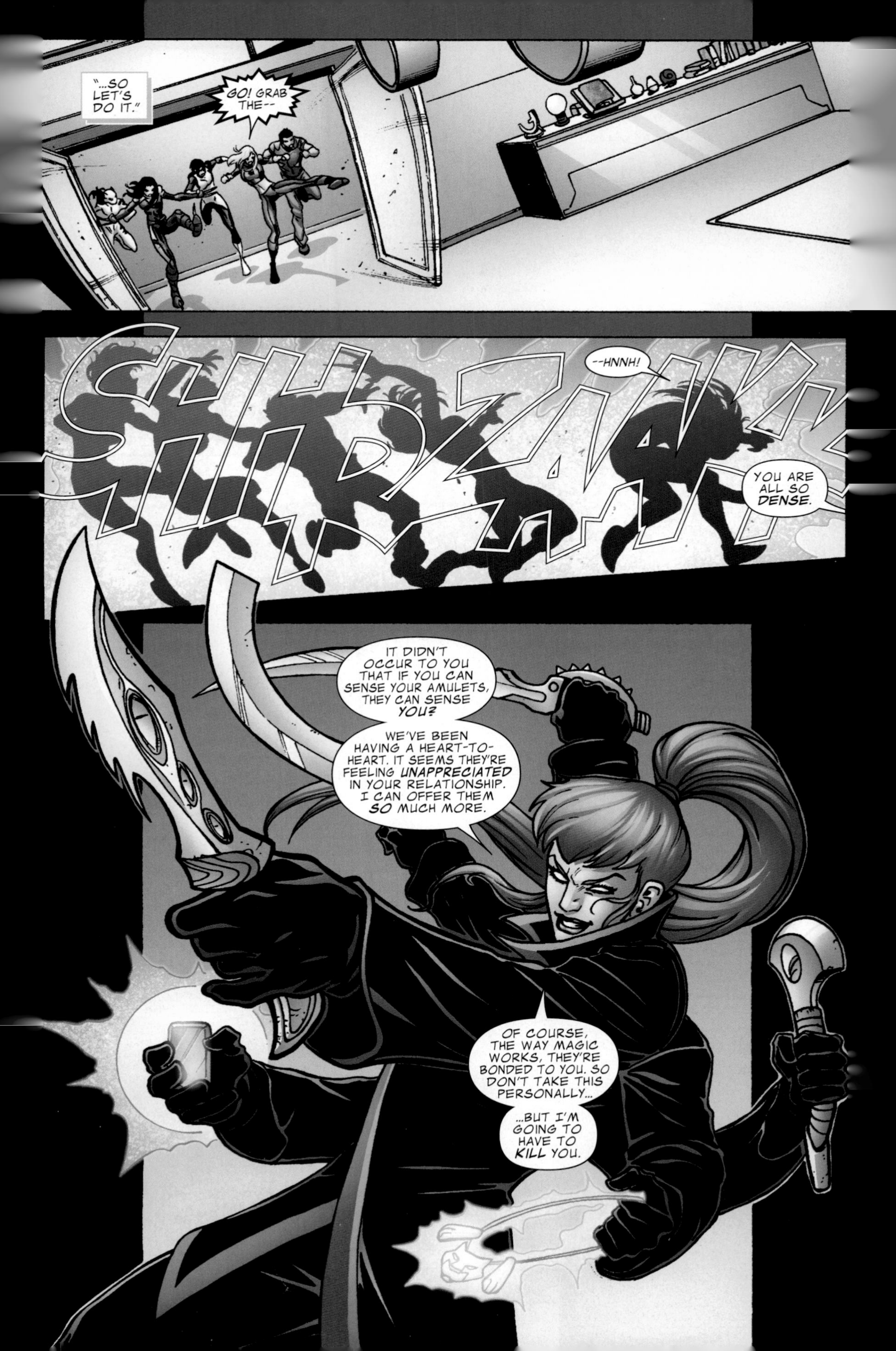
"...SO LET'S DO IT."
GO! GRAB THE--
SHHRZAAKK
--HNNH!
YOU ARE ALL SO DENSE.
IT DIDN'T OCCUR TO YOU THAT IF YOU CAN SENSE YOUR AMULETS, THEY CAN SENSE YOU?
WE'VE BEEN HAVING A HEART-TO-HEART. IT SEEMS THEY'RE FEELING UNAPPRECIATED IN YOUR RELATIONSHIP. I CAN OFFER THEM SO MUCH MORE.
OF COURSE, THE WAY MAGIC WORKS, THEY'RE BONDED TO YOU. SO DON'T TAKE THIS PERSONALLY...
...BUT I'M GOING TO HAVE TO KILL YOU.

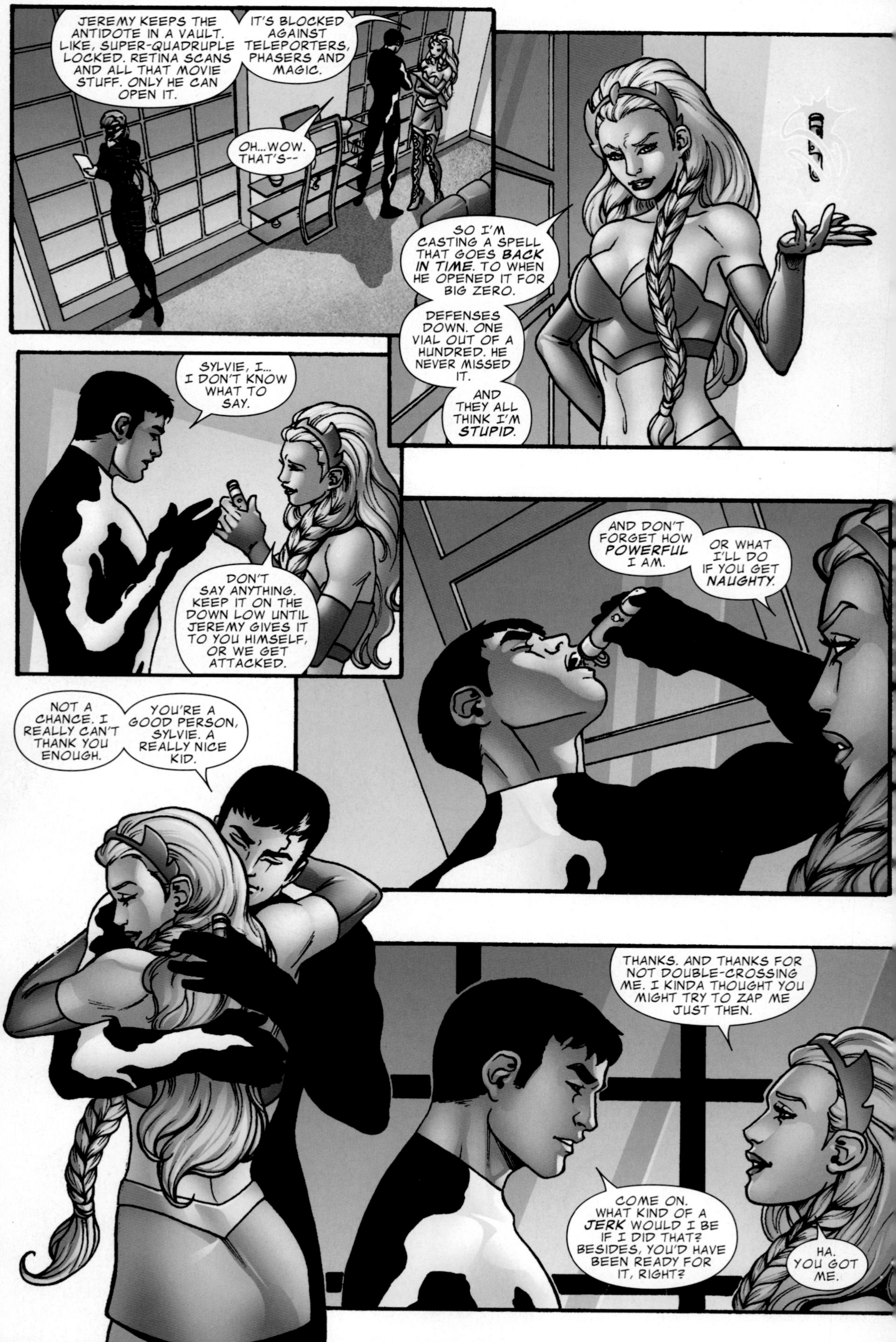
JEREMY KEEPS THE ANTIDOTE IN A VAULT. LIKE, SUPER-QUADRUPLE LOCKED. RETINA SCANS AND ALL THAT MOVIE STUFF. ONLY HE CAN OPEN IT.
IT'S BLOCKED AGAINST TELEPORTERS, PHASERS AND MAGIC.
OH...WOW. THAT'S--
SO I'M CASTING A SPELL THAT GOES BACK IN TIME. TO WHEN HE OPENED IT FOR BIG ZERO.
DEFENSES DOWN. ONE VIAL OUT OF A HUNDRED. HE NEVER MISSED IT.
AND THEY ALL THINK I'M STUPID.
SYLVIE, I... I DON'T KNOW WHAT TO SAY.
DON'T SAY ANYTHING. KEEP IT ON THE DOWN LOW UNTIL JEREMY GIVES IT TO YOU HIMSELF, OR WE GET ATTACKED.
AND DON'T FORGET HOW POWERFUL I AM.
OR WHAT I'LL DO IF YOU GET NAUGHTY.
NOT A CHANCE. I REALLY CAN'T THANK YOU ENOUGH.
YOU'RE A GOOD PERSON, SYLVIE. A REALLY NICE KID.
THANKS. AND THANKS FOR NOT DOUBLE-CROSSING ME. I KINDA THOUGHT YOU MIGHT TRY TO ZAP ME JUST THEN.
COME ON. WHAT KIND OF A JERK WOULD I BE IF I DID THAT? BESIDES, YOU'D HAVE BEEN READY FOR IT, RIGHT?
HA. YOU GOT ME.

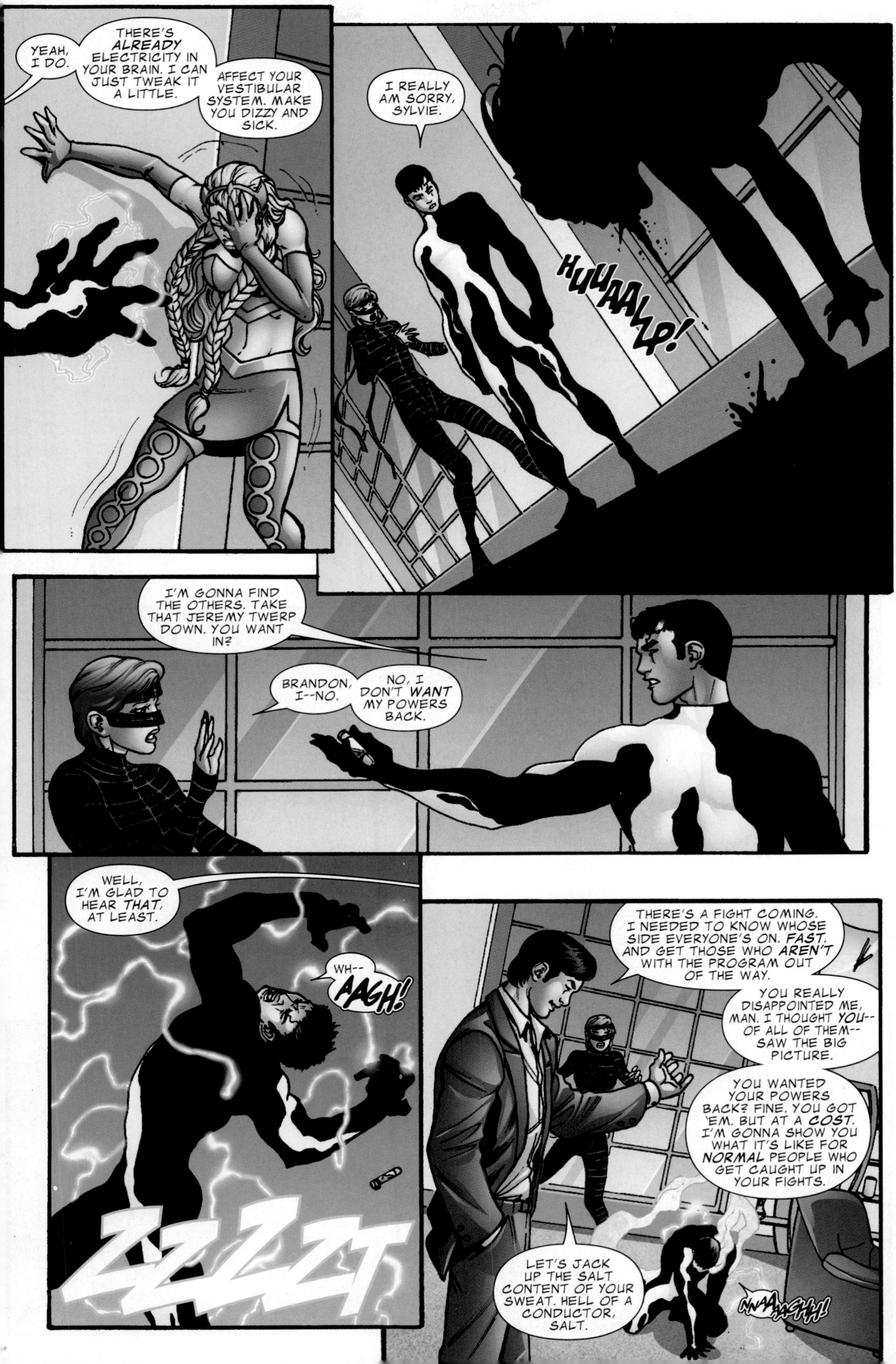
YEAH, I DO.
THERE'S ALREADY ELECTRICITY IN YOUR BRAIN. I CAN JUST TWEAK IT A LITTLE.
AFFECT YOUR VESTIBULAR SYSTEM. MAKE YOU DIZZY AND SICK.
I REALLY AM SORRY, SYLVIE.
HUUAAALP!
I'M GONNA FIND THE OTHERS. TAKE THAT JEREMY TWERP DOWN. YOU WANT IN?
BRANDON, I--NO.
NO, I DON'T WANT MY POWERS BACK.
WELL, I'M GLAD TO HEAR THAT, AT LEAST.
WH--
AAGH!
ZZZZT
THERE'S A FIGHT COMING. I NEEDED TO KNOW WHOSE SIDE EVERYONE'S ON. FAST. AND GET THOSE WHO AREN'T WITH THE PROGRAM OUT OF THE WAY.
YOU REALLY DISAPPOINTED ME, MAN. I THOUGHT YOU-- OF ALL OF THEM-- SAW THE BIG PICTURE.
YOU WANTED YOUR POWERS BACK? FINE. YOU GOT 'EM. BUT AT A COST. I'M GONNA SHOW YOU WHAT IT'S LIKE FOR NORMAL PEOPLE WHO GET CAUGHT UP IN YOUR FIGHTS.
LET'S JACK UP THE SALT CONTENT OF YOUR SWEAT. HELL OF A CONDUCTOR, SALT.
NNAAAAGHH!

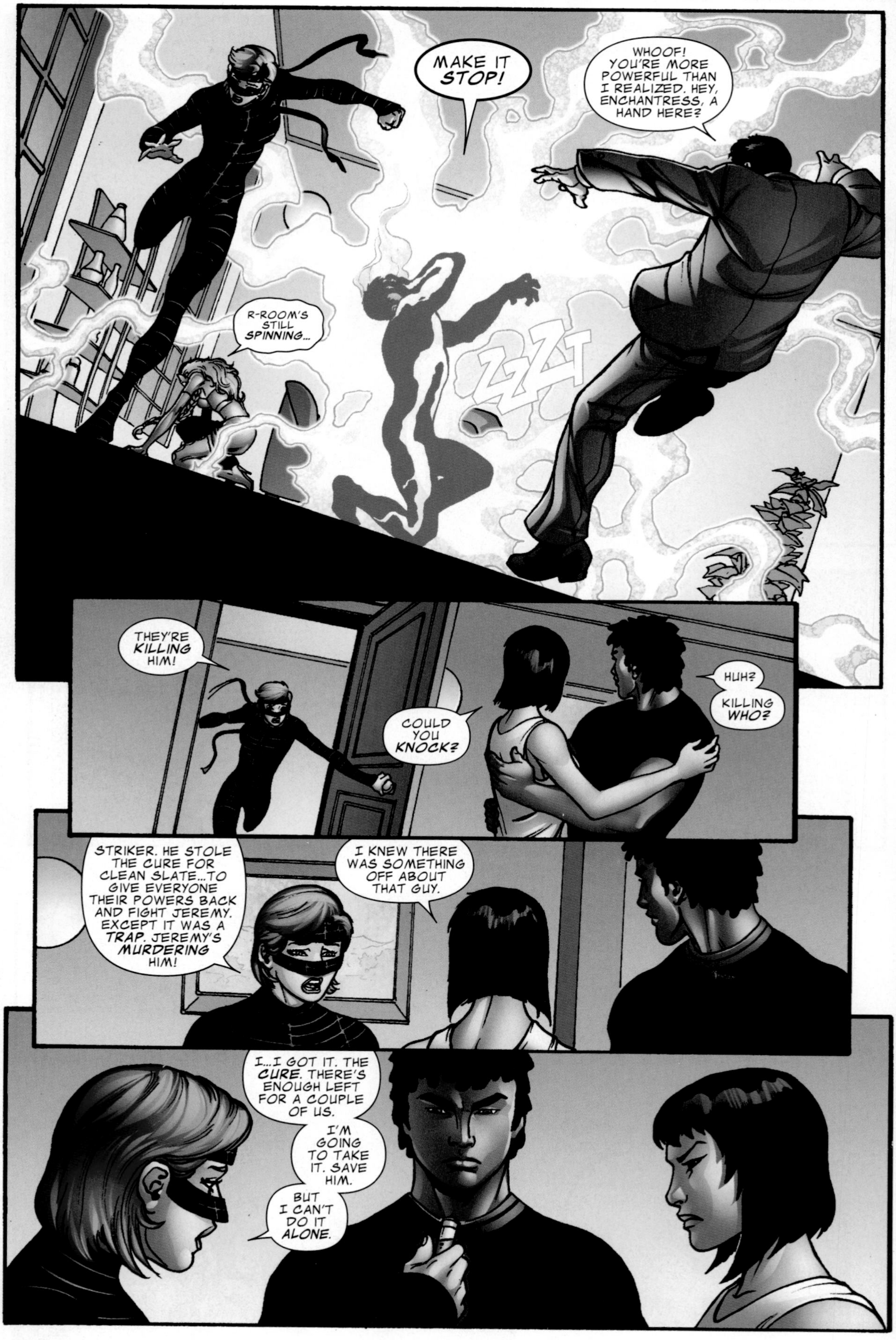
MAKE IT STOP!
WHOOF! YOU'RE MORE POWERFUL THAN I REALIZED. HEY, ENCHANTRESS, A HAND HERE?
R-ROOM'S STILL SPINNING...
ZZZT
THEY'RE KILLING HIM!
COULD YOU KNOCK?
HUH?
KILLING WHO?
STRIKER. HE STOLE THE CURE FOR CLEAN SLATE...TO GIVE EVERYONE THEIR POWERS BACK AND FIGHT JEREMY. EXCEPT IT WAS A TRAP. JEREMY'S MURDERING HIM!
I KNEW THERE WAS SOMETHING OFF ABOUT THAT GUY.
I...I GOT IT. THE CURE. THERE'S ENOUGH LEFT FOR A COUPLE OF US.
I'M GOING TO TAKE IT. SAVE HIM.
BUT I CAN'T DO IT ALONE.

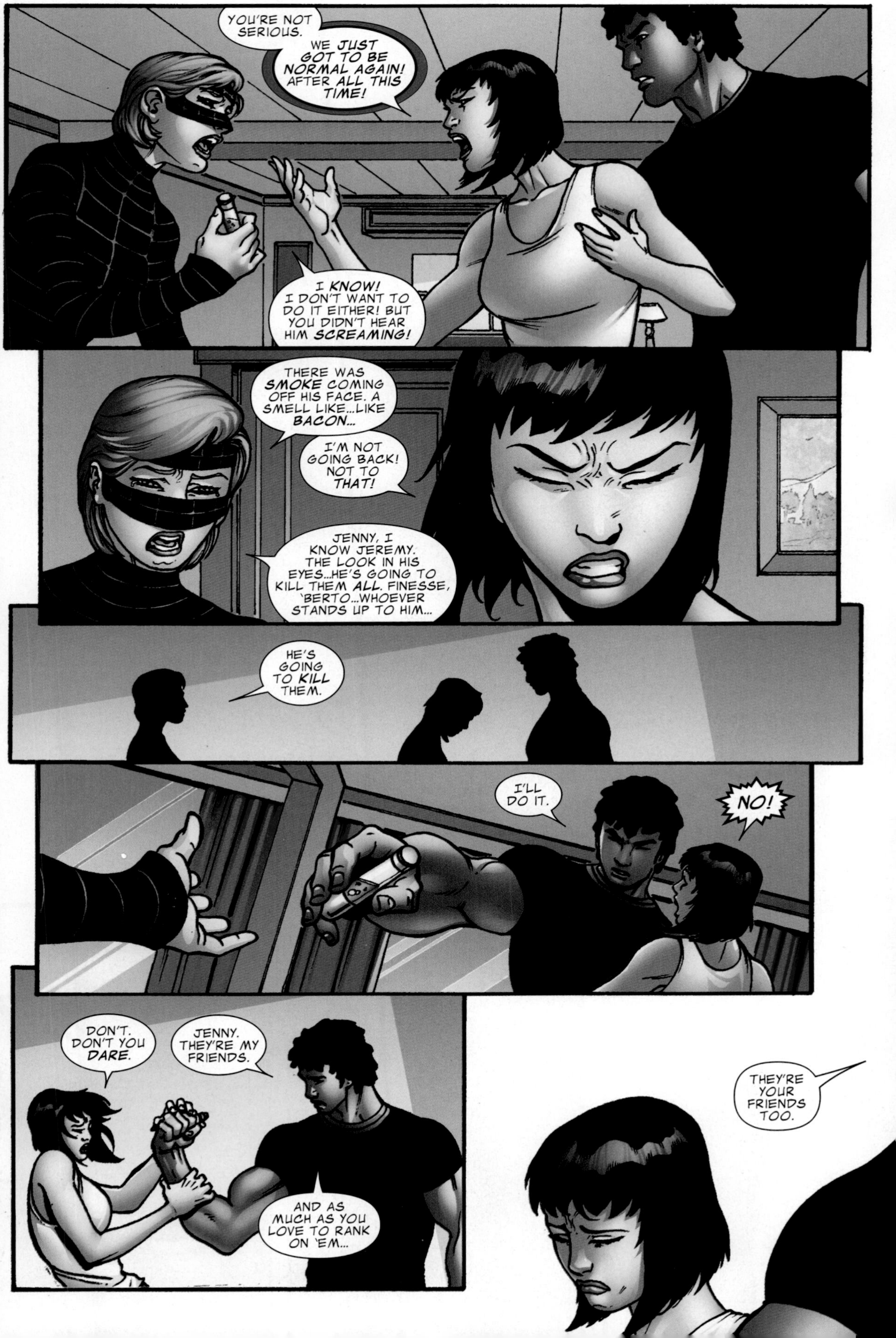
YOU'RE NOT SERIOUS.
WE JUST GOT TO BE NORMAL AGAIN! AFTER ALL THIS TIME!
I KNOW! I DON'T WANT TO DO IT EITHER! BUT YOU DIDN'T HEAR HIM SCREAMING!
THERE WAS SMOKE COMING OFF HIS FACE. A SMELL LIKE...LIKE BACON...
I'M NOT GOING BACK! NOT TO THAT!
JENNY, I KNOW JEREMY. THE LOOK IN HIS EYES...HE'S GOING TO KILL THEM ALL. FINESSE, 'BERTO...WHOEVER STANDS UP TO HIM...
HE'S GOING TO KILL THEM.
I'LL DO IT.
NO!
DON'T. DON'T YOU DARE.
JENNY. THEY'RE MY FRIENDS.
AND AS MUCH AS YOU LOVE TO RANK ON 'EM...
THEY'RE YOUR FRIENDS TOO.

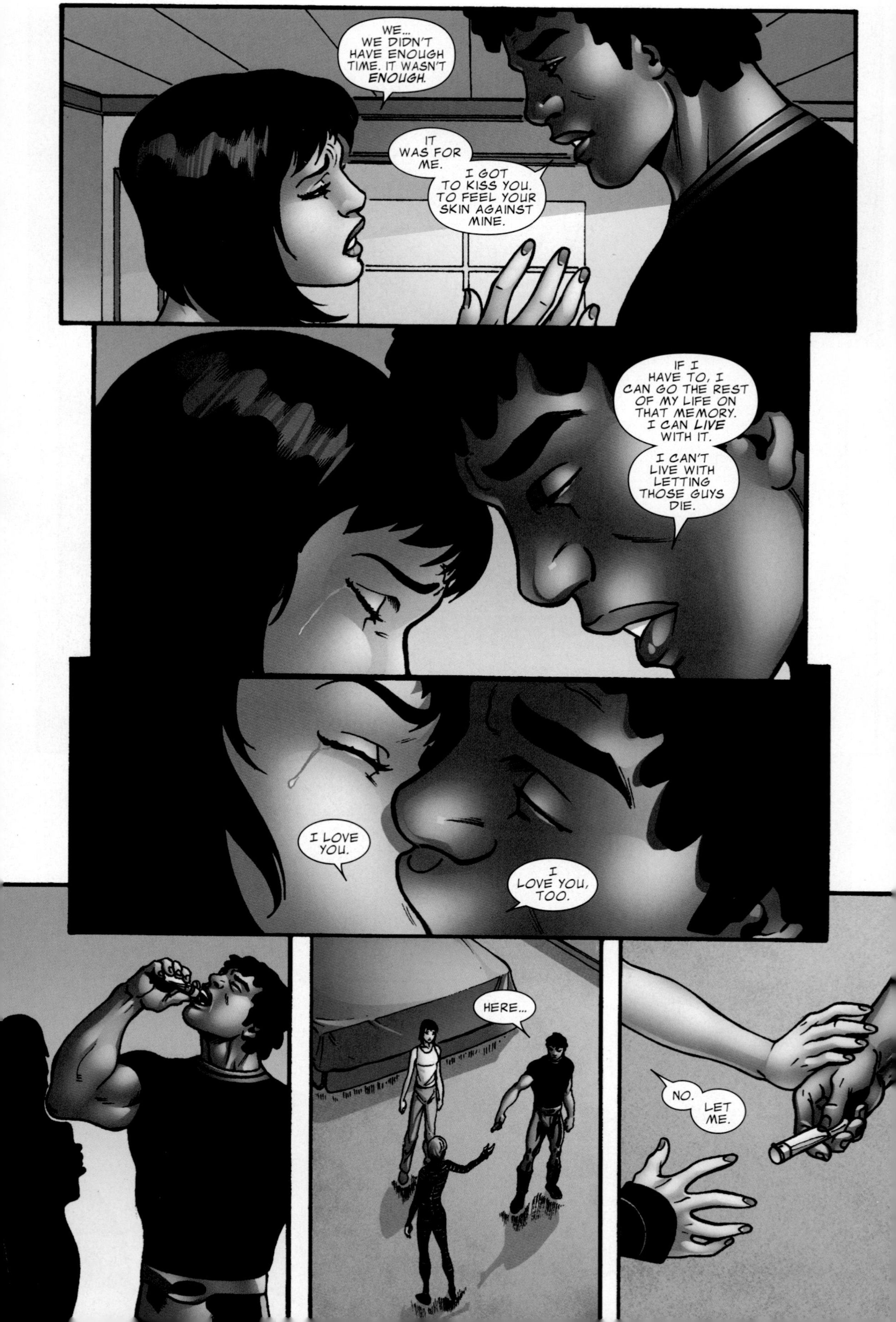
WE... WE DIDN'T HAVE ENOUGH TIME. IT WASN'T ENOUGH.
IT WAS FOR ME.
I GOT TO KISS YOU. TO FEEL YOUR SKIN AGAINST MINE.
IF I HAVE TO, I CAN GO THE REST OF MY LIFE ON THAT MEMORY. I CAN LIVE WITH IT.
I CAN'T LIVE WITH LETTING THOSE GUYS DIE.
I LOVE YOU.
I LOVE YOU, TOO.
HERE...
NO.
LET ME.

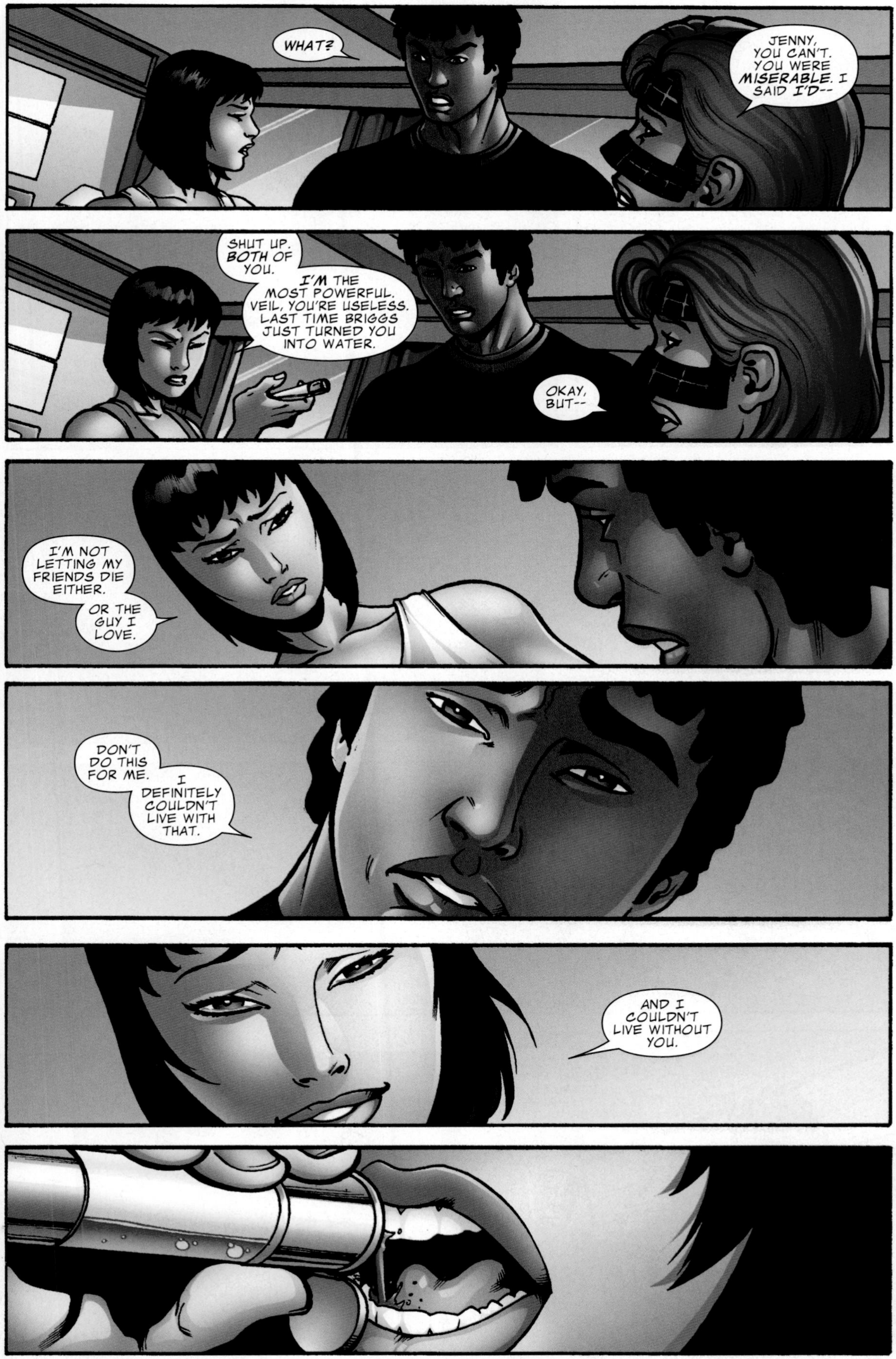
WHAT?
JENNY, YOU CAN'T. YOU WERE MISERABLE. I SAID I'D--
SHUT UP. BOTH OF YOU.
I'M THE MOST POWERFUL. VEIL, YOU'RE USELESS. LAST TIME BRIGGS JUST TURNED YOU INTO WATER.
OKAY, BUT--
I'M NOT LETTING MY FRIENDS DIE EITHER.
OR THE GUY I LOVE.
DON'T DO THIS FOR ME.
I DEFINITELY COULDN'T LIVE WITH THAT.
AND I COULDN'T LIVE WITHOUT YOU.

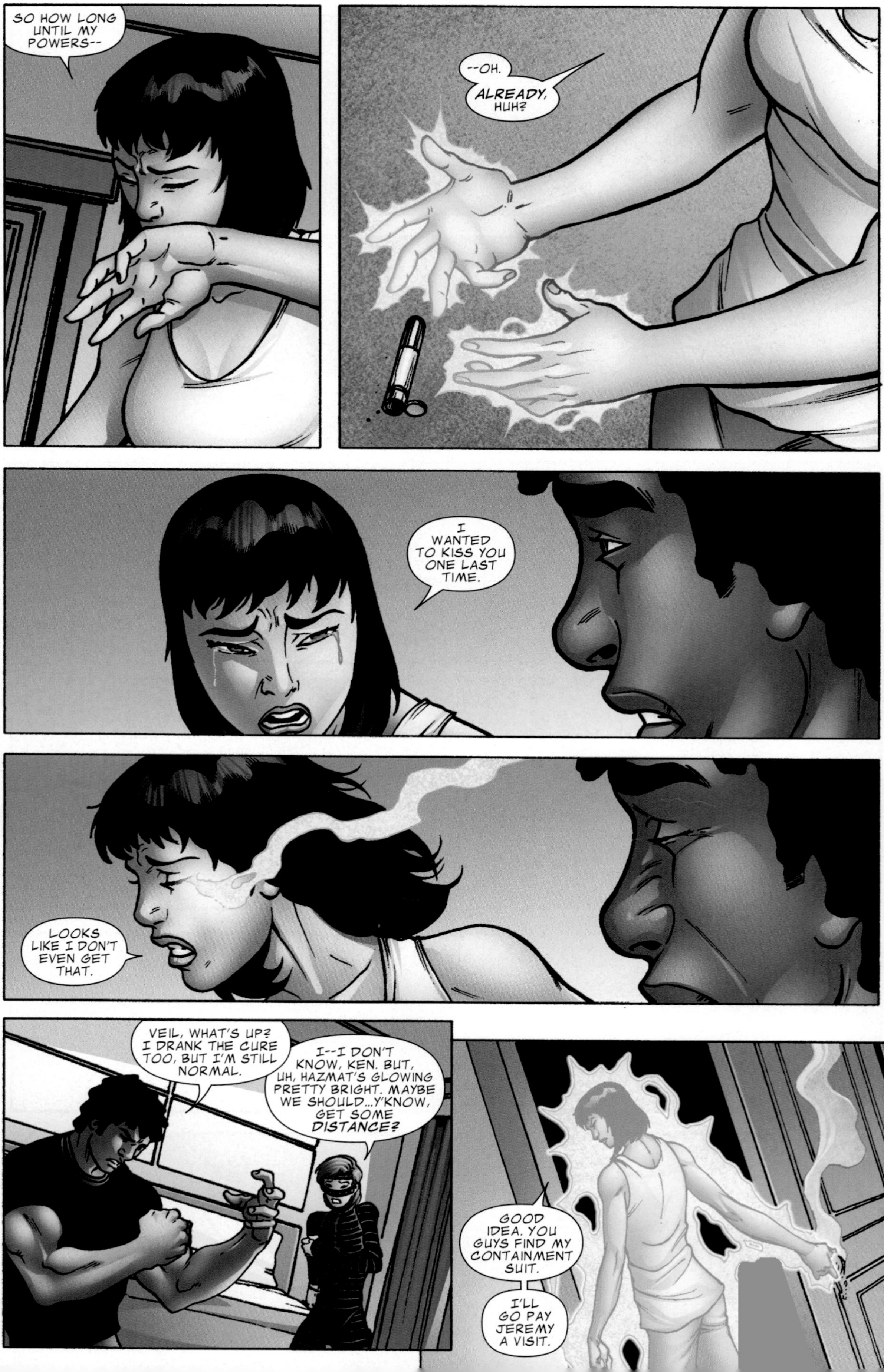
SO HOW LONG UNTIL MY POWERS--
--OH. ALREADY, HUH?
I WANTED TO KISS YOU ONE LAST TIME.
LOOKS LIKE I DON'T EVEN GET THAT.
VEIL, WHAT'S UP? I DRANK THE CURE TOO, BUT I'M STILL NORMAL.
I--I DON'T KNOW, KEN. BUT, UH, HAZMAT'S GLOWING PRETTY BRIGHT. MAYBE WE SHOULD...Y'KNOW, GET SOME DISTANCE?
GOOD IDEA. YOU GUYS FIND MY CONTAINMENT SUIT.
I'LL GO PAY JEREMY A VISIT.

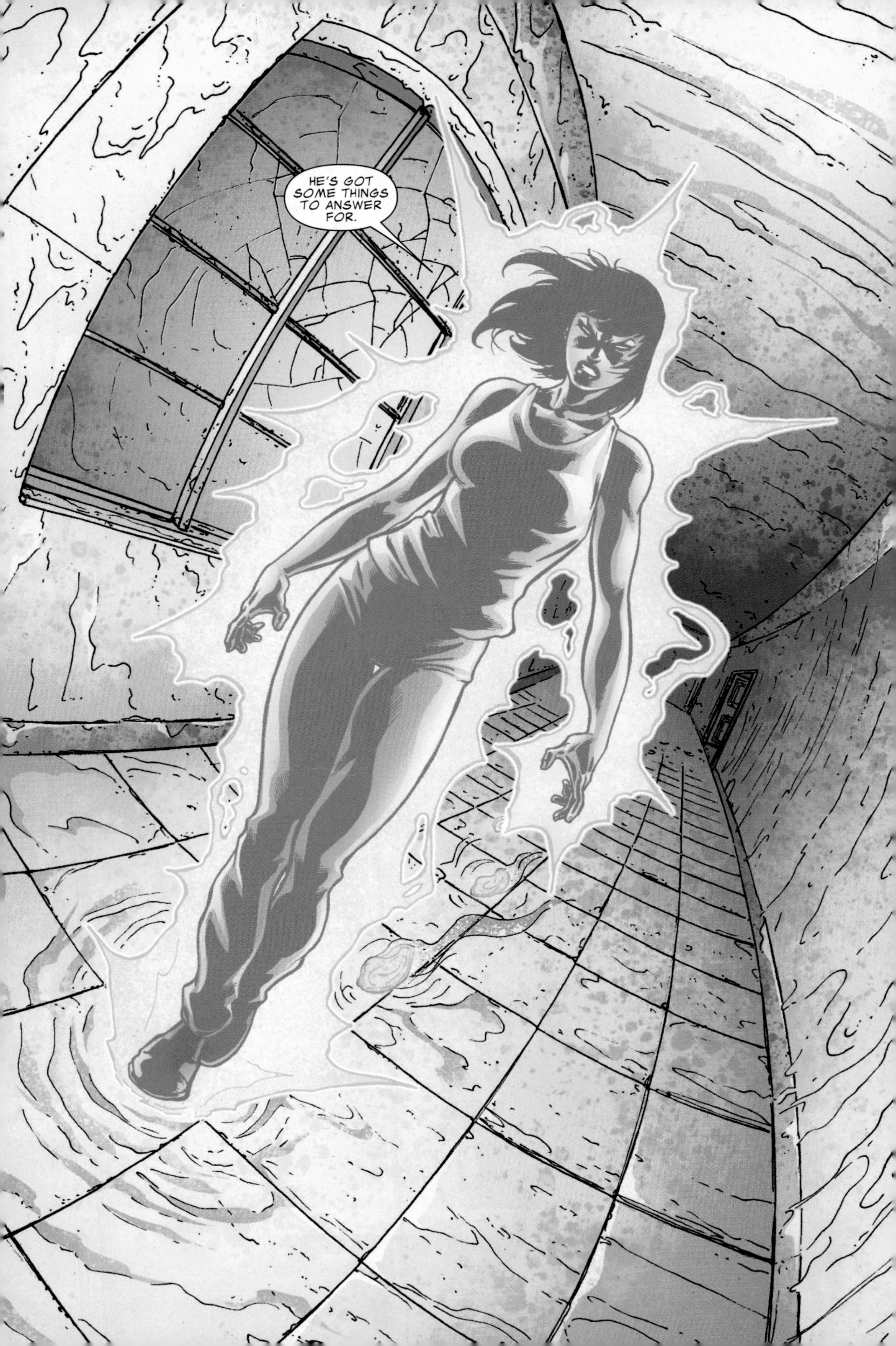
HE'S GOT SOME THINGS TO ANSWER FOR.

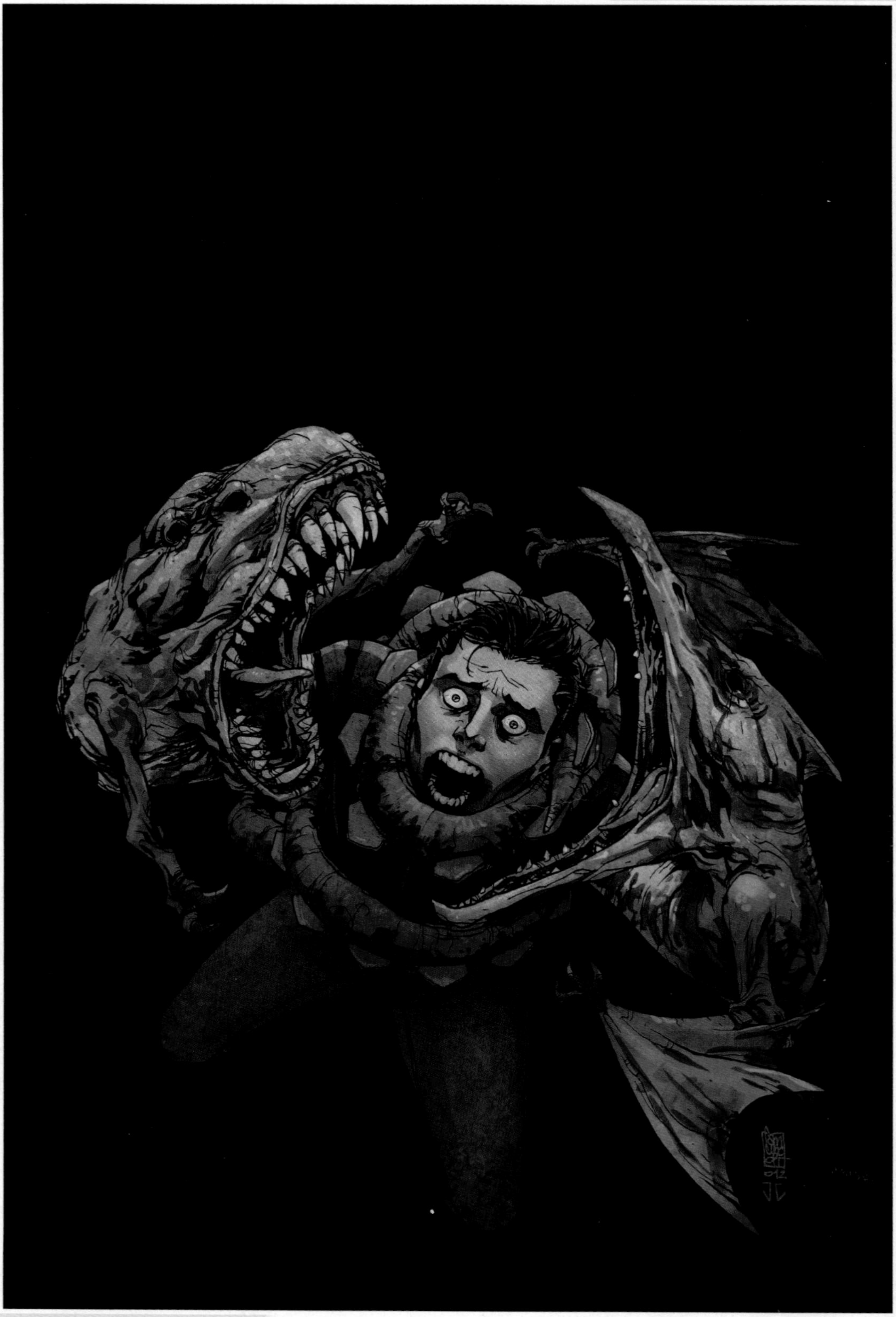

Avengers Academy #36

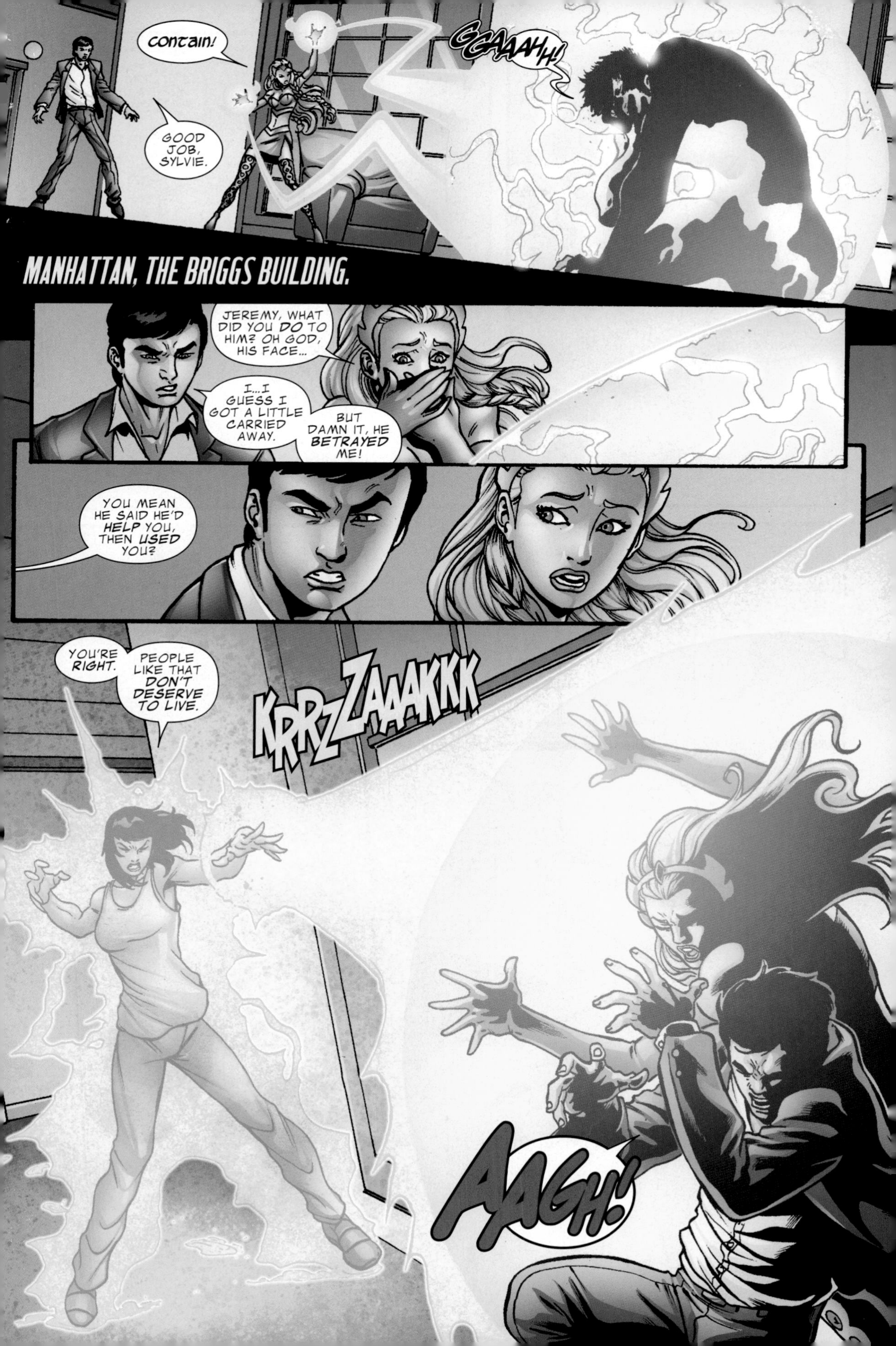
CONTAIN!
GOOD JOB, SYLVIE.
GGAAAHH!
MANHATTAN, THE BRIGGS BUILDING.
JEREMY, WHAT DID YOU DO TO HIM? OH GOD, HIS FACE...
I...I GUESS I GOT A LITTLE CARRIED AWAY.
BUT DAMN IT, HE BETRAYED ME!
YOU MEAN HE SAID HE'D HELP YOU, THEN USED YOU?
YOU'RE RIGHT.
PEOPLE LIKE THAT DON'T DESERVE TO LIVE.
KRRZZAAAKKK
AAGH!

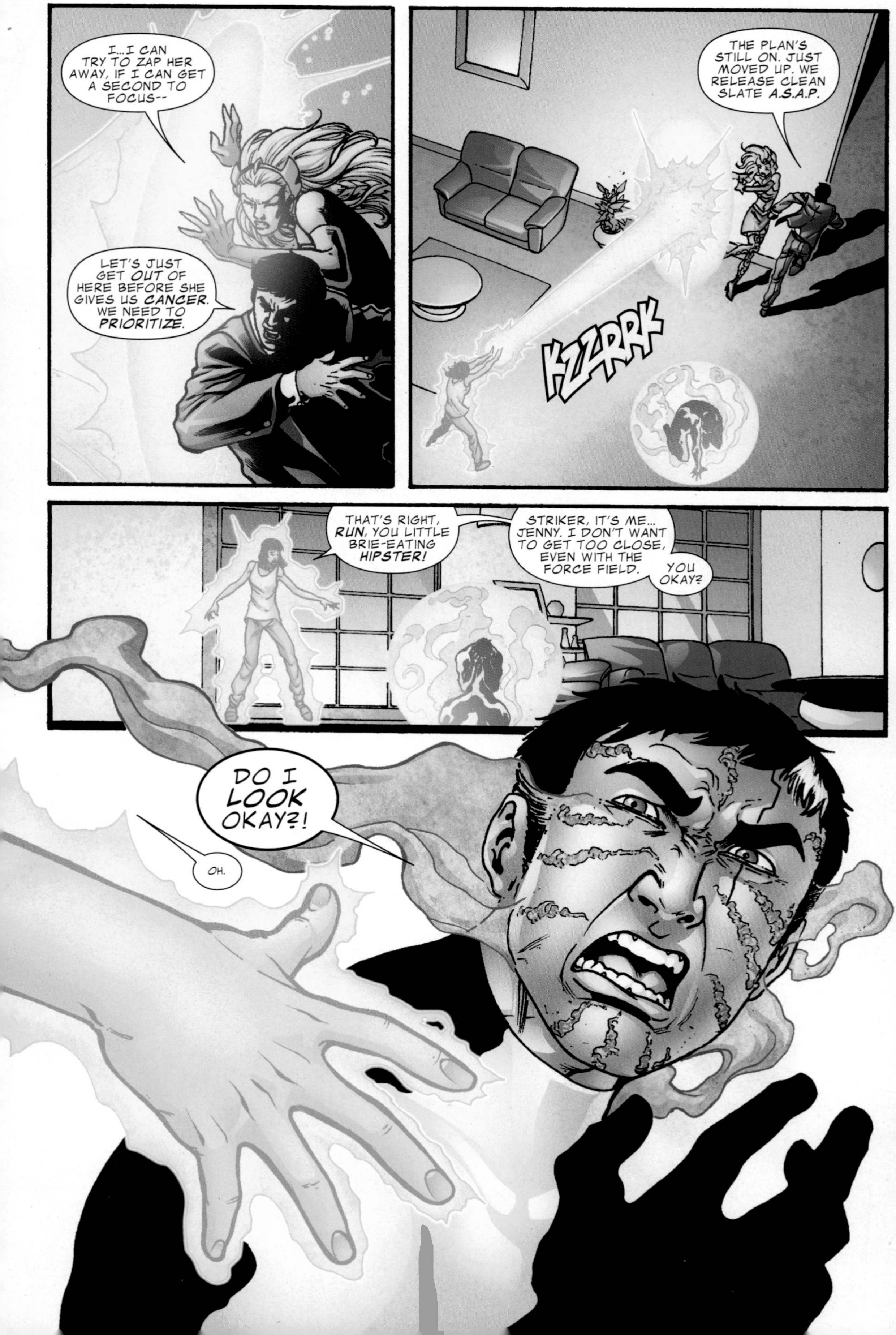
I...I CAN TRY TO ZAP HER AWAY, IF I CAN GET A SECOND TO FOCUS--
LET'S JUST GET OUT OF HERE BEFORE SHE GIVES US CANCER. WE NEED TO PRIORITIZE.
THE PLAN'S STILL ON. JUST MOVED UP. WE RELEASE CLEAN SLATE A.S.A.P.
KZZRRK
THAT'S RIGHT, RUN, YOU LITTLE BRIE-EATING HIPSTER!
STRIKER, IT'S ME... JENNY. I DON'T WANT TO GET TOO CLOSE, EVEN WITH THE FORCE FIELD.
YOU OKAY?
DO I LOOK OKAY?!
OH.

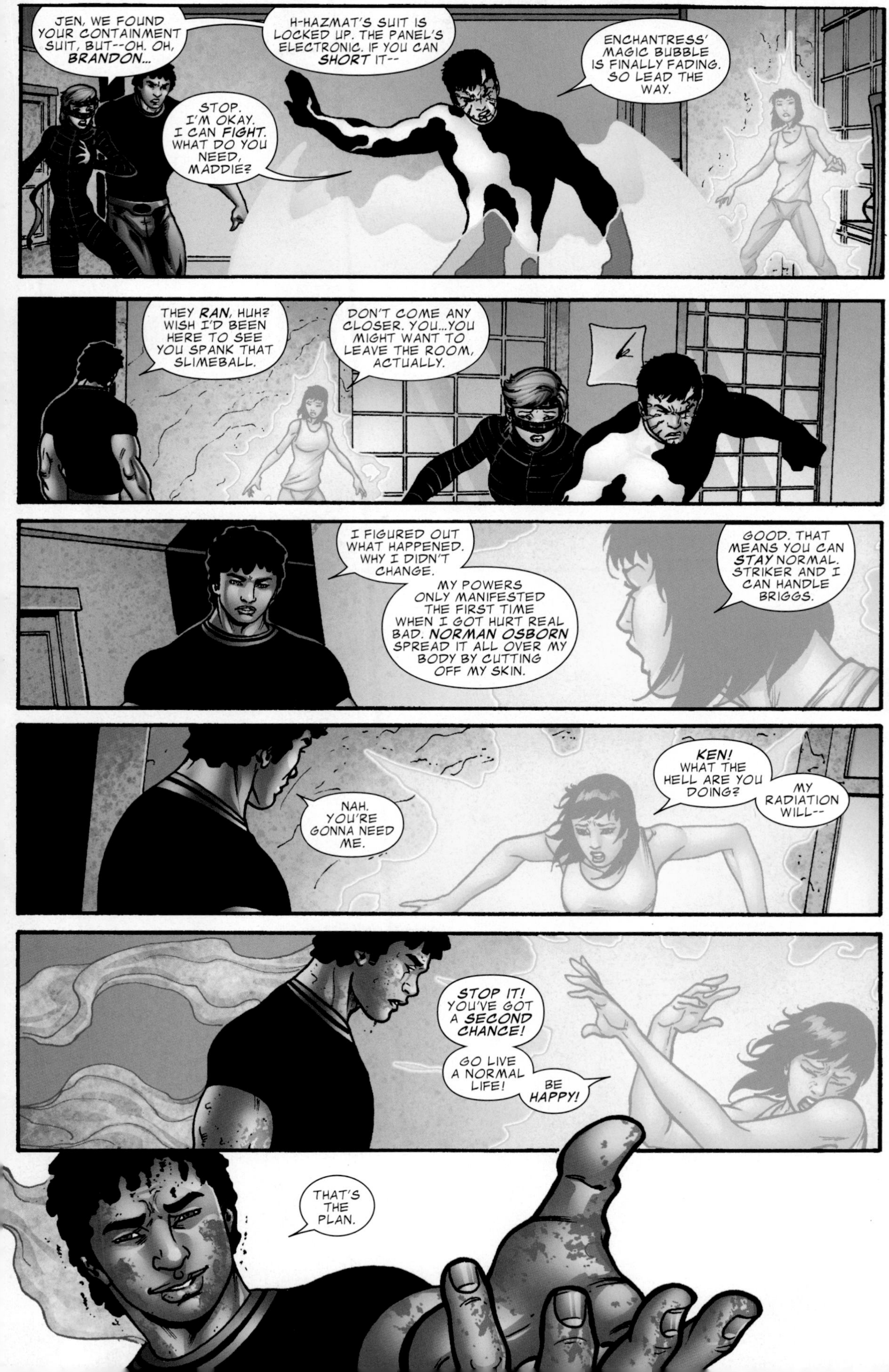
JEN, WE FOUND YOUR CONTAINMENT SUIT, BUT--OH. OH, BRANDON...
H-HAZMAT'S SUIT IS LOCKED UP. THE PANEL'S ELECTRONIC. IF YOU CAN SHORT IT--
STOP. I'M OKAY. I CAN FIGHT. WHAT DO YOU NEED, MADDIE?
ENCHANTRESS' MAGIC BUBBLE IS FINALLY FADING. SO LEAD THE WAY.
THEY RAN, HUH? WISH I'D BEEN HERE TO SEE YOU SPANK THAT SLIMEBALL.
DON'T COME ANY CLOSER. YOU...YOU MIGHT WANT TO LEAVE THE ROOM, ACTUALLY.
I FIGURED OUT WHAT HAPPENED. WHY I DIDN'T CHANGE.
MY POWERS ONLY MANIFESTED THE FIRST TIME WHEN I GOT HURT REAL BAD. NORMAN OSBORN SPREAD IT ALL OVER MY BODY BY CUTTING OFF MY SKIN.
GOOD. THAT MEANS YOU CAN STAY NORMAL. STRIKER AND I CAN HANDLE BRIGGS.
NAH. YOU'RE GONNA NEED ME.
KEN! WHAT THE HELL ARE YOU DOING?
MY RADIATION WILL--
STOP IT! YOU'VE GOT A SECOND CHANCE!
GO LIVE A NORMAL LIFE!
BE HAPPY!
THAT'S THE PLAN.

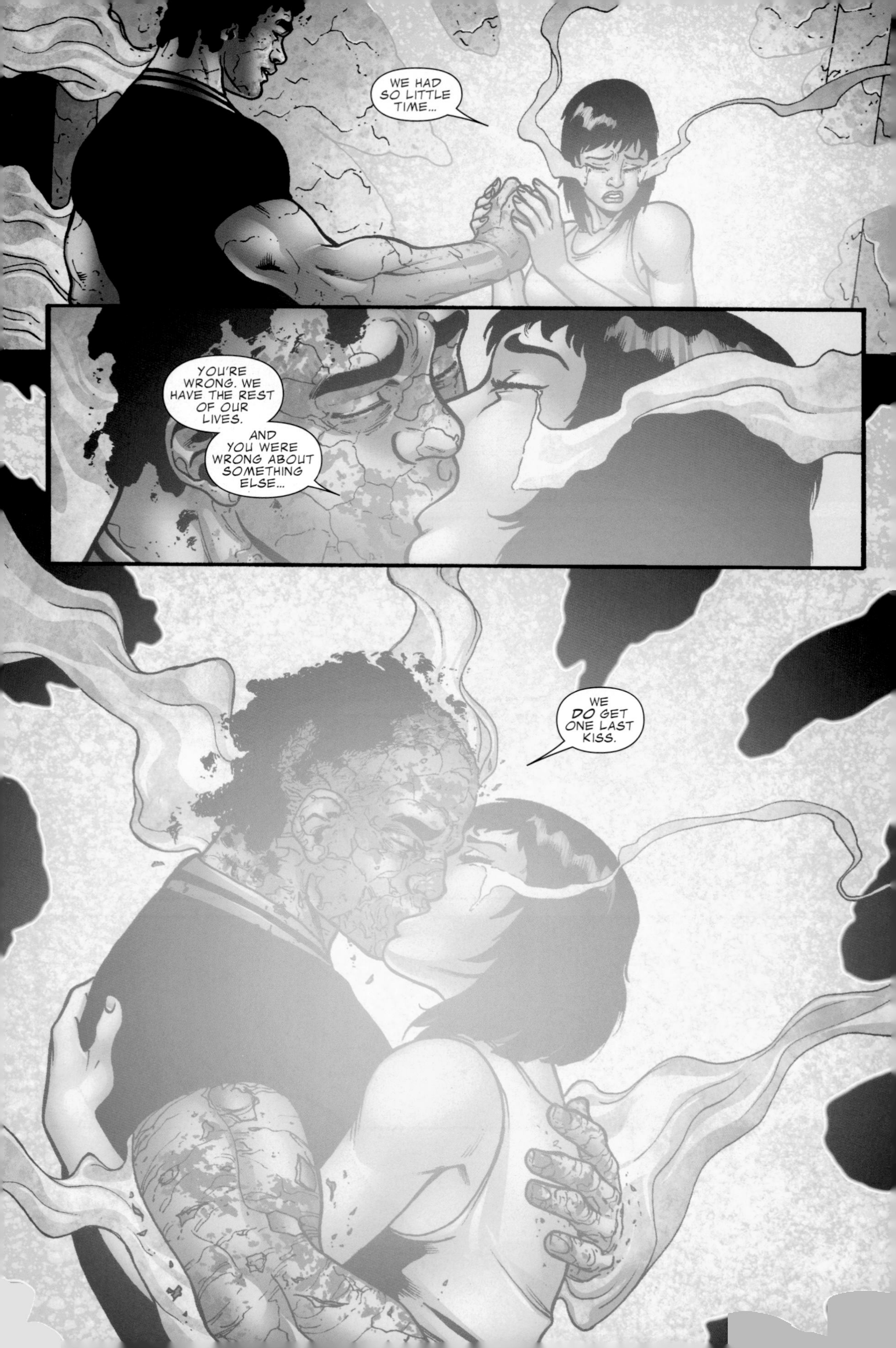
WE HAD SO LITTLE TIME...
YOU'RE WRONG. WE HAVE THE REST OF OUR LIVES.
AND YOU WERE WRONG ABOUT SOMETHING ELSE...
WE DO GET ONE LAST KISS.

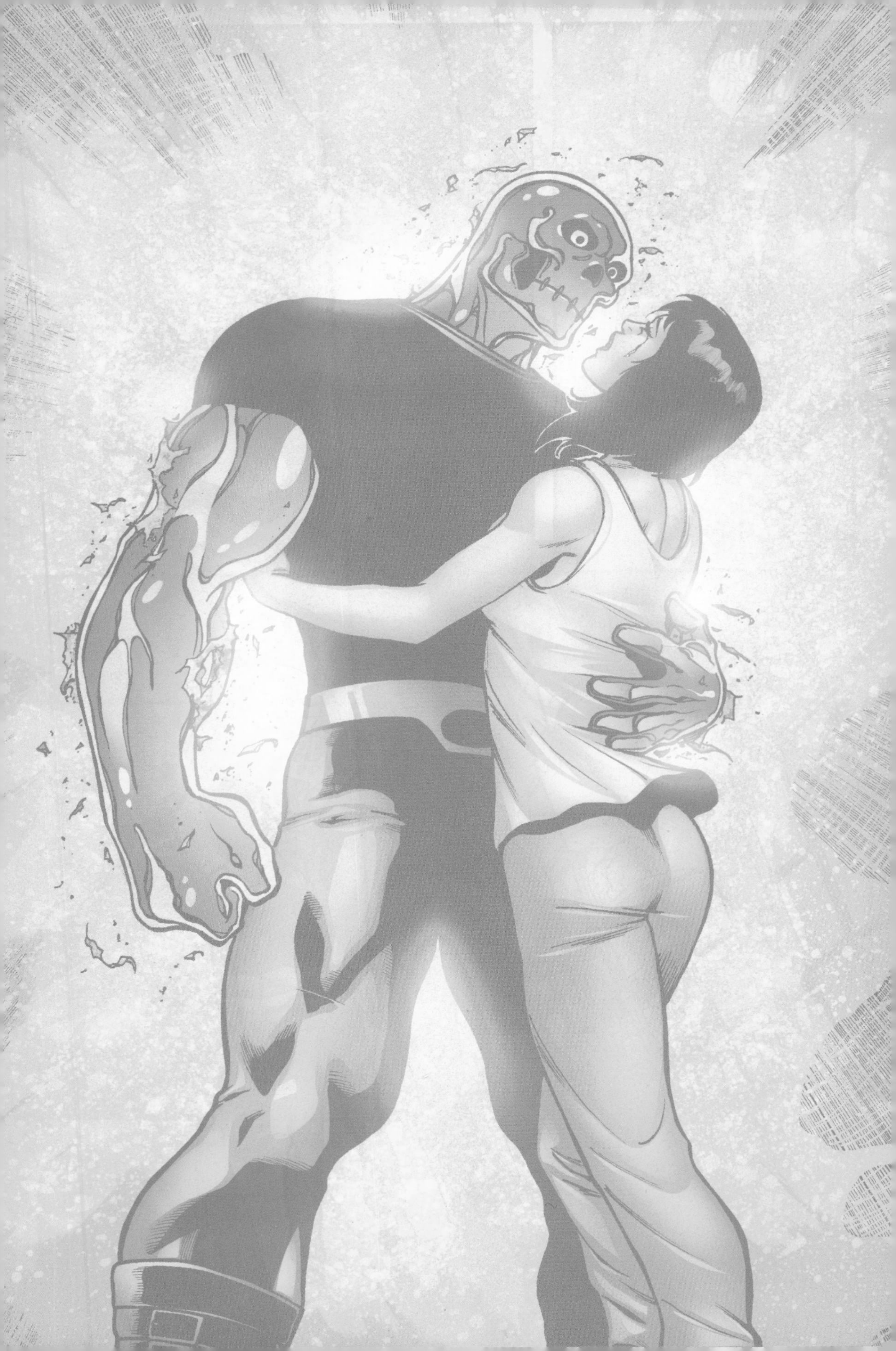

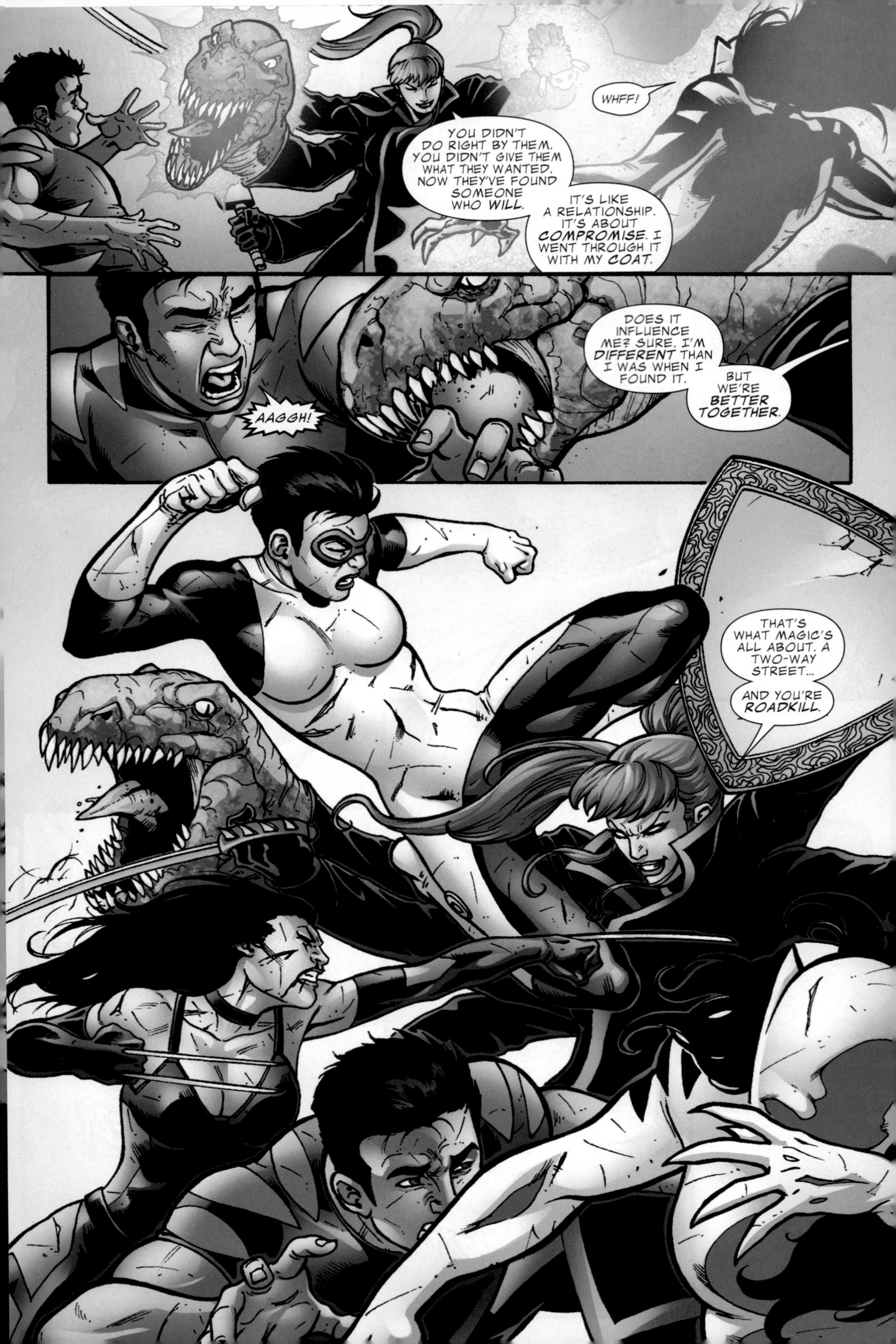
WHFF!
YOU DIDN'T DO RIGHT BY THEM. YOU DIDN'T GIVE THEM WHAT THEY WANTED. NOW THEY'VE FOUND SOMEONE WHO WILL.
IT'S LIKE A RELATIONSHIP. IT'S ABOUT COMPROMISE. I WENT THROUGH IT WITH MY COAT.
AAGGH!
DOES IT INFLUENCE ME? SURE. I'M DIFFERENT THAN I WAS WHEN I FOUND IT.
BUT WE'RE BETTER TOGETHER.
THAT'S WHAT MAGIC'S ALL ABOUT. A TWO-WAY STREET...
AND YOU'RE ROADKILL.

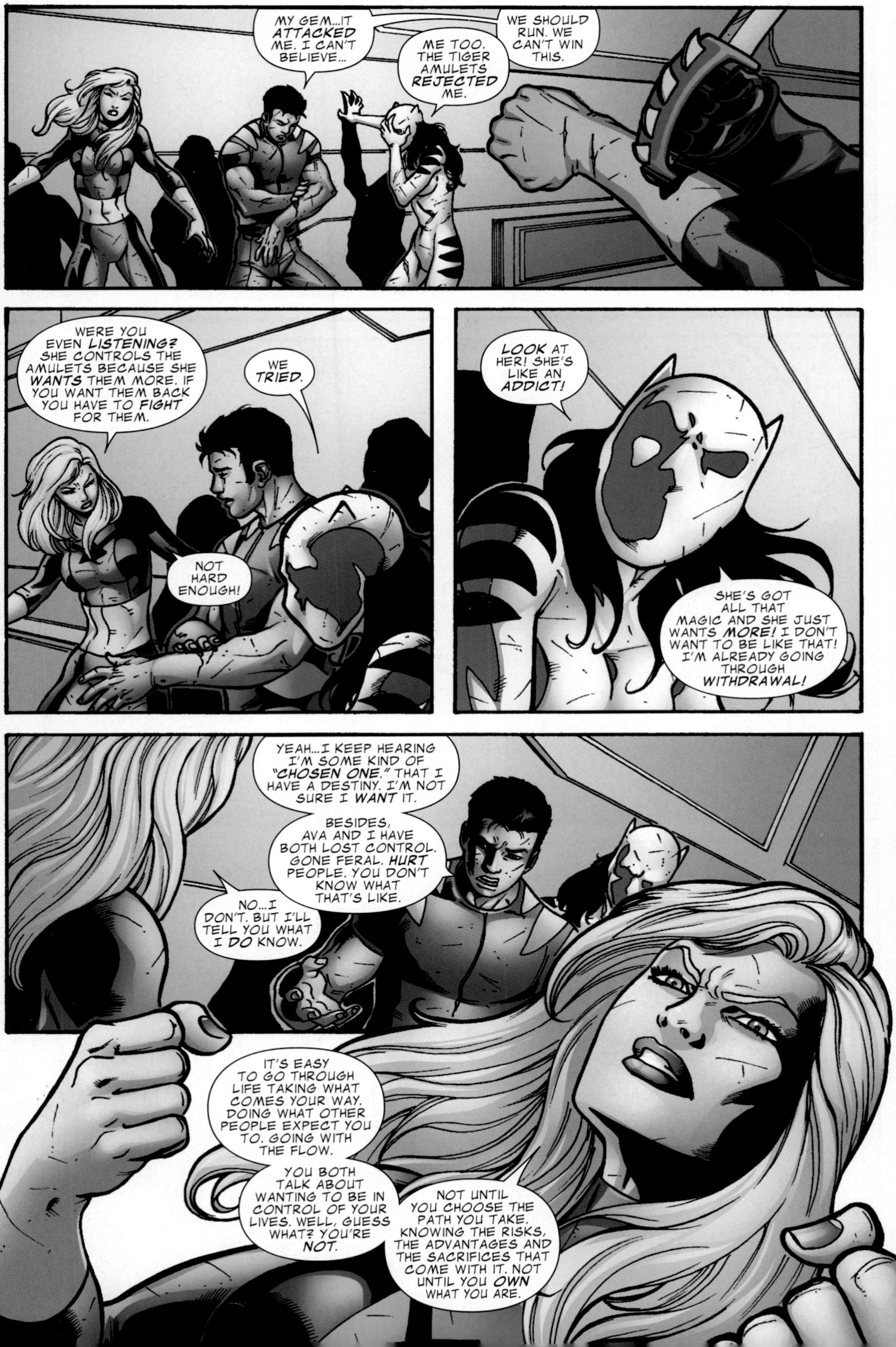
MY GEM...IT ATTACKED ME. I CAN'T BELIEVE...
ME TOO. THE TIGER AMULETS REJECTED ME.
WE SHOULD RUN. WE CAN'T WIN THIS.
WERE YOU EVEN LISTENING? SHE CONTROLS THE AMULETS BECAUSE SHE WANTS THEM MORE. IF YOU WANT THEM BACK YOU HAVE TO FIGHT FOR THEM.
WE TRIED.
NOT HARD ENOUGH!
LOOK AT HER! SHE'S LIKE AN ADDICT!
SHE'S GOT ALL THAT MAGIC AND SHE JUST WANTS MORE! I DON'T WANT TO BE LIKE THAT! I'M ALREADY GOING THROUGH WITHDRAWAL!
YEAH...I KEEP HEARING I'M SOME KIND OF "CHOSEN ONE," THAT I HAVE A DESTINY. I'M NOT SURE I WANT IT.
BESIDES, AVA AND I HAVE BOTH LOST CONTROL. GONE FERAL. HURT PEOPLE. YOU DON'T KNOW WHAT THAT'S LIKE.
NO...I DON'T. BUT I'LL TELL YOU WHAT I DO KNOW.
IT'S EASY TO GO THROUGH LIFE TAKING WHAT COMES YOUR WAY. DOING WHAT OTHER PEOPLE EXPECT YOU TO. GOING WITH THE FLOW.
YOU BOTH TALK ABOUT WANTING TO BE IN CONTROL OF YOUR LIVES. WELL, GUESS WHAT? YOU'RE NOT.
NOT UNTIL YOU CHOOSE THE PATH YOU TAKE. KNOWING THE RISKS, THE ADVANTAGES AND THE SACRIFICES THAT COME WITH IT. NOT UNTIL YOU OWN WHAT YOU ARE.

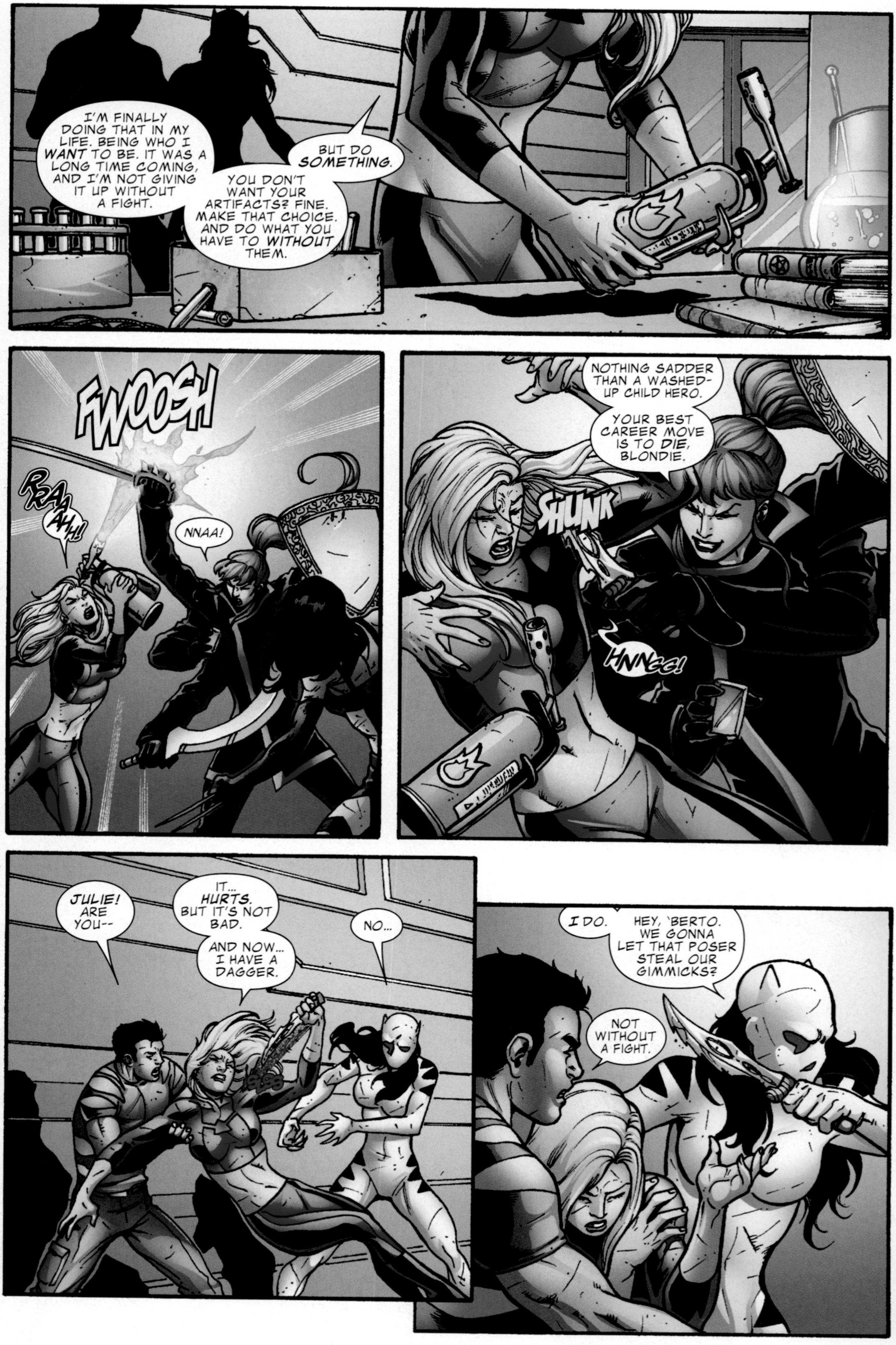
I'M FINALLY DOING THAT IN MY LIFE. BEING WHO I WANT TO BE. IT WAS A LONG TIME COMING, AND I'M NOT GIVING IT UP WITHOUT A FIGHT.
BUT DO SOMETHING.
YOU DON'T WANT YOUR ARTIFACTS? FINE. MAKE THAT CHOICE. AND DO WHAT YOU HAVE TO WITHOUT THEM.
FWOOSH
RRAAAHH!
NNAA!
NOTHING SADDER THAN A WASHED-UP CHILD HERO.
YOUR BEST CAREER MOVE IS TO DIE, BLONDIE.
SHUNK
HNNGG!
JULIE! ARE YOU--
IT... HURTS. BUT IT'S NOT BAD.
AND NOW... I HAVE A DAGGER.
NO...
I DO.
HEY, 'BERTO. WE GONNA LET THAT POSER STEAL OUR GIMMICKS?
NOT WITHOUT A FIGHT.

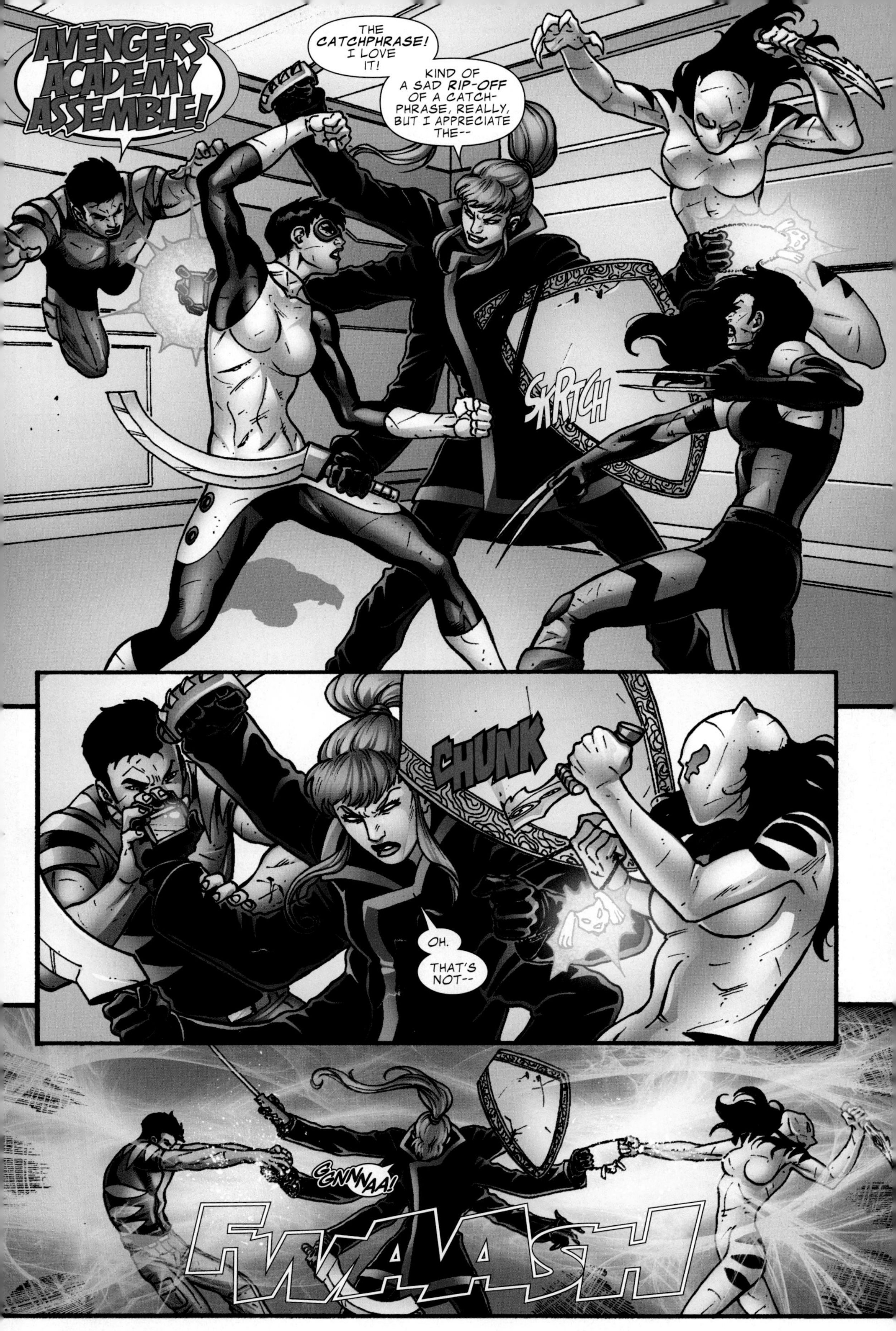
AVENGERS ACADEMY ASSEMBLE!
THE CATCHPHRASE! I LOVE IT!
KIND OF A SAD RIP-OFF OF A CATCH-PHRASE, REALLY, BUT I APPRECIATE THE--
SKRTCH
CHUNK
OH.
THAT'S NOT--
GNNNAA!
FWAASH

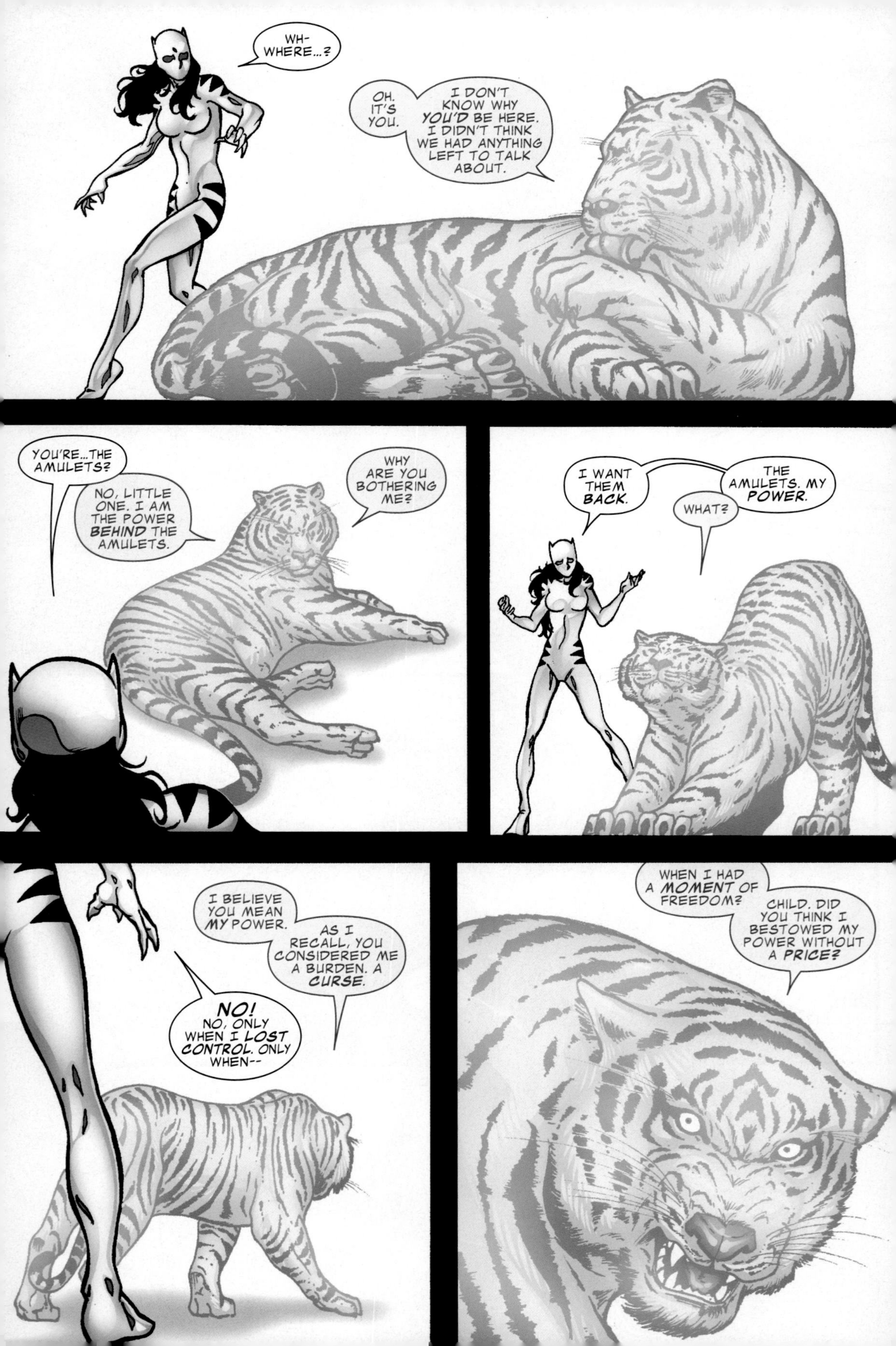
WH- WHERE...?
OH. IT'S YOU.
I DON'T KNOW WHY YOU'D BE HERE. I DIDN'T THINK WE HAD ANYTHING LEFT TO TALK ABOUT.
YOU'RE...THE AMULETS?
NO, LITTLE ONE. I AM THE POWER BEHIND THE AMULETS.
WHY ARE YOU BOTHERING ME?
I WANT THEM BACK.
THE AMULETS. MY POWER.
WHAT?
I BELIEVE YOU MEAN MY POWER.
AS I RECALL, YOU CONSIDERED ME A BURDEN. A CURSE.
NO! NO, ONLY WHEN I LOST CONTROL. ONLY WHEN--
WHEN I HAD A MOMENT OF FREEDOM?
CHILD. DID YOU THINK I BESTOWED MY POWER WITHOUT A PRICE?

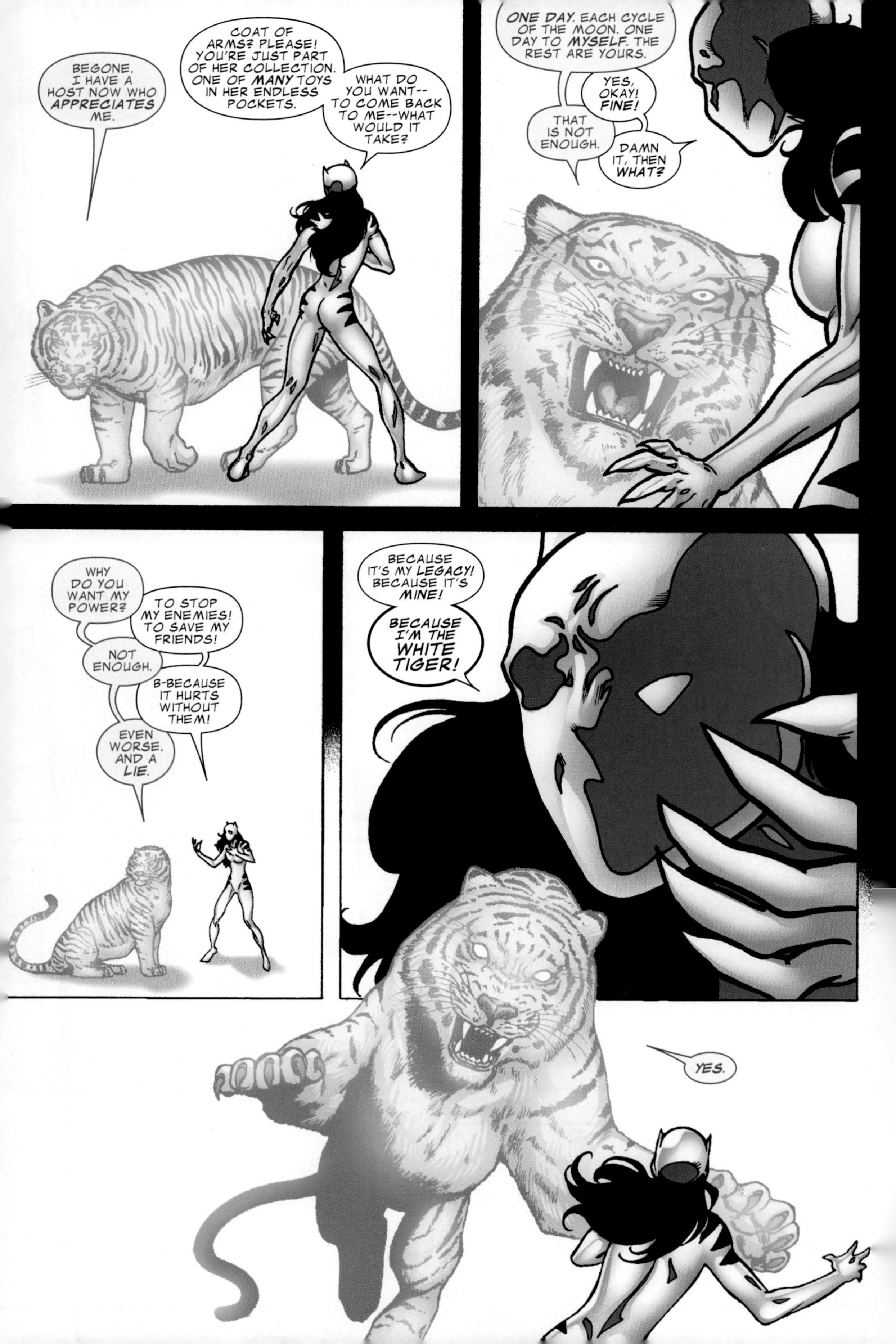
BEGONE. I HAVE A HOST NOW WHO APPRECIATES ME.
COAT OF ARMS? PLEASE! YOU'RE JUST PART OF HER COLLECTION. ONE OF MANY TOYS IN HER ENDLESS POCKETS.
WHAT DO YOU WANT-- TO COME BACK TO ME--WHAT WOULD IT TAKE?
ONE DAY. EACH CYCLE OF THE MOON. ONE DAY TO MYSELF. THE REST ARE YOURS.
THAT IS NOT ENOUGH.
YES, OKAY! FINE!
DAMN IT, THEN WHAT?
WHY DO YOU WANT MY POWER?
TO STOP MY ENEMIES! TO SAVE MY FRIENDS!
NOT ENOUGH.
B-BECAUSE IT HURTS WITHOUT THEM!
EVEN WORSE. AND A LIE.
BECAUSE IT'S MY LEGACY! BECAUSE IT'S MINE!
BECAUSE I'M THE WHITE TIGER!
YES.

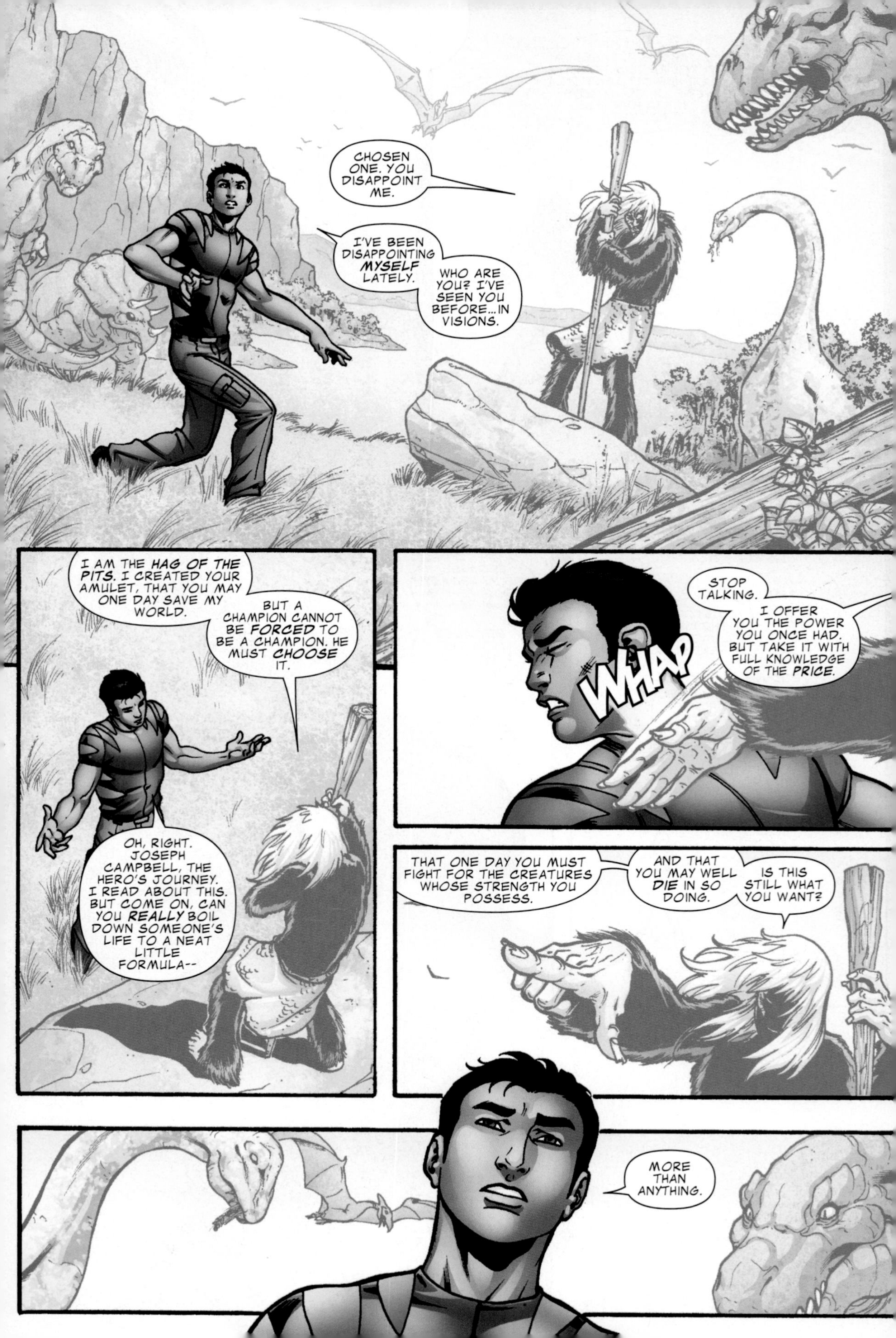

CHOSEN ONE. YOU DISAPPOINT ME.
I'VE BEEN DISAPPOINTING MYSELF LATELY.
WHO ARE YOU? I'VE SEEN YOU BEFORE...IN VISIONS.
I AM THE HAG OF THE PITS. I CREATED YOUR AMULET, THAT YOU MAY ONE DAY SAVE MY WORLD.
BUT A CHAMPION CANNOT BE FORCED TO BE A CHAMPION. HE MUST CHOOSE IT.
OH, RIGHT. JOSEPH CAMPBELL, THE HERO'S JOURNEY. I READ ABOUT THIS. BUT COME ON, CAN YOU REALLY BOIL DOWN SOMEONE'S LIFE TO A NEAT LITTLE FORMULA--
WHAP
STOP TALKING.
I OFFER YOU THE POWER YOU ONCE HAD. BUT TAKE IT WITH FULL KNOWLEDGE OF THE PRICE.
THAT ONE DAY YOU MUST FIGHT FOR THE CREATURES WHOSE STRENGTH YOU POSSESS.
AND THAT YOU MAY WELL DIE IN SO DOING.
IS THIS STILL WHAT YOU WANT?
MORE THAN ANYTHING.

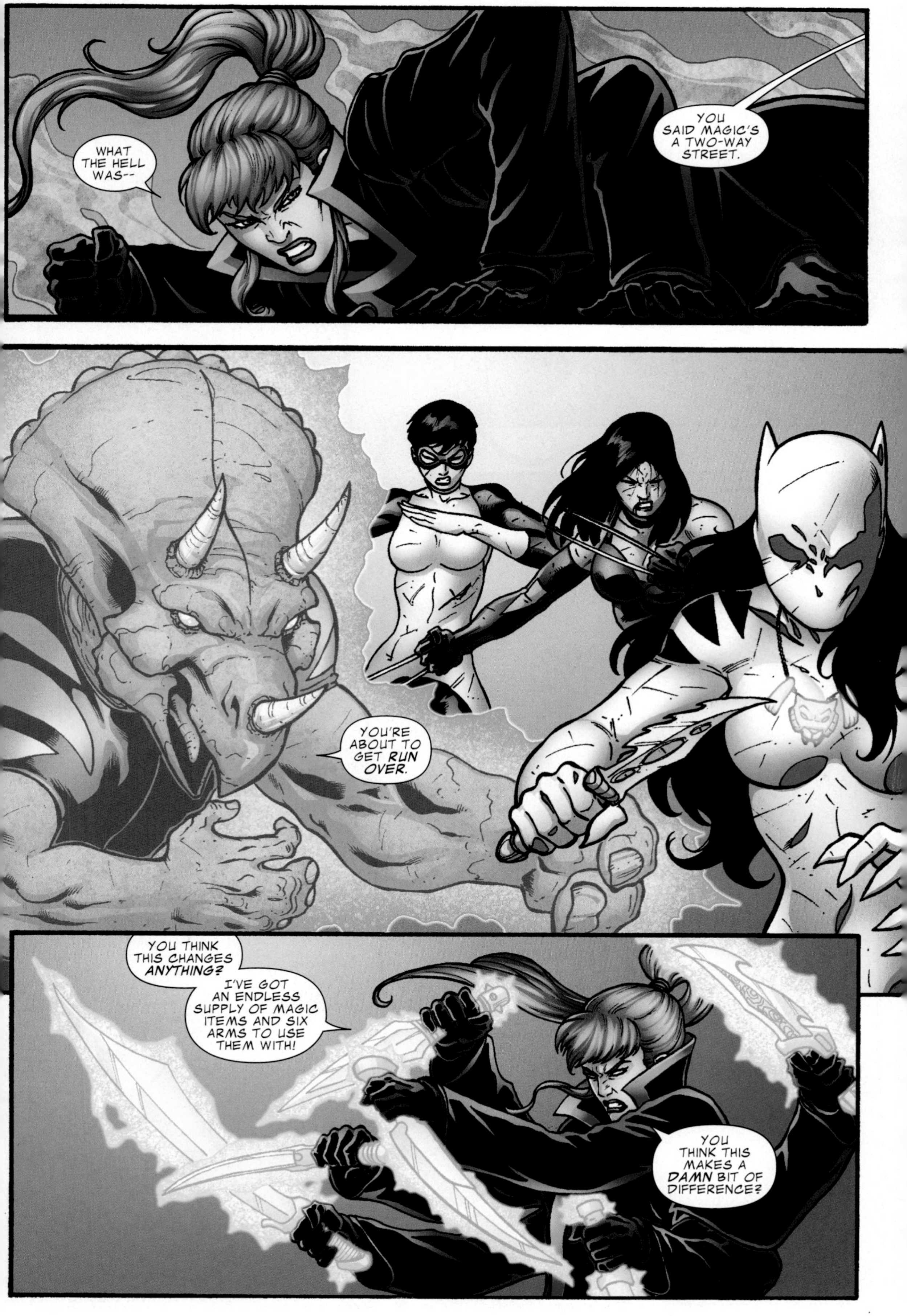
WHAT THE HELL WAS--
YOU SAID MAGIC'S A TWO-WAY STREET.
YOU'RE ABOUT TO GET RUN OVER.
YOU THINK THIS CHANGES ANYTHING?
I'VE GOT AN ENDLESS SUPPLY OF MAGIC ITEMS AND SIX ARMS TO USE THEM WITH!
YOU THINK THIS MAKES A DAMN BIT OF DIFFERENCE?

SHRRIPP
SLSSH

THWAAMMMM

YEAH.
I'D SAY IT
DOES.

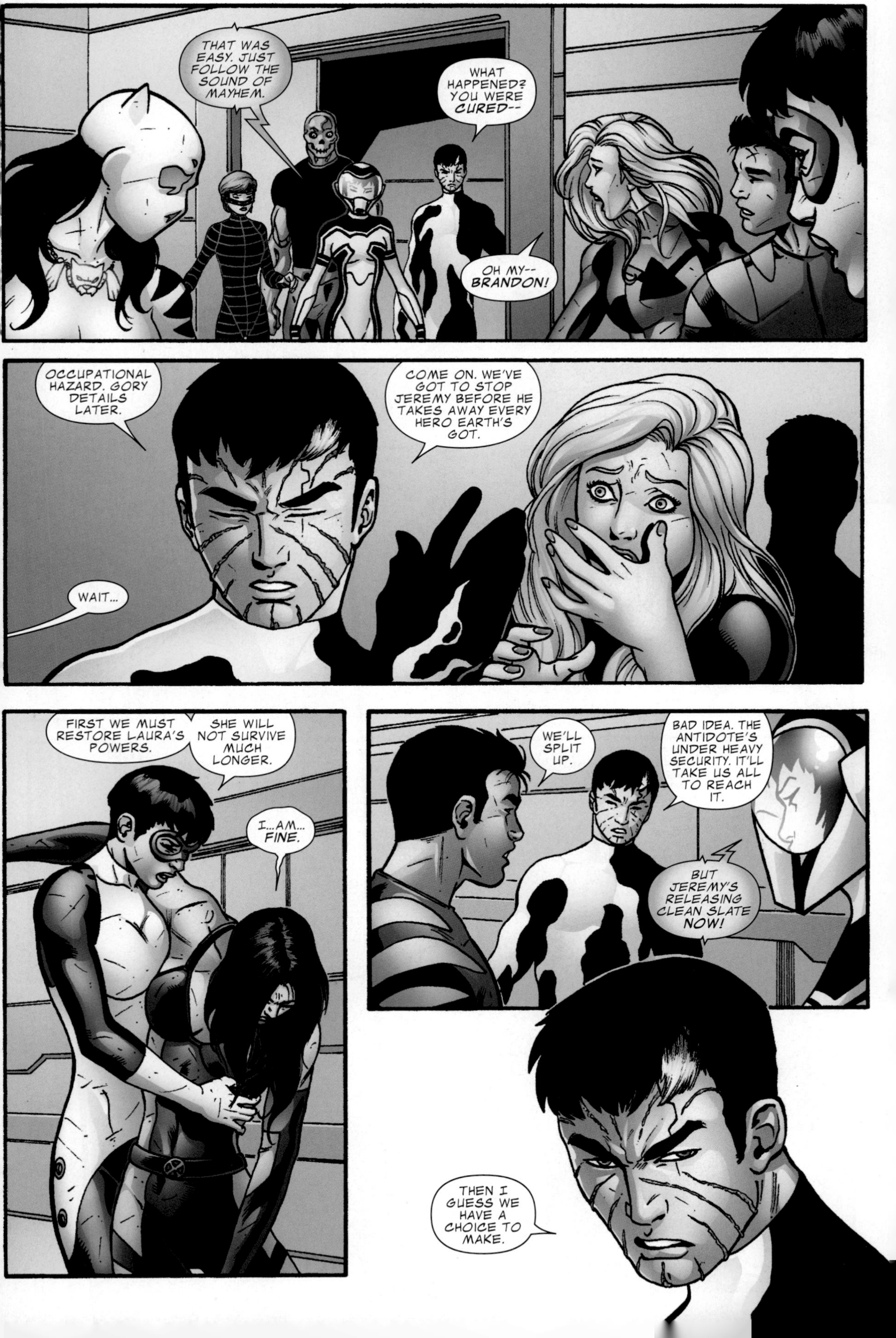

THAT WAS EASY. JUST FOLLOW THE SOUND OF MAYHEM.
WHAT HAPPENED? YOU WERE CURED--
OH MY-- BRANDON!
OCCUPATIONAL HAZARD. GORY DETAILS LATER.
COME ON. WE'VE GOT TO STOP JEREMY BEFORE HE TAKES AWAY EVERY HERO EARTH'S GOT.
WAIT...
FIRST WE MUST RESTORE LAURA'S POWERS.
SHE WILL NOT SURVIVE MUCH LONGER.
I...AM... FINE.
WE'LL SPLIT UP.
BAD IDEA. THE ANTIDOTE'S UNDER HEAVY SECURITY. IT'LL TAKE US ALL TO REACH IT.
BUT JEREMY'S RELEASING CLEAN SLATE NOW!
THEN I GUESS WE HAVE A CHOICE TO MAKE.

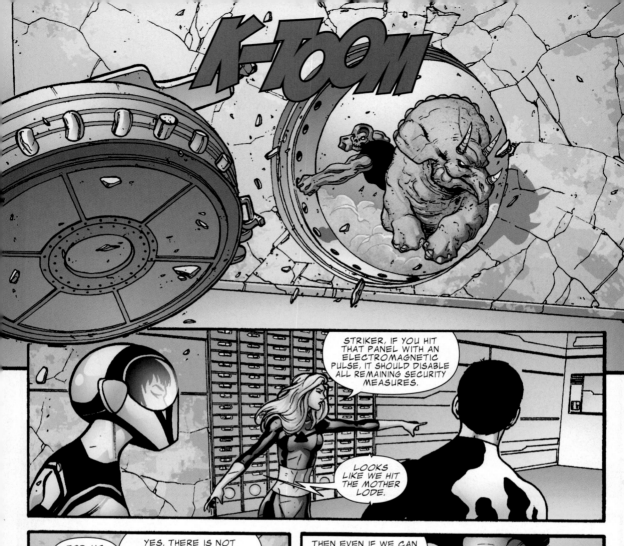

K-TOOM

STRIKER, IF YOU HIT THAT PANEL WITH AN ELECTROMAGNETIC PULSE, IT SHOULD DISABLE ALL REMAINING SECURITY MEASURES.

LOOKS LIKE WE HIT THE MOTHER LODE.

FOR *US*, SURE. BUT I SEE A PROBLEM.

YES. THERE IS NOT NEARLY ENOUGH OF THE CURE HERE TO COUNTERACT A WORLDWIDE SPREAD OF CLEAN SLATE.

JEREMY OBVIOUSLY PLANNED ON DOING A LOT LESS RE-POWERING THAN DE-POWERING.

THEN EVEN IF WE CAN MAKE MORE, MOST OF THE WORLD'S HEROES WILL BE POWERLESS FOR WHO KNOWS HOW LONG.

WHAT IF THERE'S AN ALIEN INVASION... OR SOME KIND OF COSMIC CRISIS? THE WHOLE PLANET'LL BE PRETTY MUCH *DEFENSELESS*.

THEN WE WILL MAKE SURE THAT DOES NOT HAPPEN.

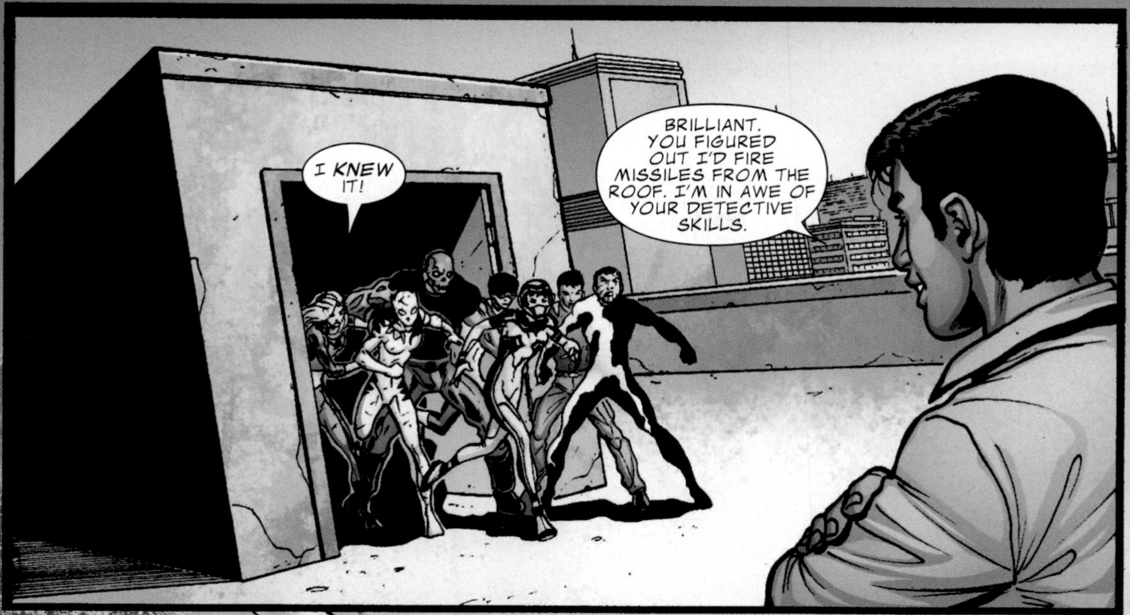
I KNEW IT!
BRILLIANT. YOU FIGURED OUT I'D FIRE MISSILES FROM THE ROOF. I'M IN AWE OF YOUR DETECTIVE SKILLS.

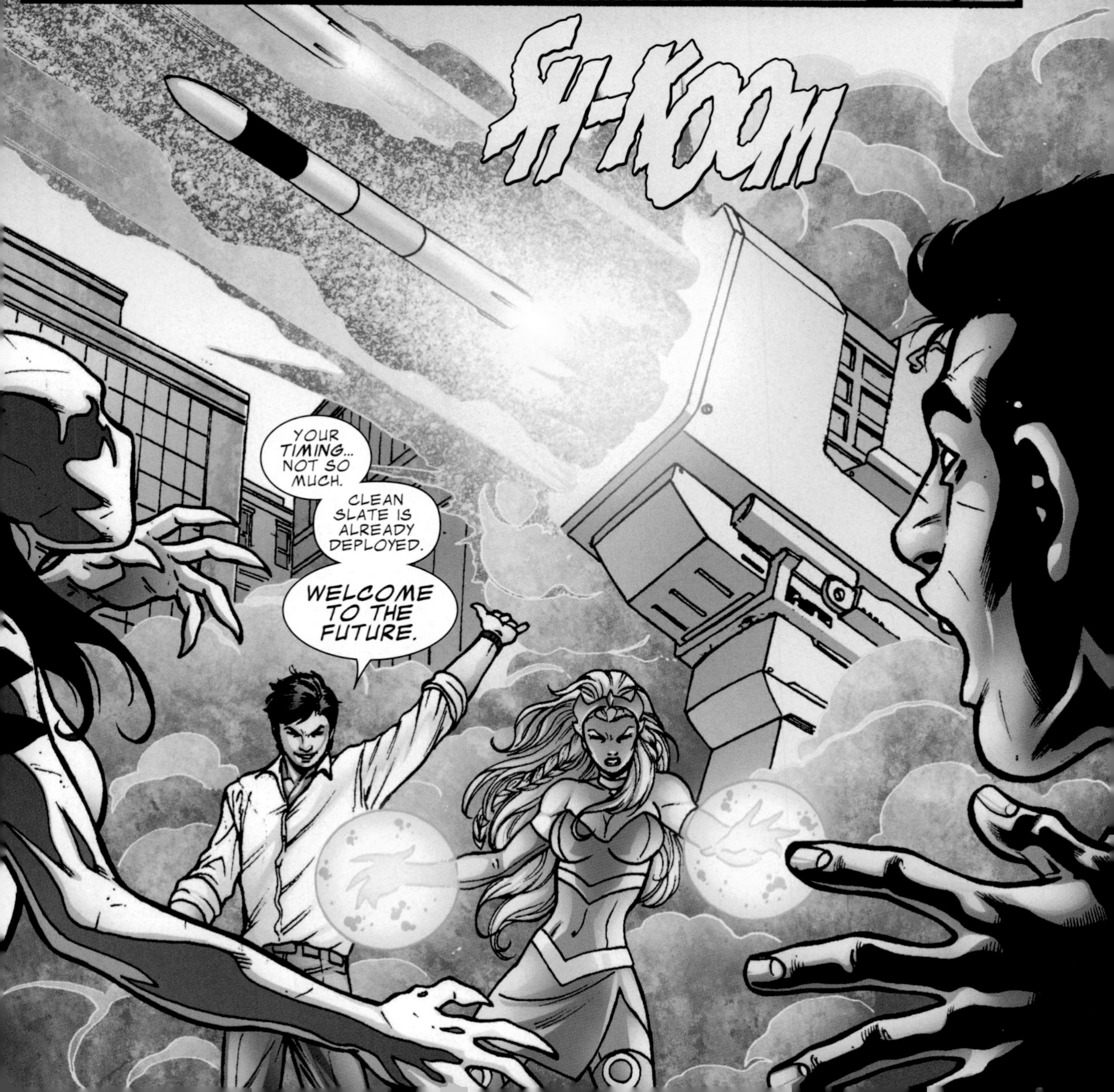
SH-KOOM
YOUR TIMING... NOT SO MUCH.
CLEAN SLATE IS ALREADY DEPLOYED.
WELCOME TO THE FUTURE.

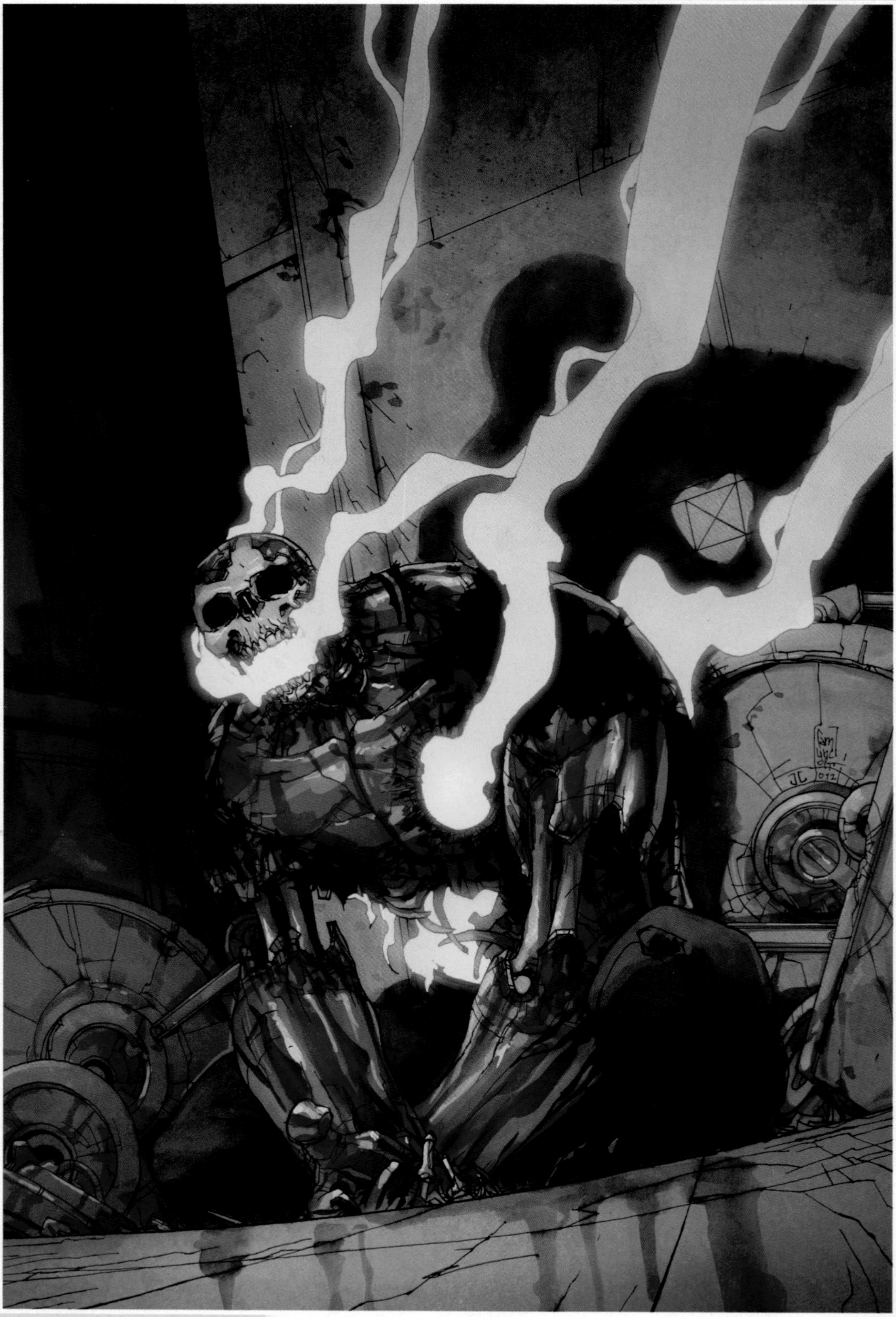

Avengers Academy #37

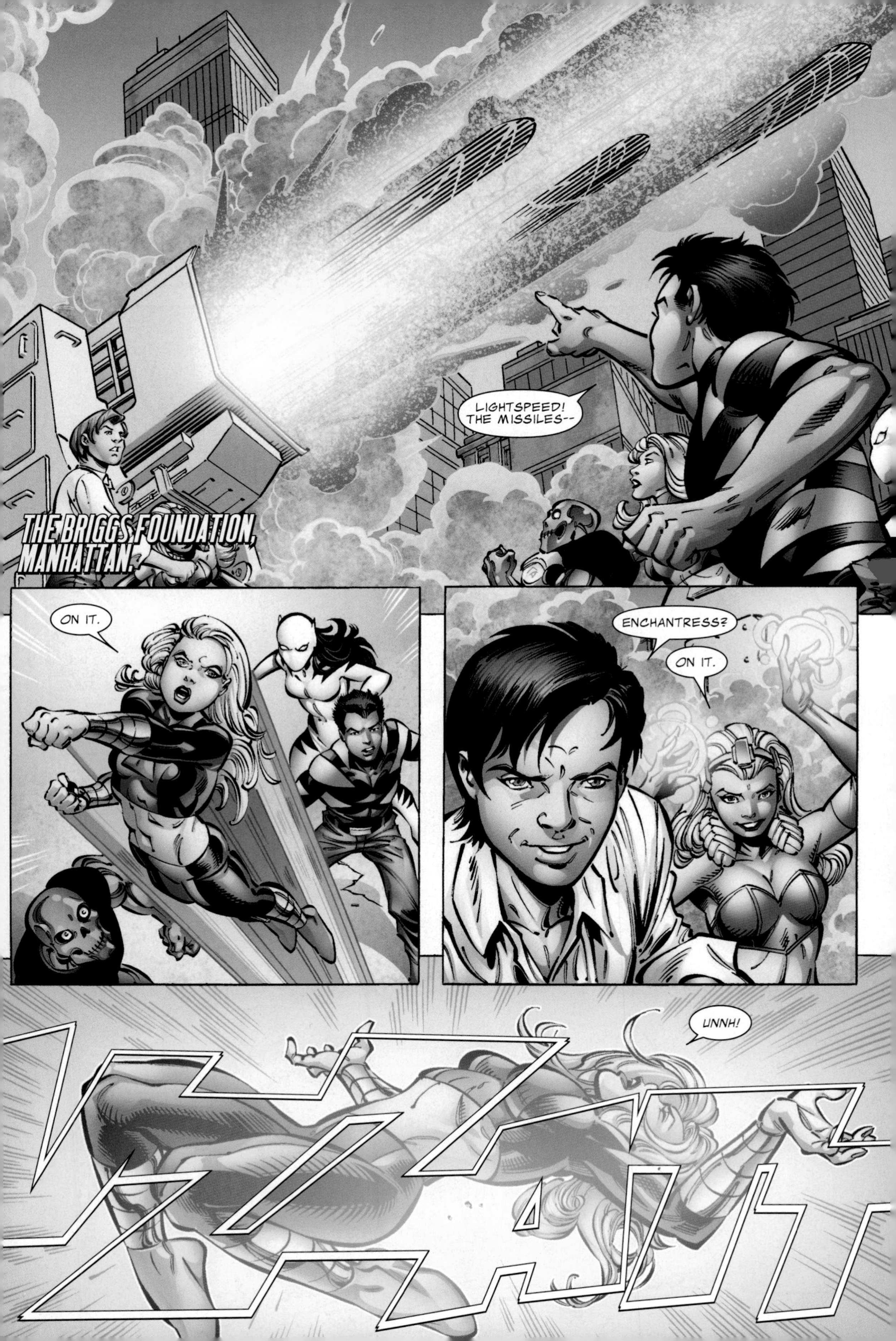
THE BRIGGS FOUNDATION, MANHATTAN.
LIGHTSPEED! THE MISSILES--
ON IT.
ENCHANTRESS?
ON IT.
UNNH!

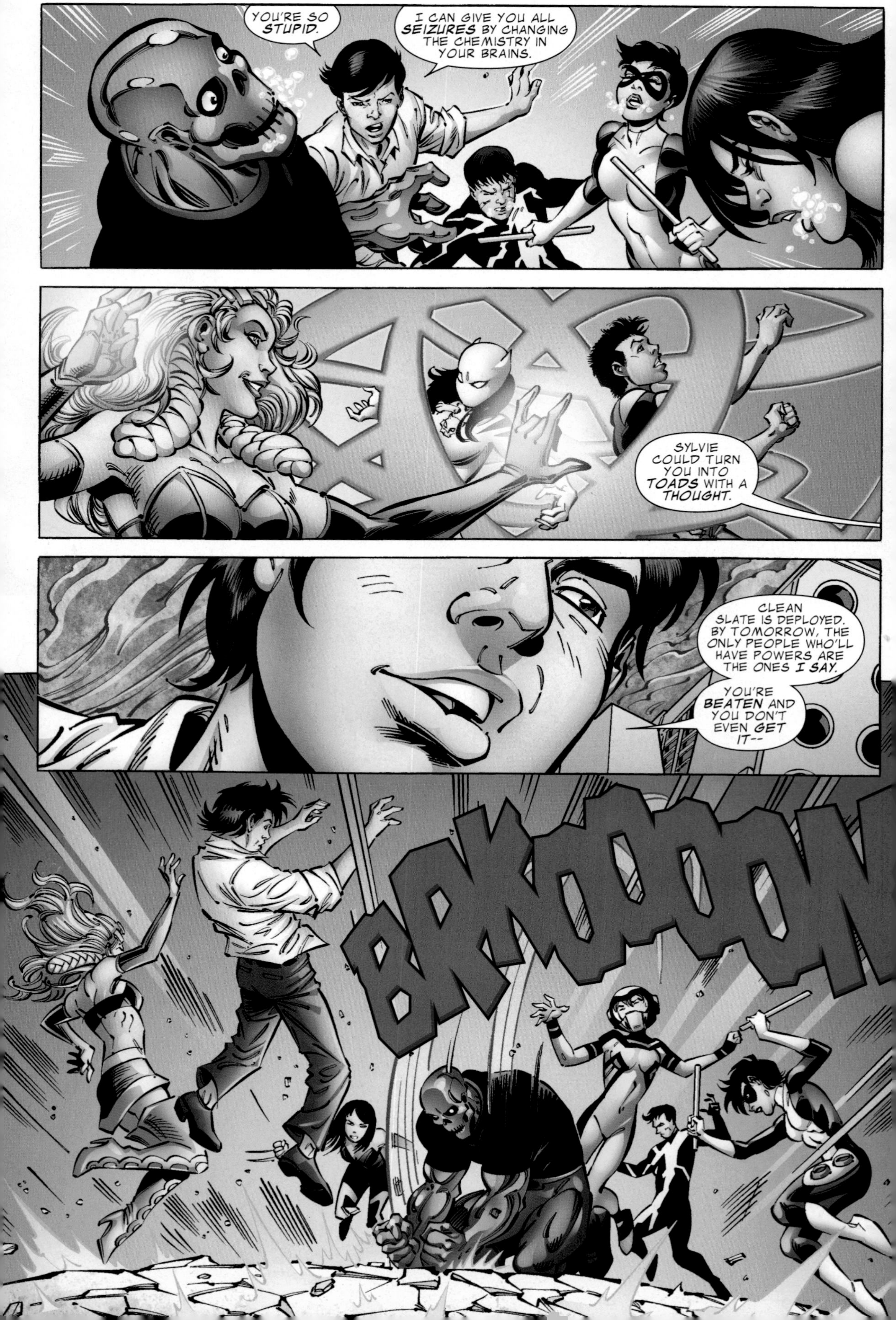
YOU'RE SO STUPID.
I CAN GIVE YOU ALL SEIZURES BY CHANGING THE CHEMISTRY IN YOUR BRAINS.
SYLVIE COULD TURN YOU INTO TOADS WITH A THOUGHT.
CLEAN SLATE IS DEPLOYED. BY TOMORROW, THE ONLY PEOPLE WHO'LL HAVE POWERS ARE THE ONES I SAY.
YOU'RE BEATEN AND YOU DON'T EVEN GET IT--
BRKOOOOM

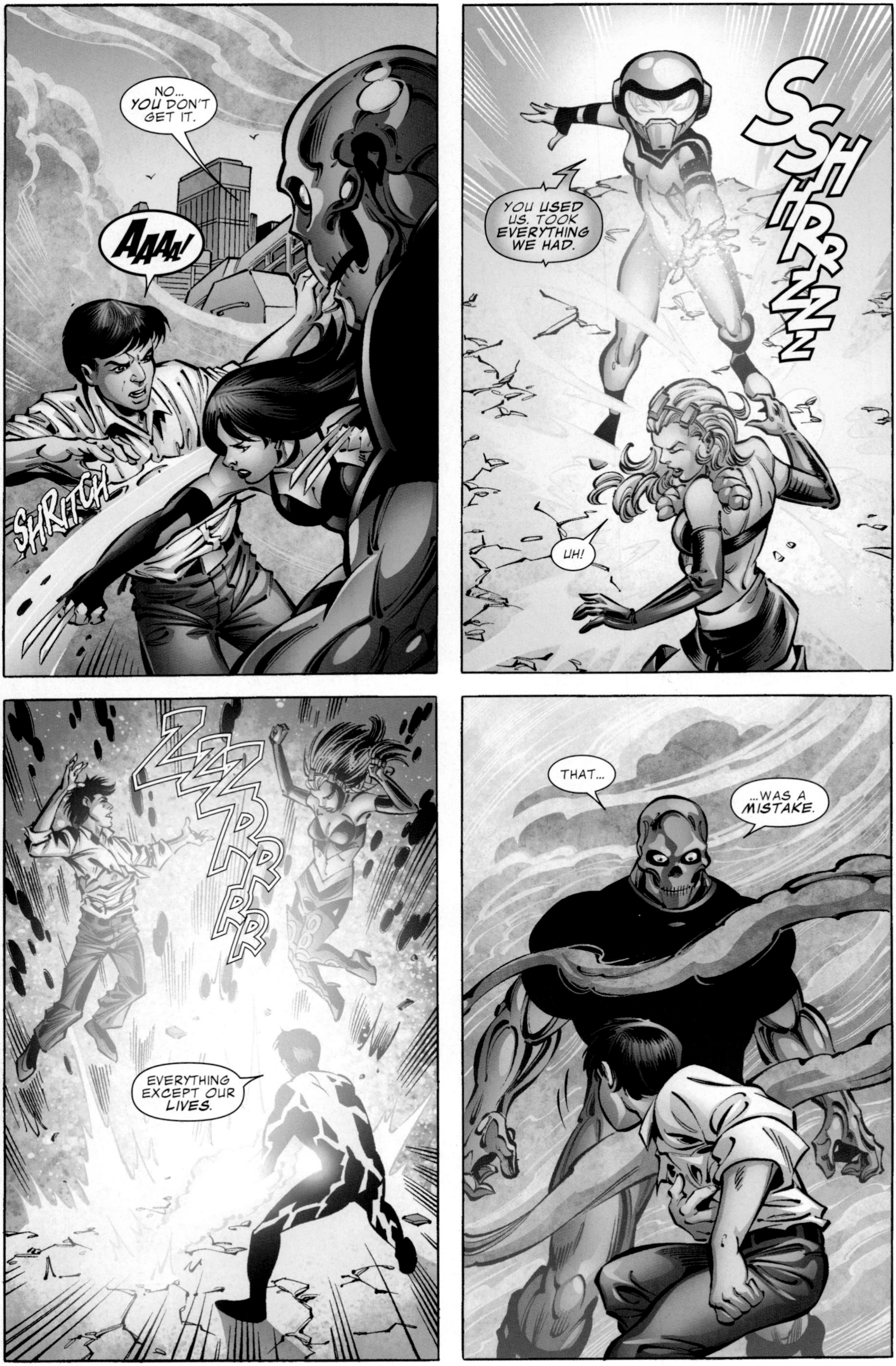
NO... YOU DON'T GET IT.
AAAA!
SHRITCH
SSHHRRZZZ
YOU USED US. TOOK EVERYTHING WE HAD.
UH!
ZZZRRRRR
EVERYTHING EXCEPT OUR LIVES.
THAT...
...WAS A MISTAKE.

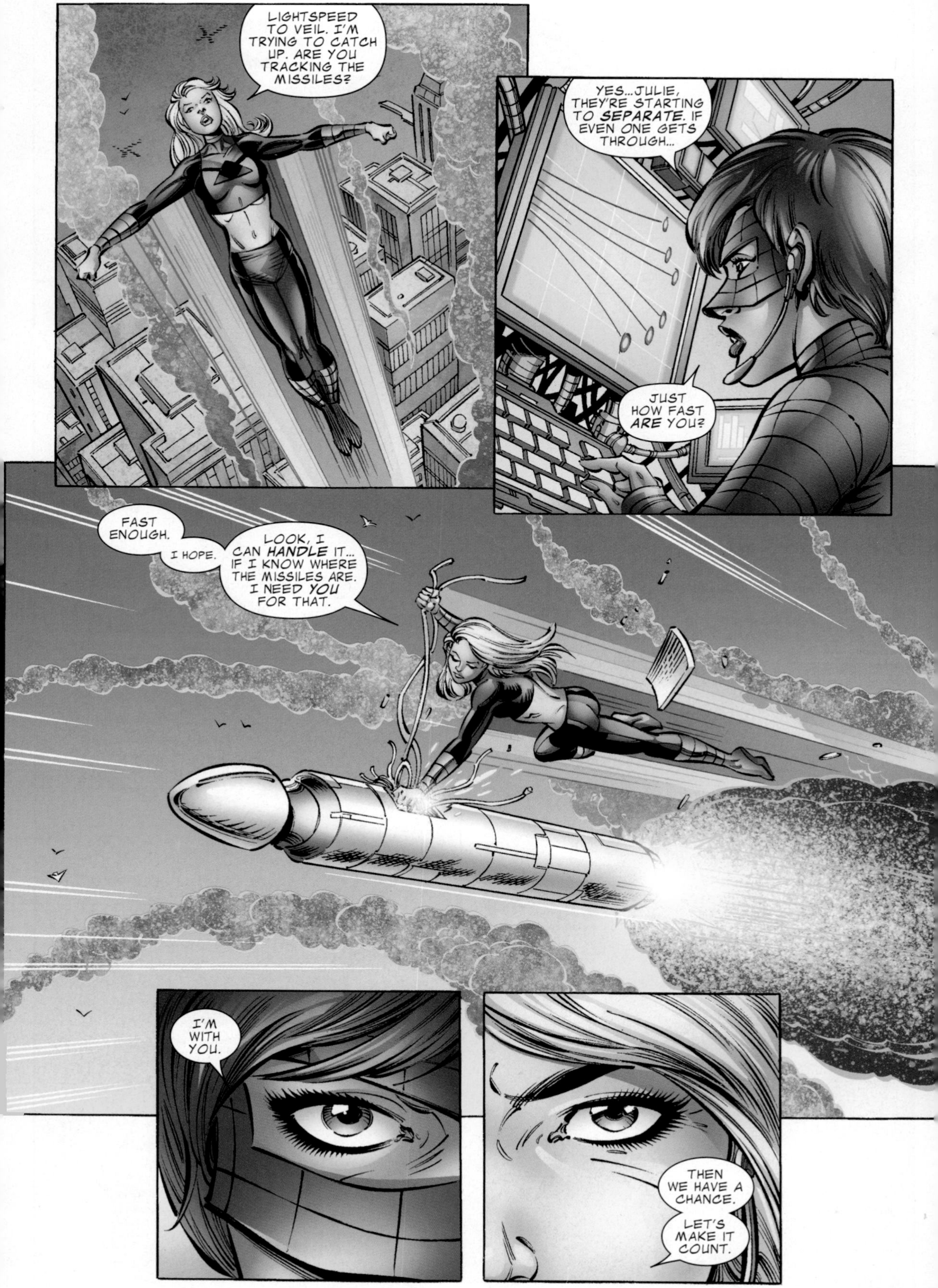

LIGHTSPEED TO VEIL. I'M TRYING TO CATCH UP. ARE YOU TRACKING THE MISSILES?
YES...JULIE, THEY'RE STARTING TO SEPARATE. IF EVEN ONE GETS THROUGH...
JUST HOW FAST ARE YOU?
FAST ENOUGH.
I HOPE.
LOOK, I CAN HANDLE IT... IF I KNOW WHERE THE MISSILES ARE. I NEED YOU FOR THAT.
I'M WITH YOU.
THEN WE HAVE A CHANCE.
LET'S MAKE IT COUNT.

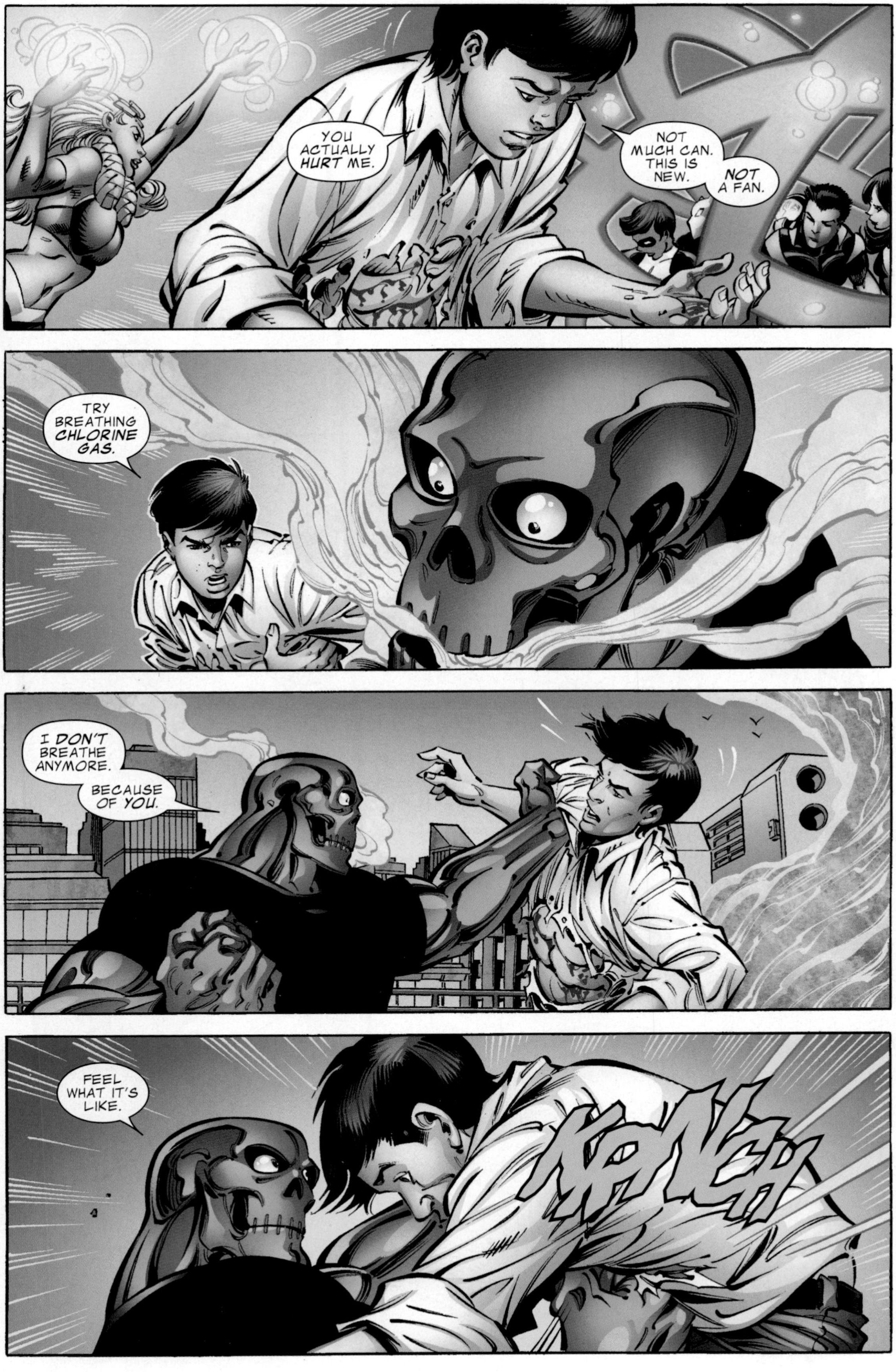
YOU ACTUALLY HURT ME.
NOT MUCH CAN. THIS IS NEW.
NOT A FAN.
TRY BREATHING CHLORINE GAS.
I DON'T BREATHE ANYMORE.
BECAUSE OF YOU.
FEEL WHAT IT'S LIKE.
KRUNCH

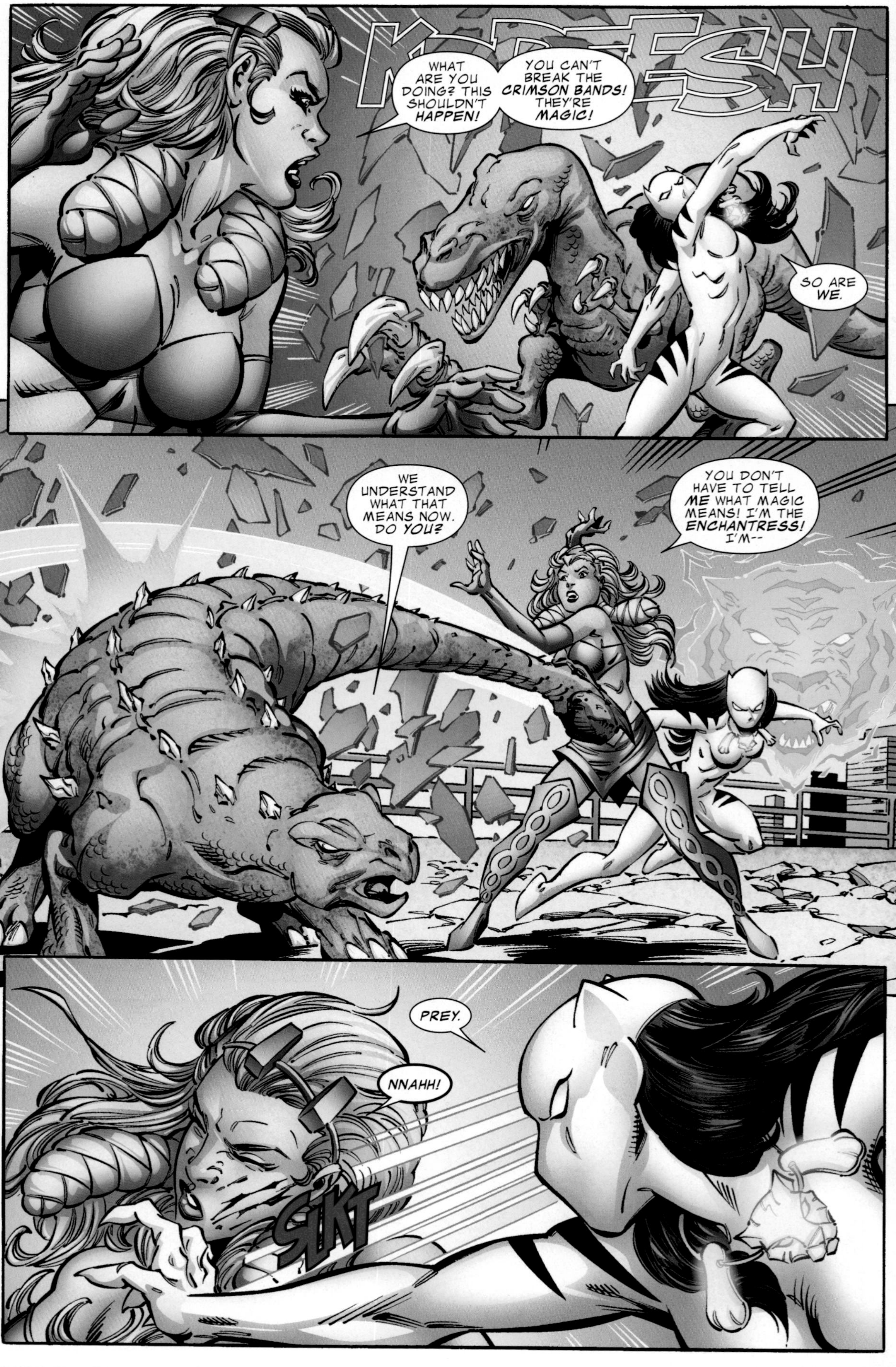

WHAT ARE YOU DOING? THIS SHOULDN'T HAPPEN!
YOU CAN'T BREAK THE CRIMSON BANDS! THEY'RE MAGIC!
SO ARE WE.
WE UNDERSTAND WHAT THAT MEANS NOW. DO YOU?
YOU DON'T HAVE TO TELL ME WHAT MAGIC MEANS! I'M THE ENCHANTRESS! I'M--
PREY.
NNAHH!
SLKT

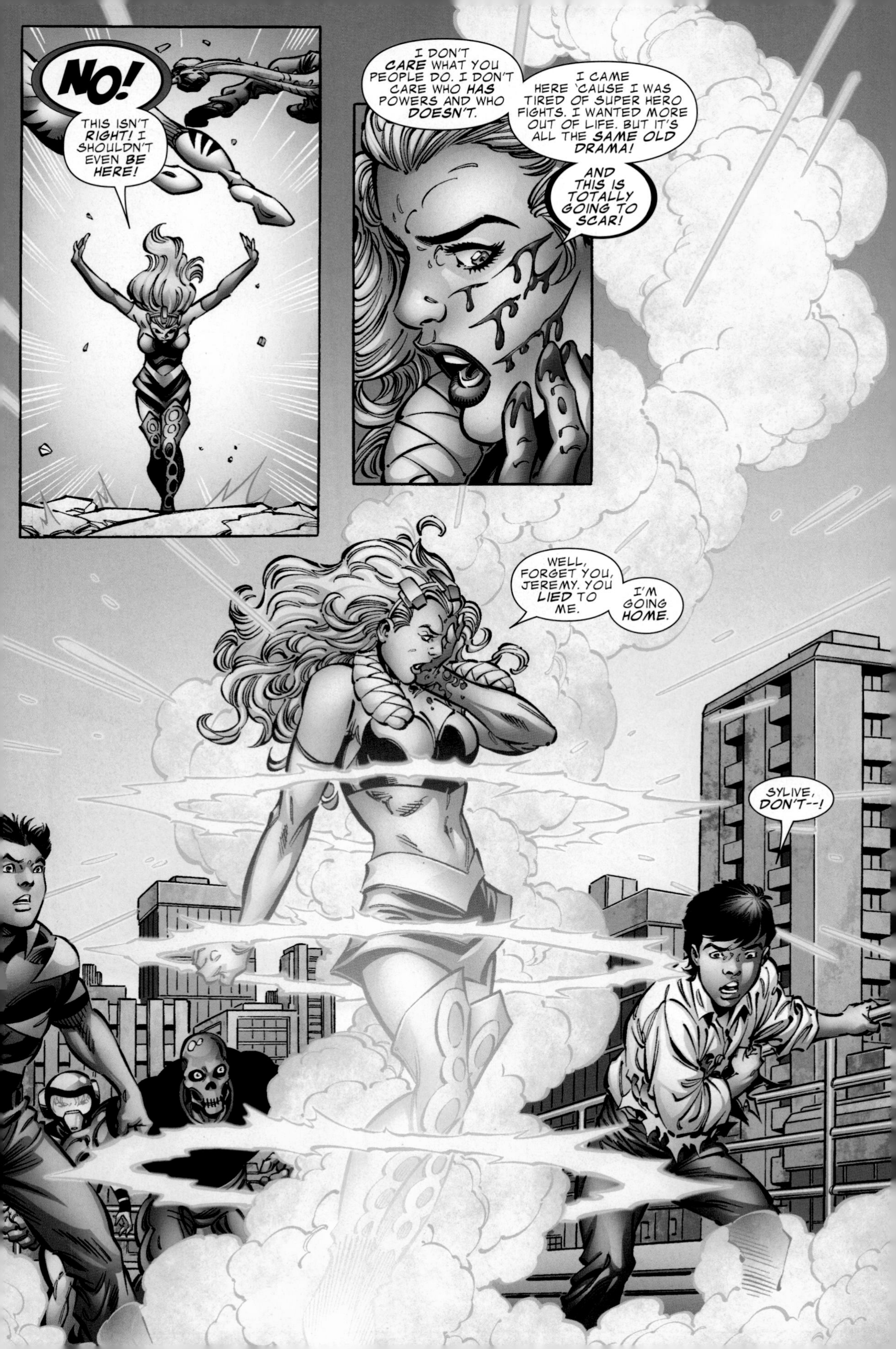
NO!
THIS ISN'T RIGHT! I SHOULDN'T EVEN BE HERE!
I DON'T CARE WHAT YOU PEOPLE DO. I DON'T CARE WHO HAS POWERS AND WHO DOESN'T.
I CAME HERE 'CAUSE I WAS TIRED OF SUPER HERO FIGHTS. I WANTED MORE OUT OF LIFE. BUT IT'S ALL THE SAME OLD DRAMA!
AND THIS IS TOTALLY GOING TO SCAR!
WELL, FORGET YOU, JEREMY. YOU LIED TO ME.
I'M GOING HOME.
SYLIVE, DON'T--!

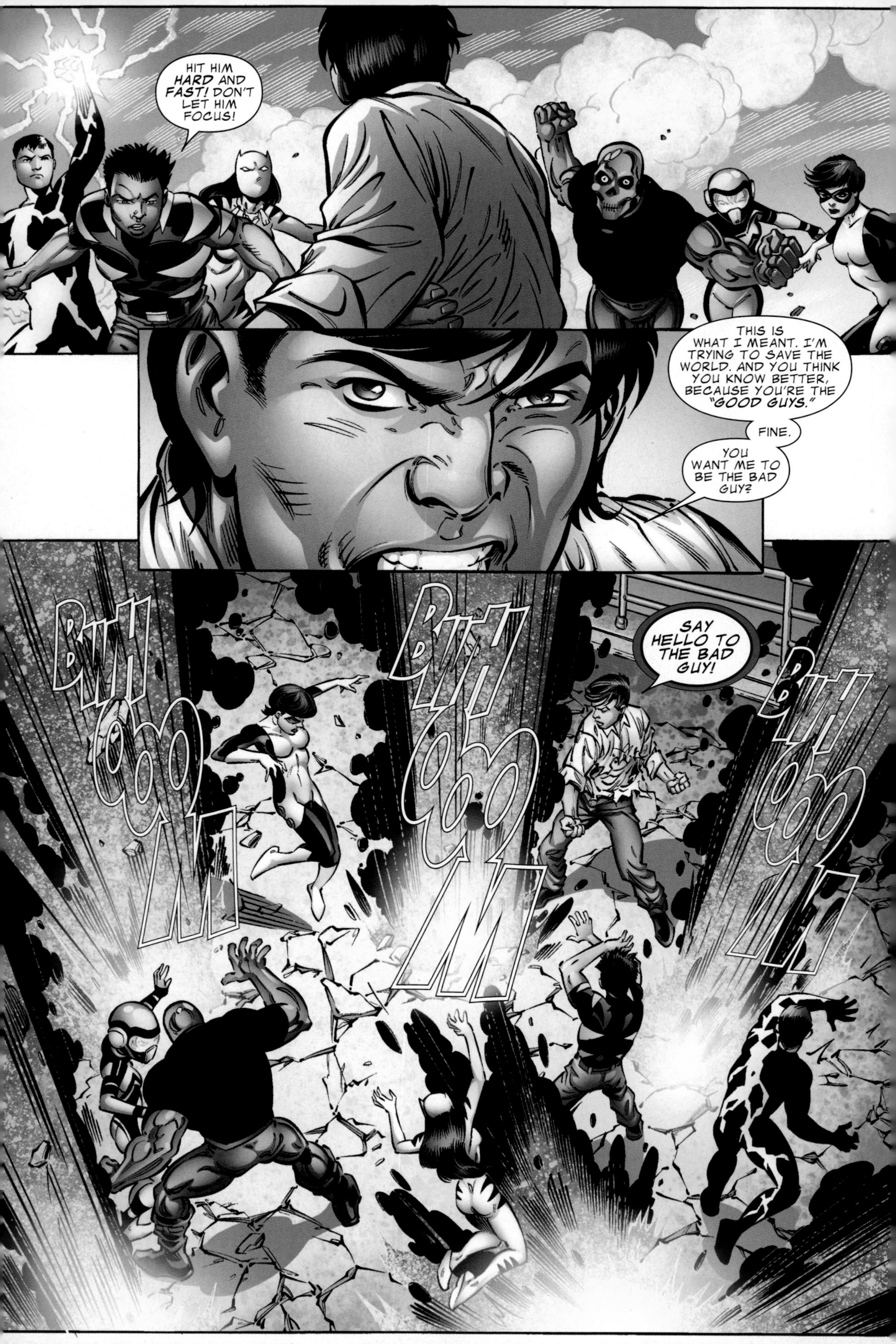
HIT HIM HARD AND FAST! DON'T LET HIM FOCUS!
THIS IS WHAT I MEANT. I'M TRYING TO SAVE THE WORLD. AND YOU THINK YOU KNOW BETTER, BECAUSE YOU'RE THE "GOOD GUYS."
FINE.
YOU WANT ME TO BE THE BAD GUY?
BWHOOOM
BWHOOOM
SAY HELLO TO THE BAD GUY!
BWHOOOM

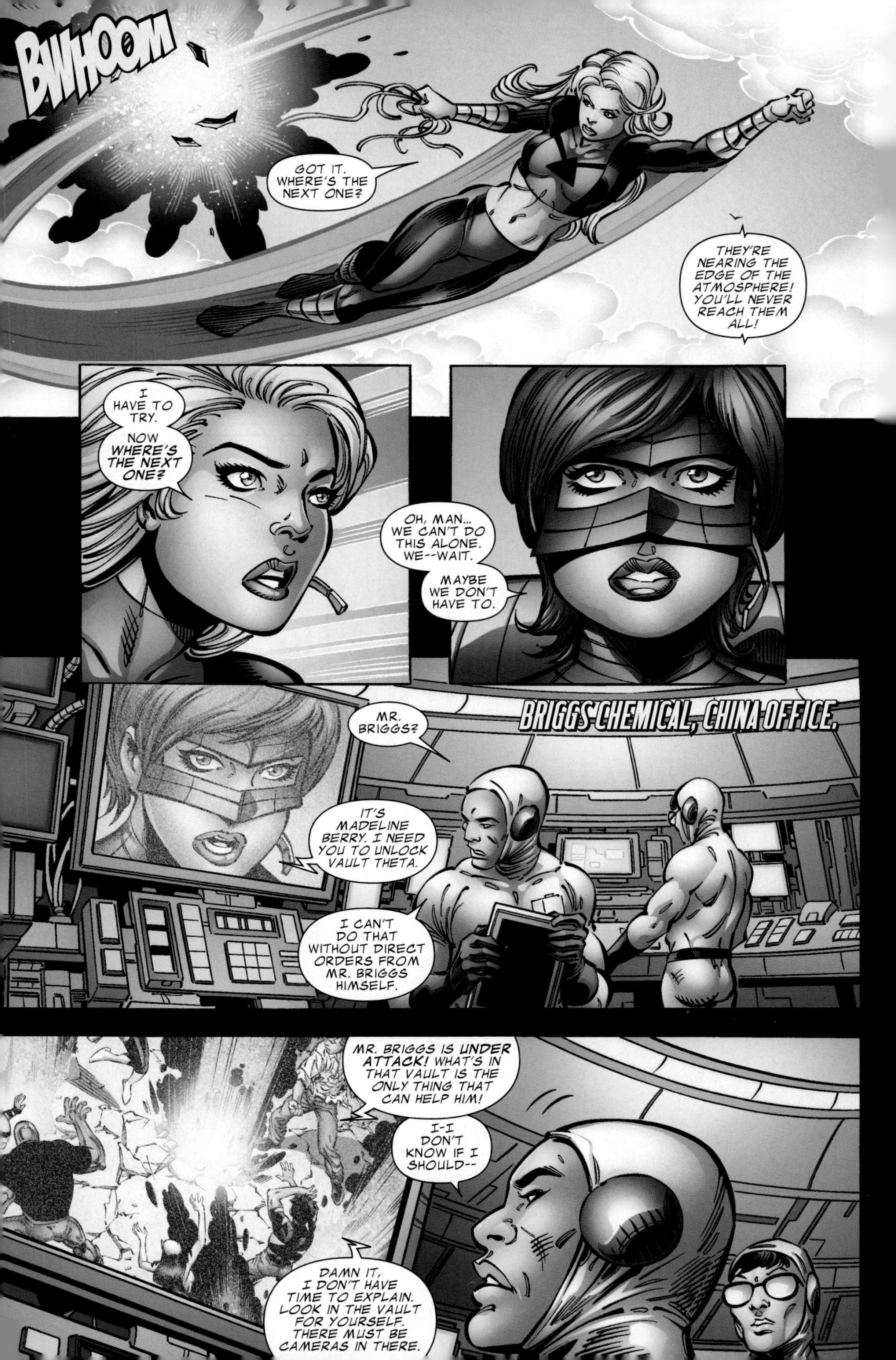
BWHOOM
GOT IT. WHERE'S THE NEXT ONE?
THEY'RE NEARING THE EDGE OF THE ATMOSPHERE! YOU'LL NEVER REACH THEM ALL!
I HAVE TO TRY.
NOW WHERE'S THE NEXT ONE?
OH, MAN... WE CAN'T DO THIS ALONE. WE--WAIT.
MAYBE WE DON'T HAVE TO.
BRIGGS CHEMICAL, CHINA OFFICE.
MR. BRIGGS?
IT'S MADELINE BERRY. I NEED YOU TO UNLOCK VAULT THETA.
I CAN'T DO THAT WITHOUT DIRECT ORDERS FROM MR. BRIGGS HIMSELF.
MR. BRIGGS IS UNDER ATTACK! WHAT'S IN THAT VAULT IS THE ONLY THING THAT CAN HELP HIM!
I-I DON'T KNOW IF I SHOULD--
DAMN IT, I DON'T HAVE TIME TO EXPLAIN. LOOK IN THE VAULT FOR YOURSELF. THERE MUST BE CAMERAS IN THERE.

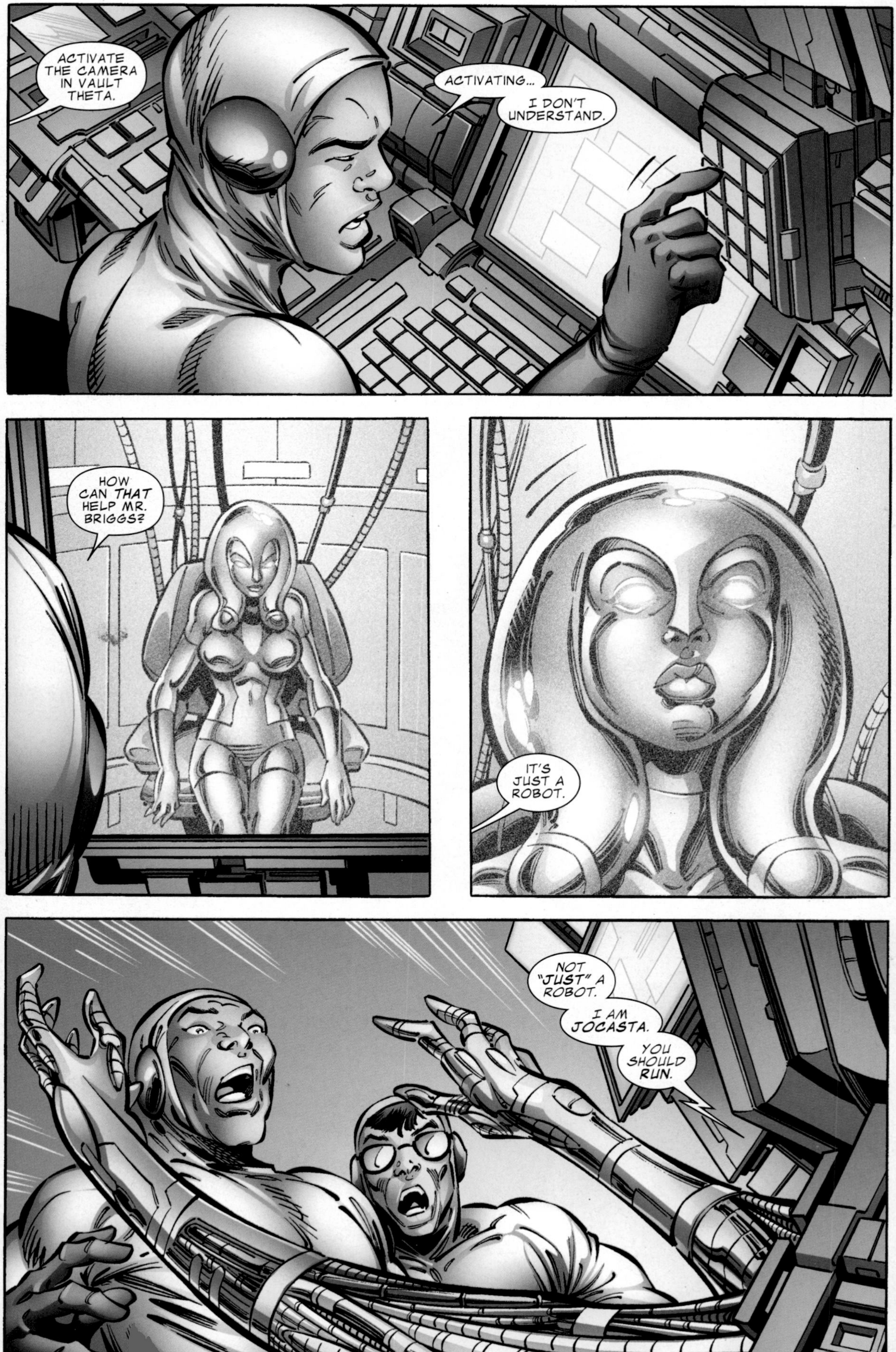
ACTIVATE THE CAMERA IN VAULT THETA.
ACTIVATING...
I DON'T UNDERSTAND.
HOW CAN *THAT* HELP MR. BRIGGS?
IT'S JUST A ROBOT.
NOT "*JUST*" A ROBOT.
I AM **JOCASTA**.
YOU SHOULD **RUN**.

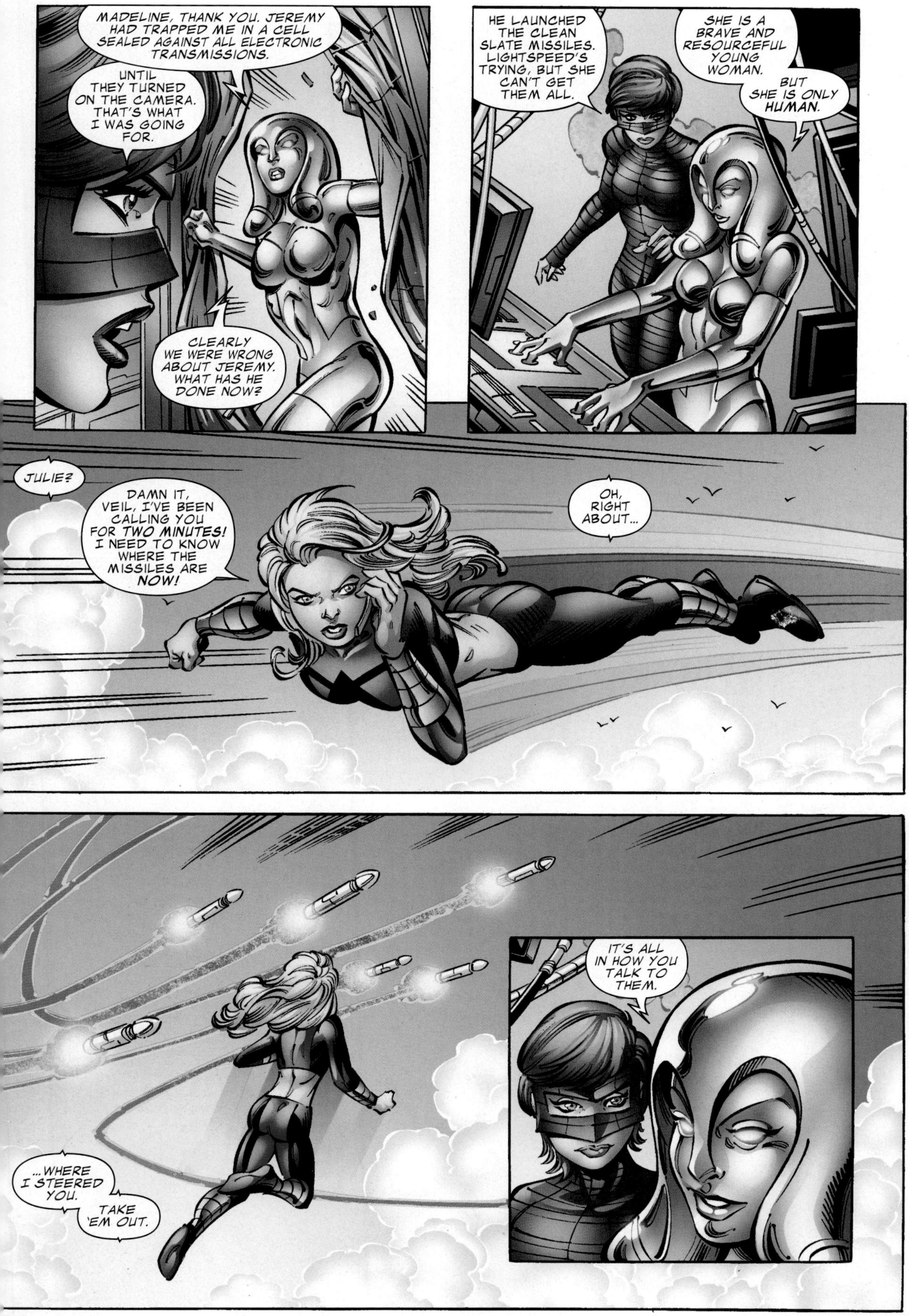
MADELINE, THANK YOU. JEREMY HAD TRAPPED ME IN A CELL SEALED AGAINST ALL ELECTRONIC TRANSMISSIONS.
UNTIL THEY TURNED ON THE CAMERA. THAT'S WHAT I WAS GOING FOR.
CLEARLY WE WERE WRONG ABOUT JEREMY. WHAT HAS HE DONE NOW?
HE LAUNCHED THE CLEAN SLATE MISSILES. LIGHTSPEED'S TRYING, BUT SHE CAN'T GET THEM ALL.
SHE IS A BRAVE AND RESOURCEFUL YOUNG WOMAN.
BUT SHE IS ONLY HUMAN.
JULIE?
DAMN IT, VEIL, I'VE BEEN CALLING YOU FOR TWO MINUTES! I NEED TO KNOW WHERE THE MISSILES ARE NOW!
OH, RIGHT ABOUT...
...WHERE I STEERED YOU.
TAKE 'EM OUT.
IT'S ALL IN HOW YOU TALK TO THEM.

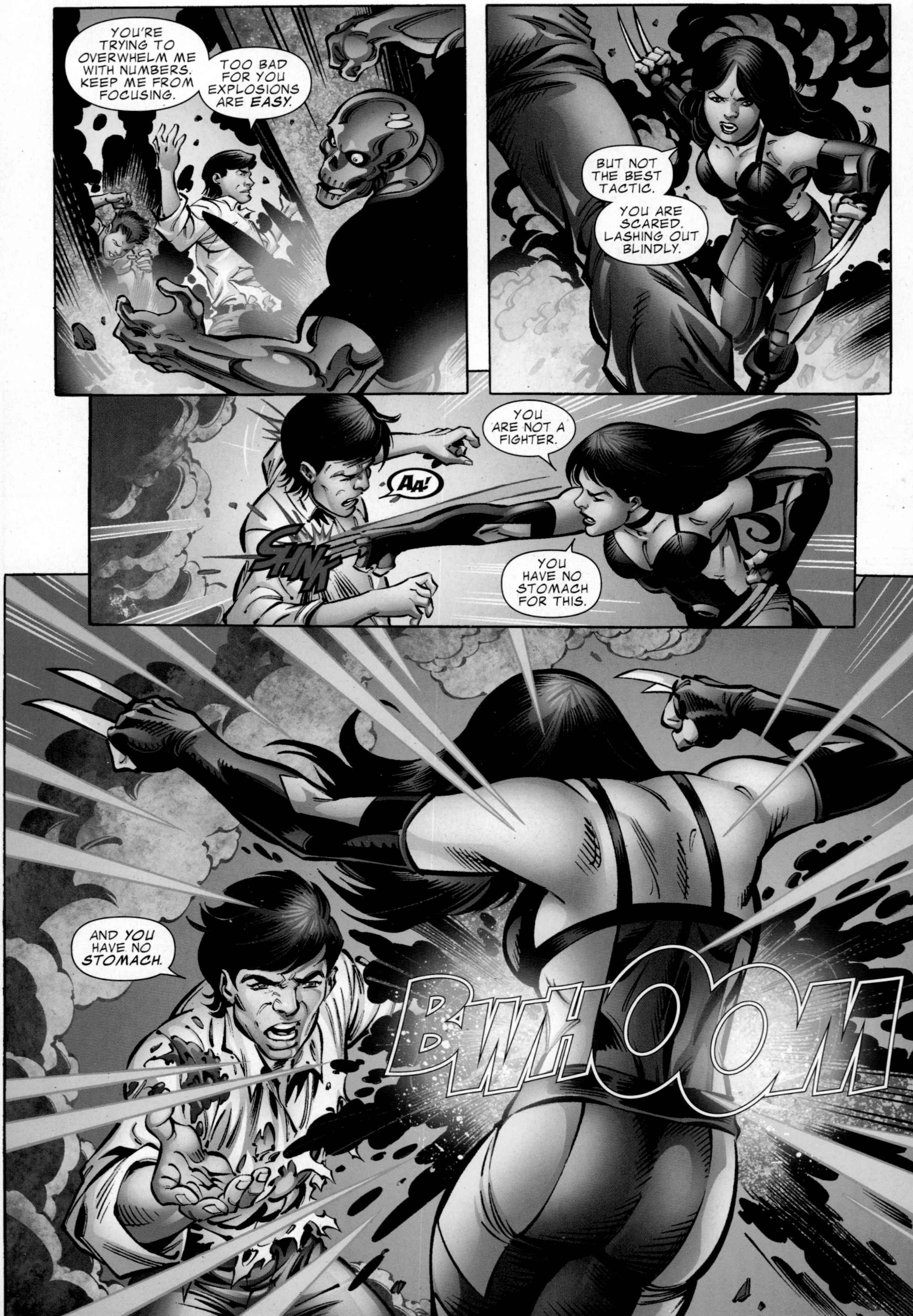

YOU'RE TRYING TO OVERWHELM ME WITH NUMBERS. KEEP ME FROM FOCUSING.
TOO BAD FOR YOU EXPLOSIONS ARE EASY.
BUT NOT THE BEST TACTIC.
YOU ARE SCARED. LASHING OUT BLINDLY.
YOU ARE NOT A FIGHTER.
AA!
SHNK
YOU HAVE NO STOMACH FOR THIS.
AND YOU HAVE NO STOMACH.
BWHOOOM

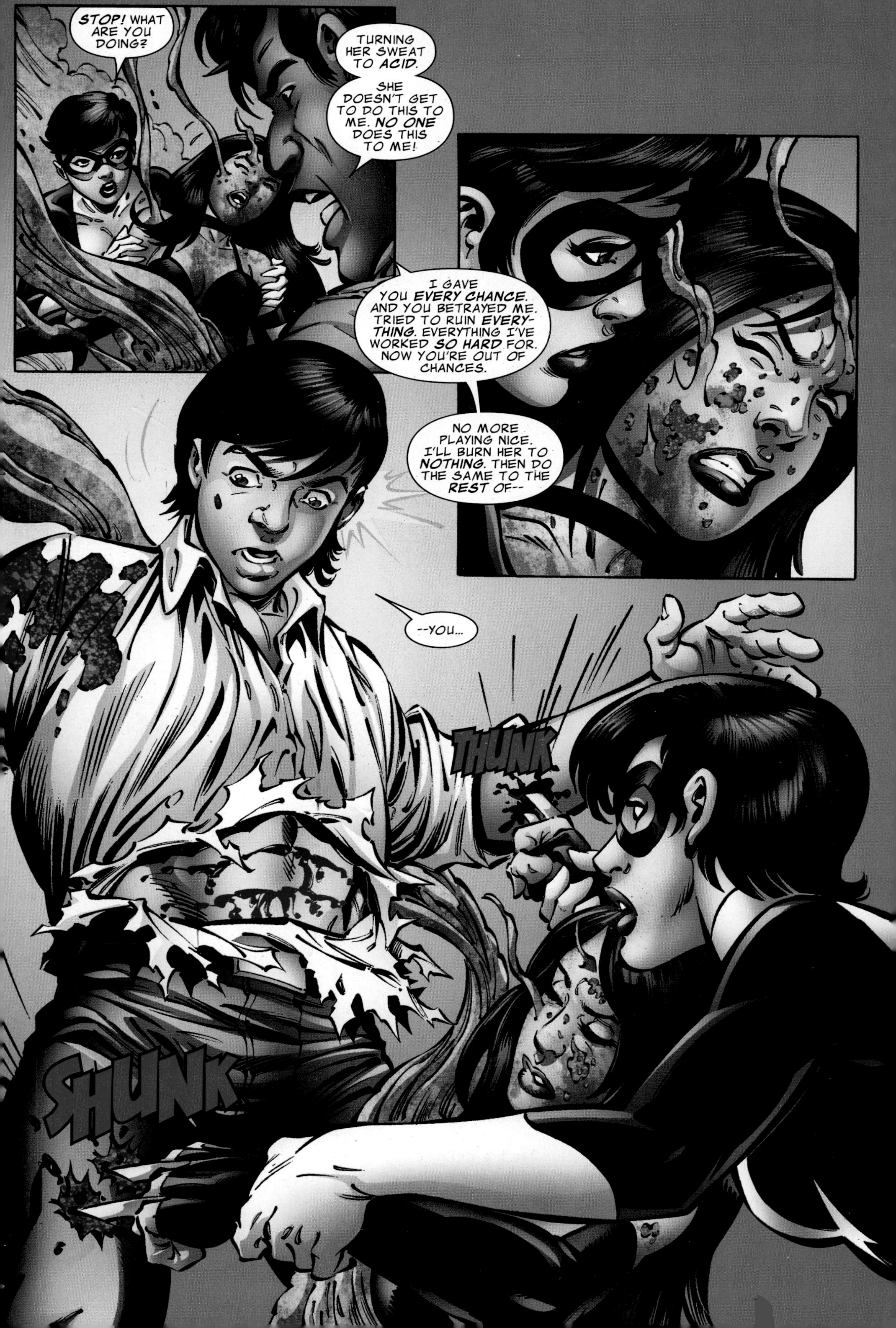
STOP! WHAT ARE YOU DOING?
TURNING HER SWEAT TO ACID.
SHE DOESN'T GET TO DO THIS TO ME. NO ONE DOES THIS TO ME!
I GAVE YOU EVERY CHANCE. AND YOU BETRAYED ME. TRIED TO RUIN EVERYTHING. EVERYTHING I'VE WORKED SO HARD FOR. NOW YOU'RE OUT OF CHANCES.
NO MORE PLAYING NICE. I'LL BURN HER TO NOTHING. THEN DO THE SAME TO THE REST OF--
--YOU...
THUNK
SHUNK

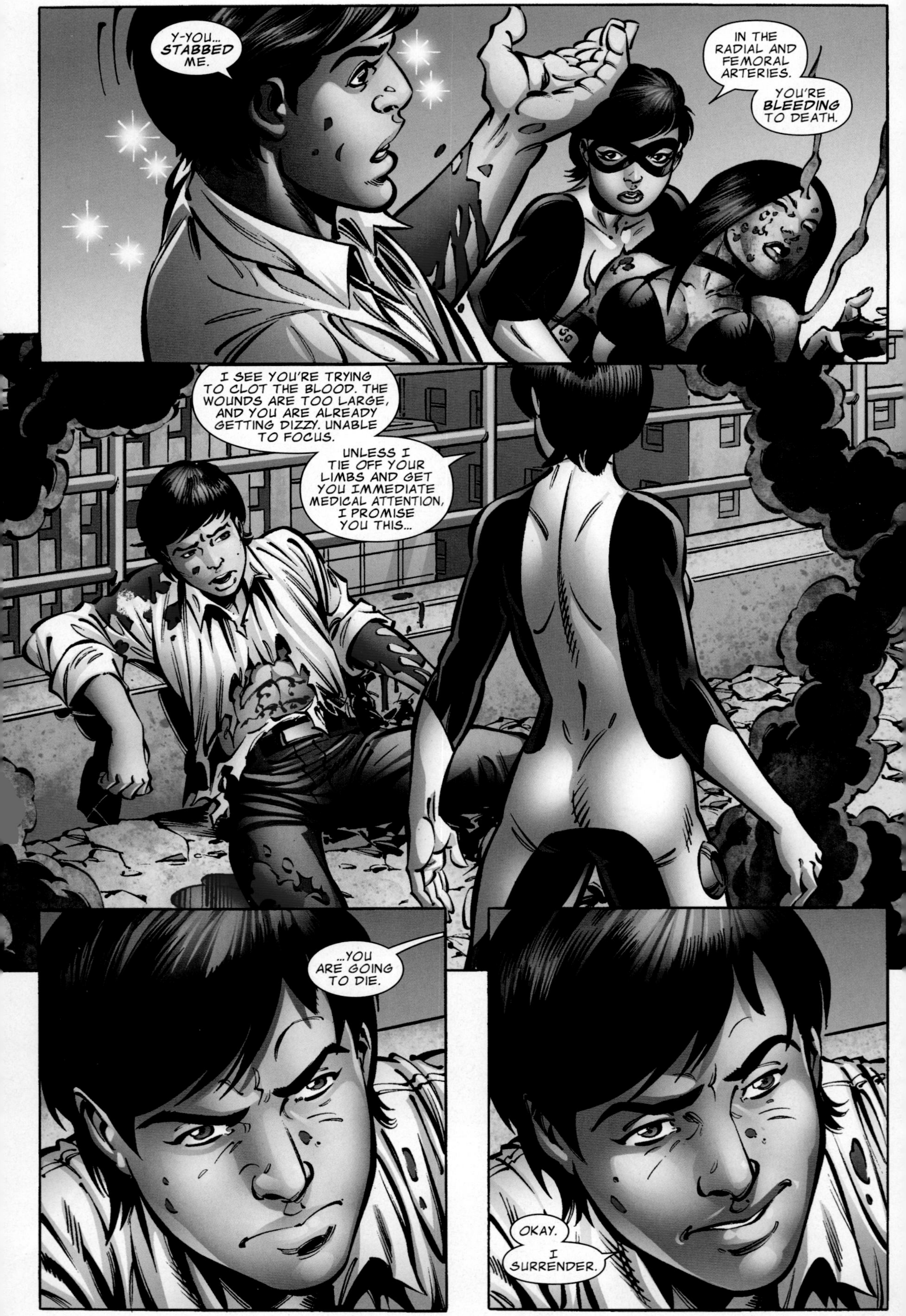
Y-YOU... STABBED ME.
IN THE RADIAL AND FEMORAL ARTERIES.
YOU'RE BLEEDING TO DEATH.
I SEE YOU'RE TRYING TO CLOT THE BLOOD. THE WOUNDS ARE TOO LARGE, AND YOU ARE ALREADY GETTING DIZZY. UNABLE TO FOCUS.
UNLESS I TIE OFF YOUR LIMBS AND GET YOU IMMEDIATE MEDICAL ATTENTION, I PROMISE YOU THIS...
...YOU ARE GOING TO DIE.
OKAY.
I SURRENDER.

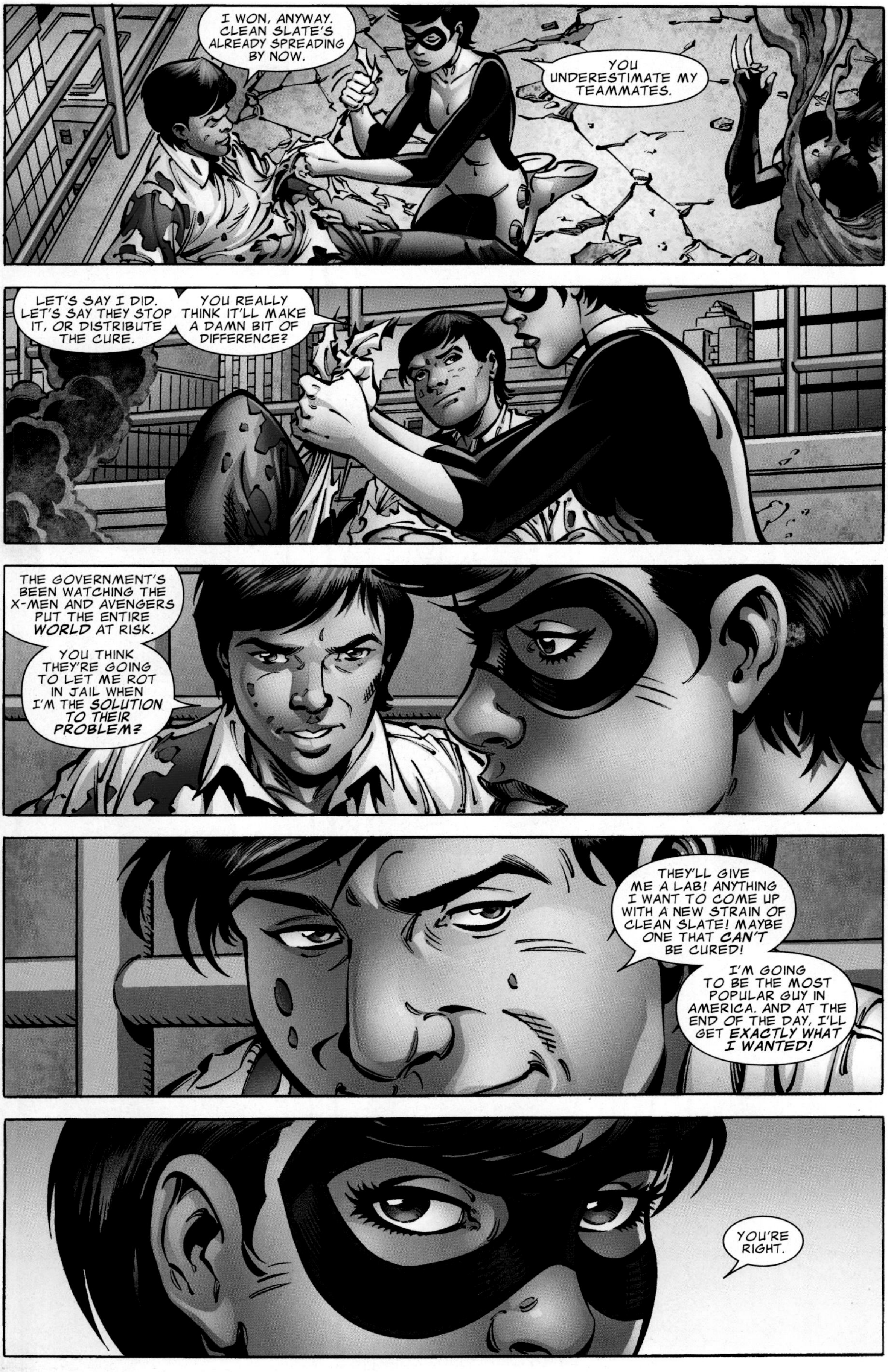

I WON, ANYWAY. CLEAN SLATE'S ALREADY SPREADING BY NOW.
YOU UNDERESTIMATE MY TEAMMATES.
LET'S SAY I DID. LET'S SAY THEY STOP IT, OR DISTRIBUTE THE CURE.
YOU REALLY THINK IT'LL MAKE A DAMN BIT OF DIFFERENCE?
THE GOVERNMENT'S BEEN WATCHING THE X-MEN AND AVENGERS PUT THE ENTIRE WORLD AT RISK.
YOU THINK THEY'RE GOING TO LET ME ROT IN JAIL WHEN I'M THE SOLUTION TO THEIR PROBLEM?
THEY'LL GIVE ME A LAB! ANYTHING I WANT TO COME UP WITH A NEW STRAIN OF CLEAN SLATE! MAYBE ONE THAT CAN'T BE CURED!
I'M GOING TO BE THE MOST POPULAR GUY IN AMERICA. AND AT THE END OF THE DAY, I'LL GET EXACTLY WHAT I WANTED!
YOU'RE RIGHT.

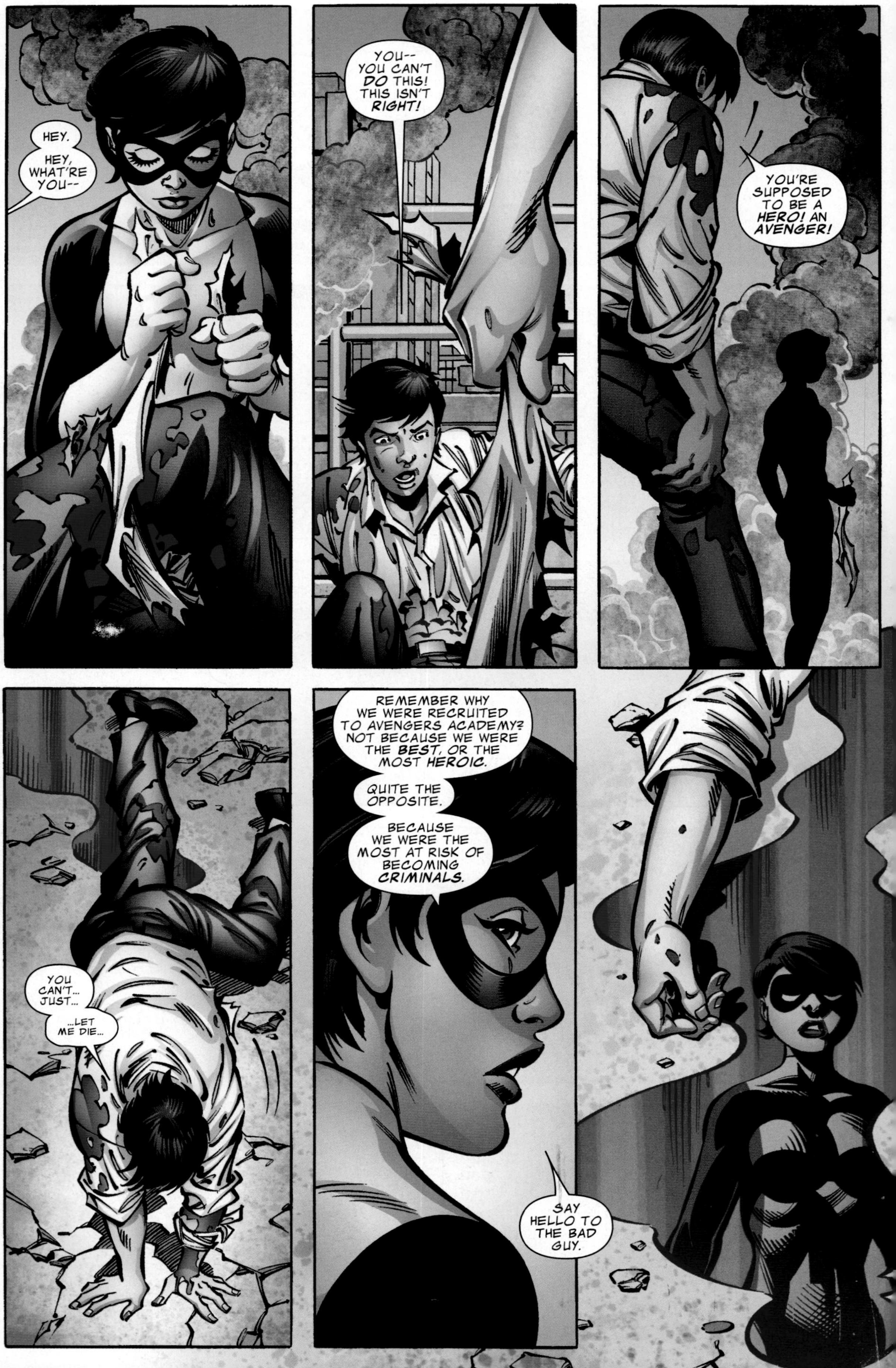
HEY.
HEY, WHAT'RE YOU--
YOU-- YOU CAN'T DO THIS! THIS ISN'T RIGHT!
YOU'RE SUPPOSED TO BE A HERO! AN AVENGER!
YOU CAN'T... JUST...
...LET ME DIE...
REMEMBER WHY WE WERE RECRUITED TO AVENGERS ACADEMY? NOT BECAUSE WE WERE THE BEST, OR THE MOST HEROIC.
QUITE THE OPPOSITE.
BECAUSE WE WERE THE MOST AT RISK OF BECOMING CRIMINALS.
SAY HELLO TO THE BAD GUY.

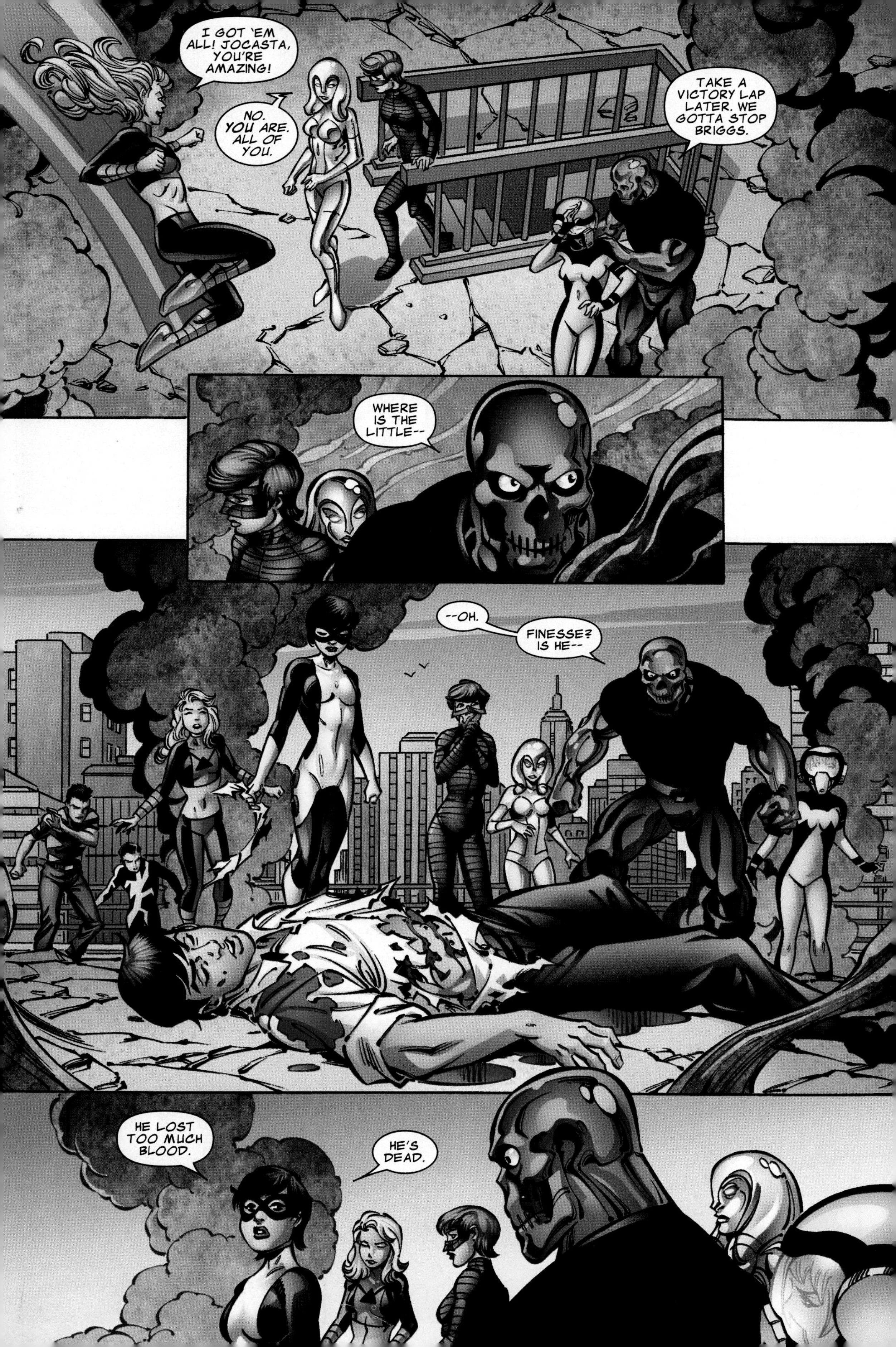
I GOT 'EM ALL! JOCASTA, YOU'RE AMAZING!
NO. YOU ARE. ALL OF YOU.
TAKE A VICTORY LAP LATER. WE GOTTA STOP BRIGGS.
WHERE IS THE LITTLE--
--OH.
FINESSE? IS HE--
HE LOST TOO MUCH BLOOD.
HE'S DEAD.

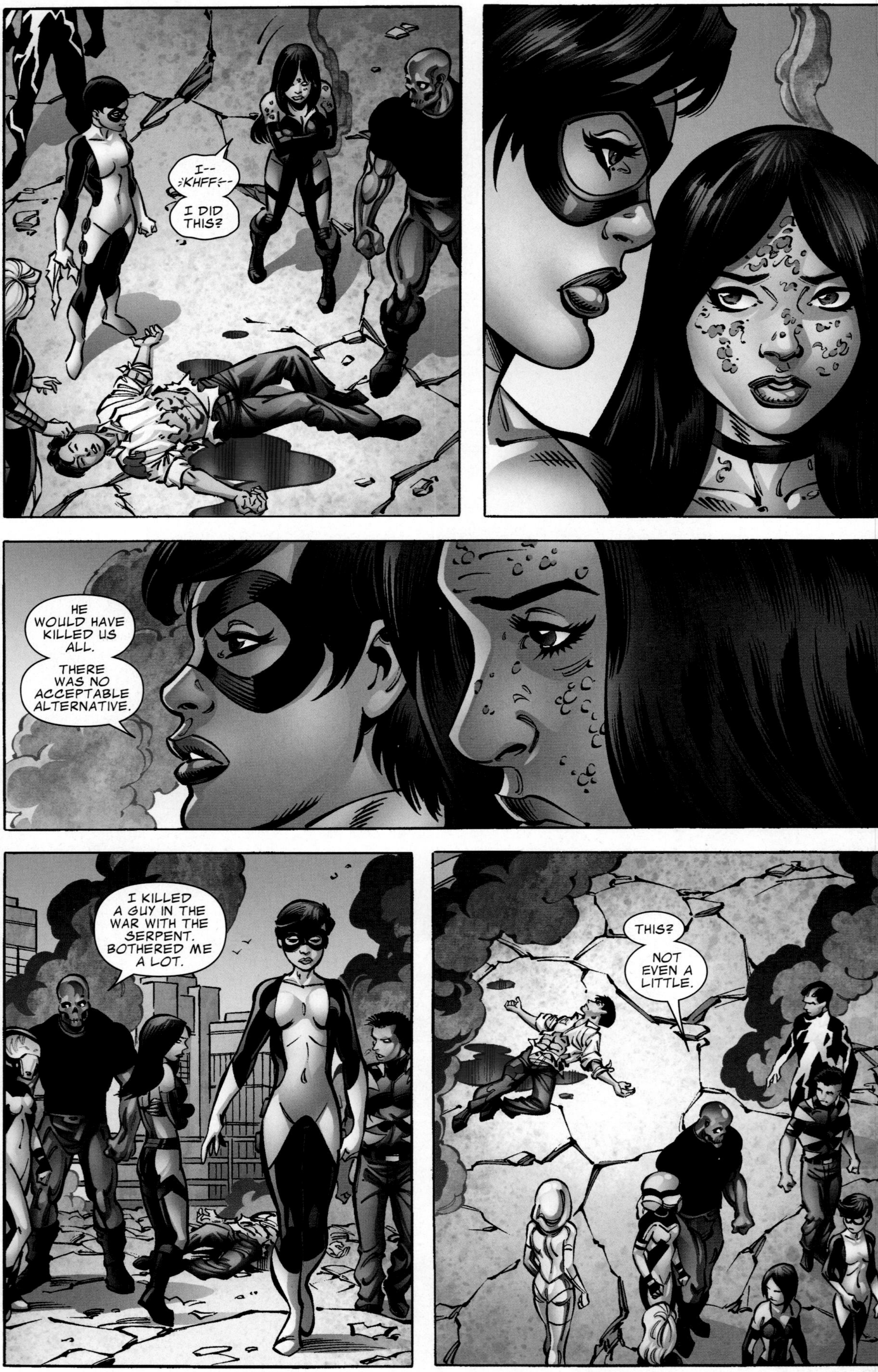
I-- ≯KHFF≮-- I DID THIS?
HE WOULD HAVE KILLED US ALL.
THERE WAS NO ACCEPTABLE ALTERNATIVE.
I KILLED A GUY IN THE WAR WITH THE SERPENT. BOTHERED ME A LOT.
THIS?
NOT EVEN A LITTLE.

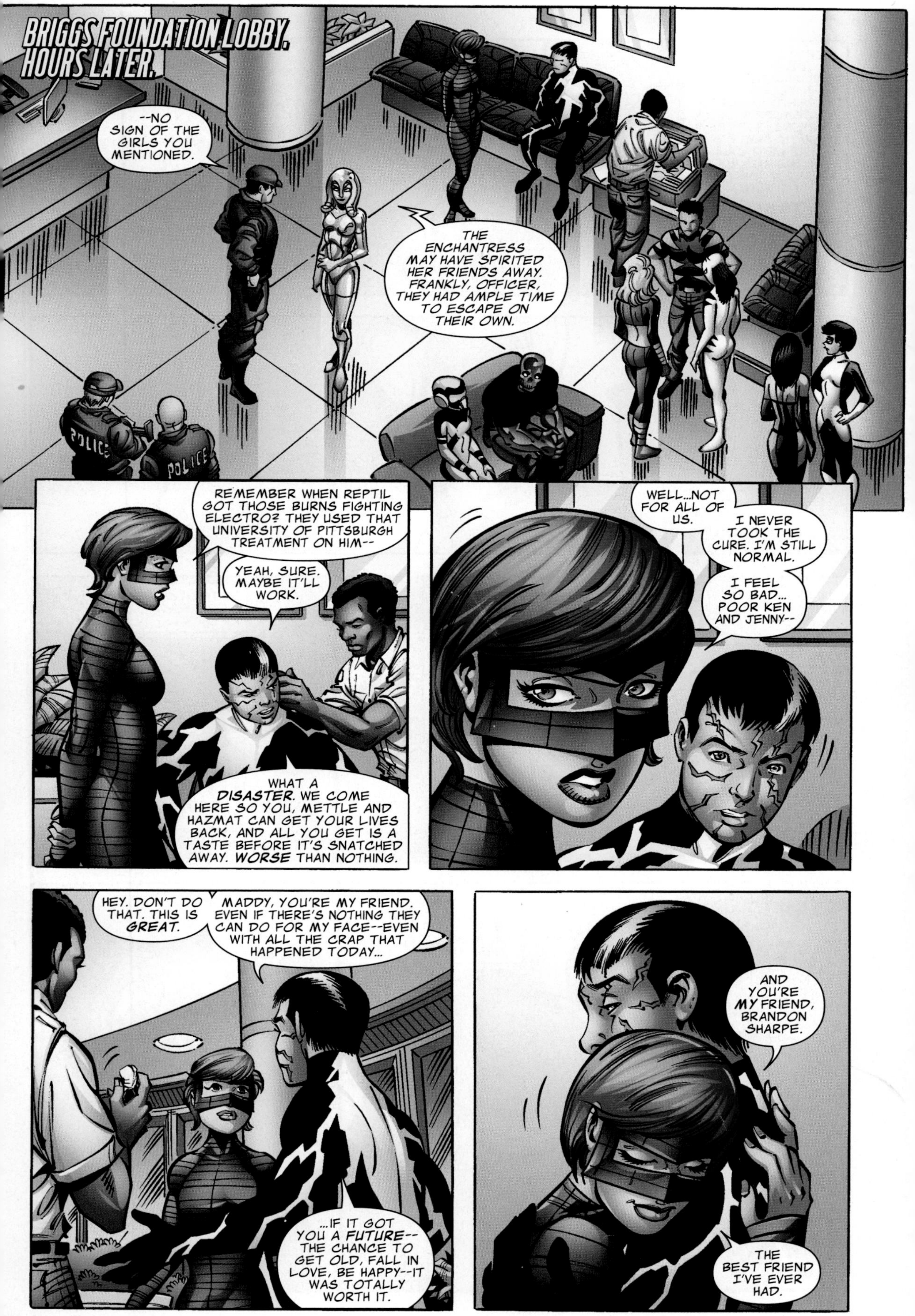
BRIGGS FOUNDATION LOBBY. HOURS LATER.
--NO SIGN OF THE GIRLS YOU MENTIONED.
THE ENCHANTRESS MAY HAVE SPIRITED HER FRIENDS AWAY. FRANKLY, OFFICER, THEY HAD AMPLE TIME TO ESCAPE ON THEIR OWN.
POLICE
POLICE
REMEMBER WHEN REPTIL GOT THOSE BURNS FIGHTING ELECTRO? THEY USED THAT UNIVERSITY OF PITTSBURGH TREATMENT ON HIM--
YEAH, SURE. MAYBE IT'LL WORK.
WHAT A DISASTER. WE COME HERE SO YOU, METTLE AND HAZMAT CAN GET YOUR LIVES BACK, AND ALL YOU GET IS A TASTE BEFORE IT'S SNATCHED AWAY. WORSE THAN NOTHING.
WELL...NOT FOR ALL OF US.
I NEVER TOOK THE CURE. I'M STILL NORMAL.
I FEEL SO BAD... POOR KEN AND JENNY--
HEY. DON'T DO THAT. THIS IS GREAT.
MADDY, YOU'RE MY FRIEND. EVEN IF THERE'S NOTHING THEY CAN DO FOR MY FACE--EVEN WITH ALL THE CRAP THAT HAPPENED TODAY...
...IF IT GOT YOU A FUTURE--THE CHANCE TO GET OLD, FALL IN LOVE, BE HAPPY--IT WAS TOTALLY WORTH IT.
AND YOU'RE MY FRIEND, BRANDON SHARPE.
THE BEST FRIEND I'VE EVER HAD.

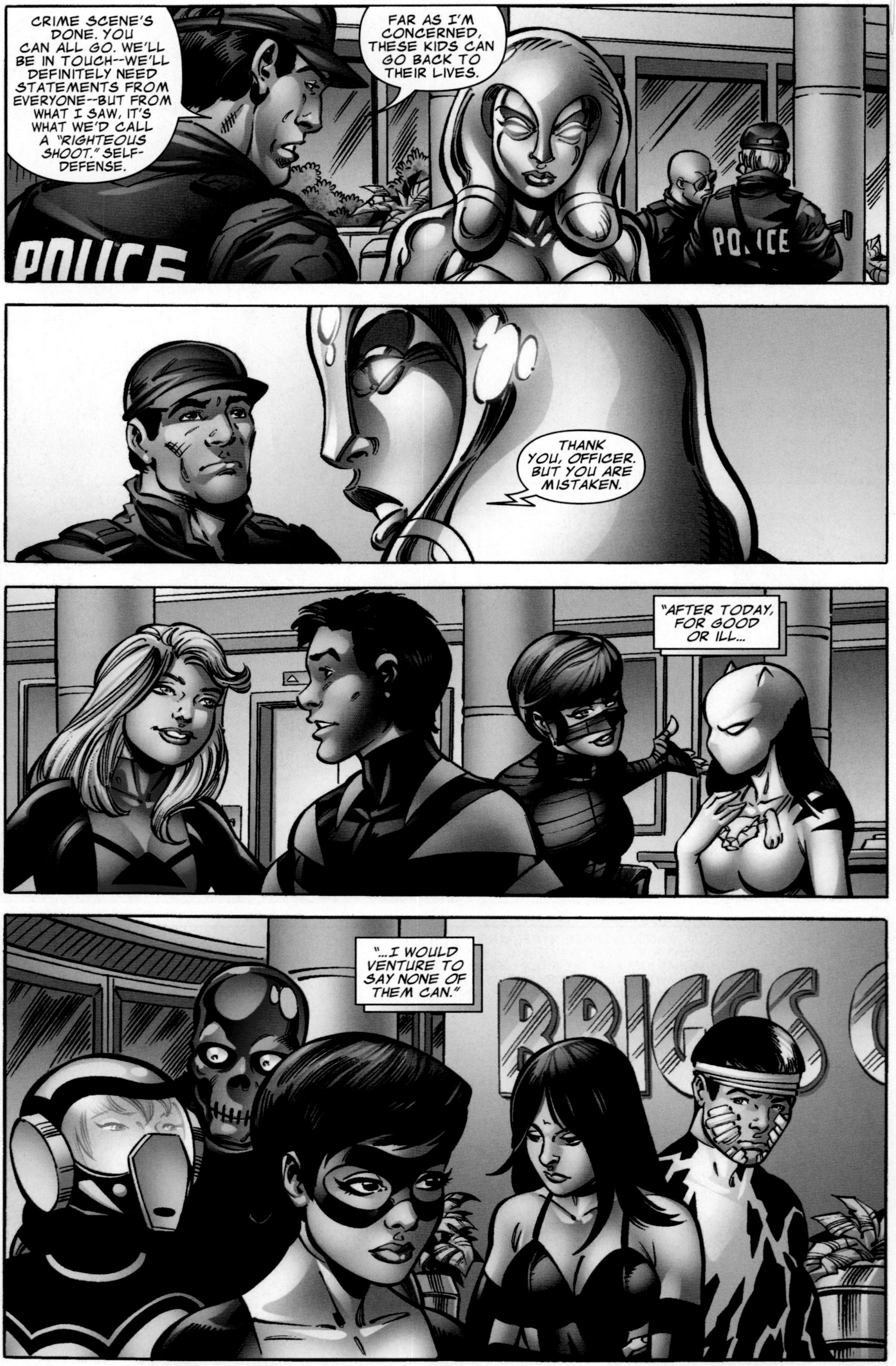
CRIME SCENE'S DONE. YOU CAN ALL GO. WE'LL BE IN TOUCH--WE'LL DEFINITELY NEED STATEMENTS FROM EVERYONE--BUT FROM WHAT I SAW, IT'S WHAT WE'D CALL A "RIGHTEOUS SHOOT." SELF-DEFENSE.
FAR AS I'M CONCERNED, THESE KIDS CAN GO BACK TO THEIR LIVES.
POLICE
POLICE
THANK YOU, OFFICER. BUT YOU ARE MISTAKEN.
"AFTER TODAY, FOR GOOD OR ILL...
"...I WOULD VENTURE TO SAY NONE OF THEM CAN."

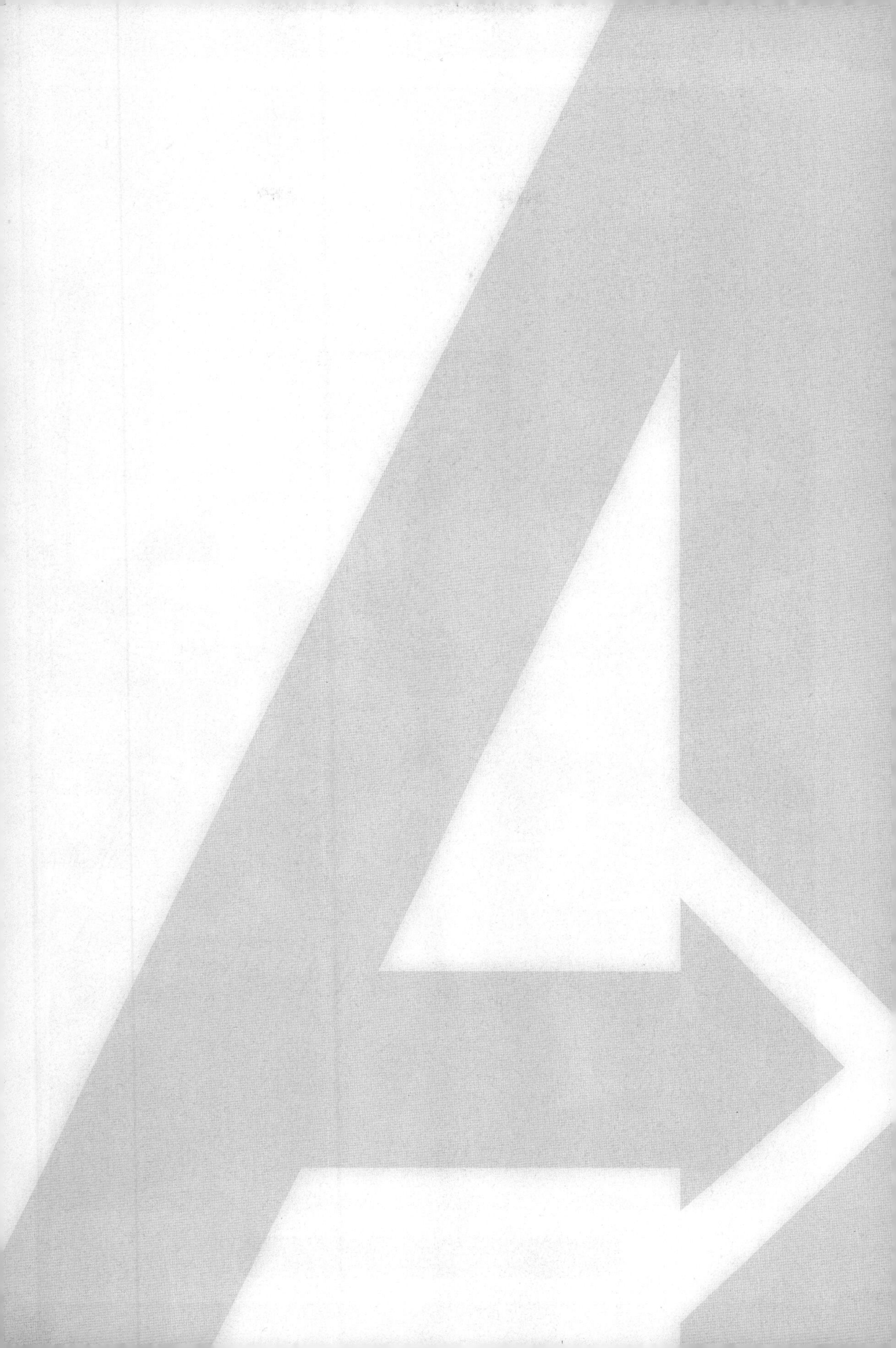

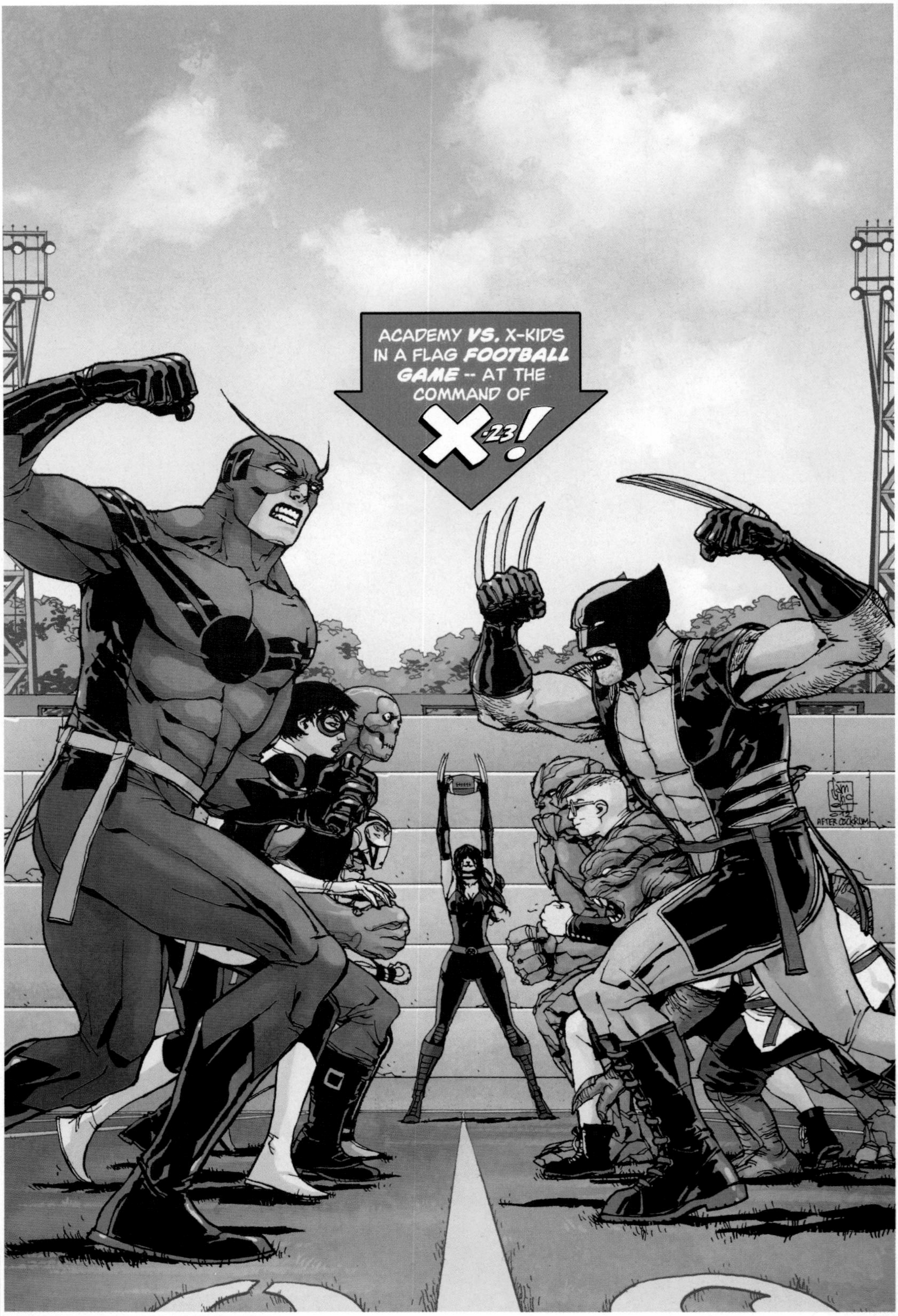
ACADEMY VS. X-KIDS IN A FLAG FOOTBALL GAME -- AT THE COMMAND OF X-23!
AFTER COCKRUM

Avengers Academy #38

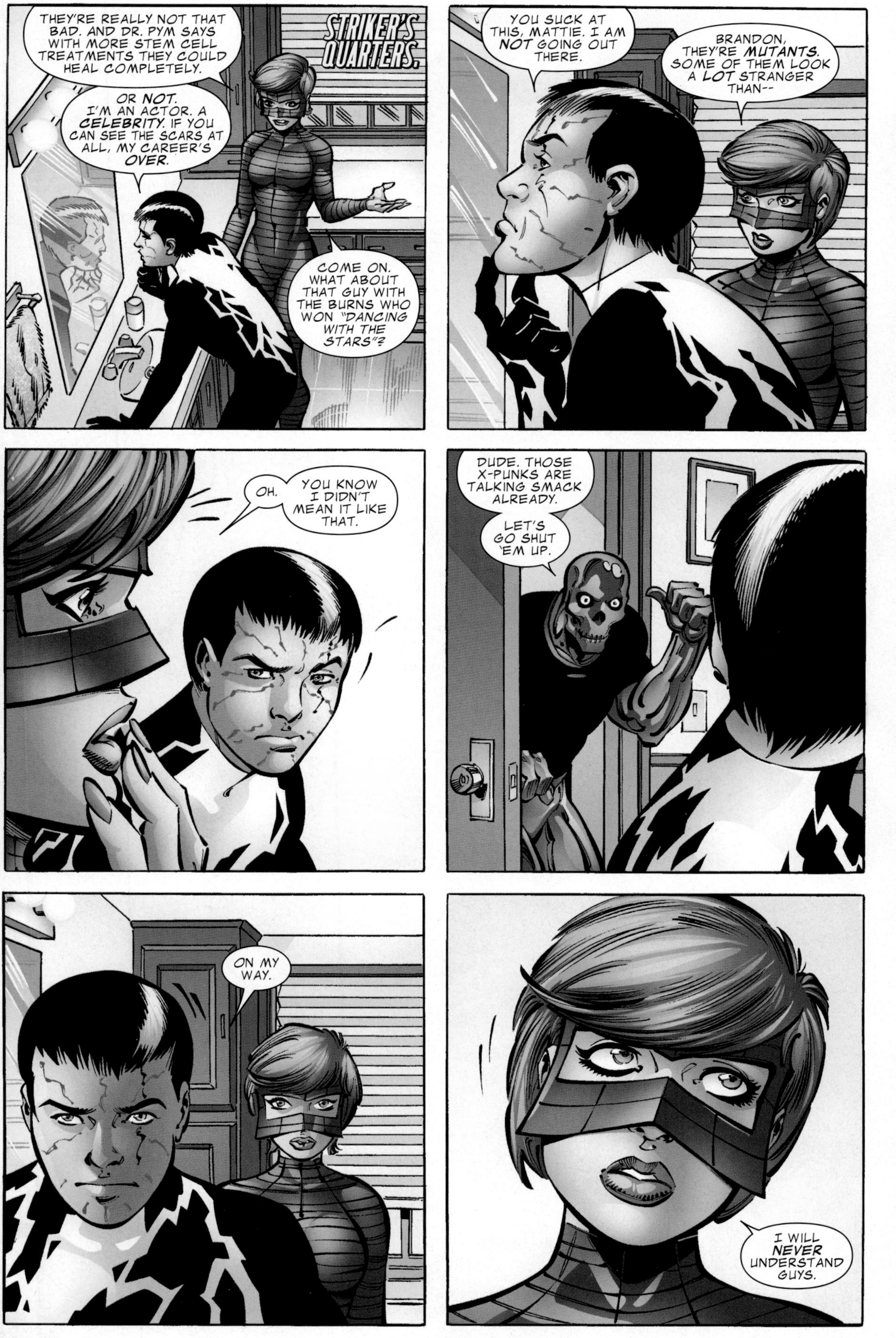

THEY'RE REALLY NOT THAT BAD. AND DR. PYM SAYS WITH MORE STEM CELL TREATMENTS THEY COULD HEAL COMPLETELY.
STRIKER'S QUARTERS.
OR NOT. I'M AN ACTOR. A CELEBRITY. IF YOU CAN SEE THE SCARS AT ALL, MY CAREER'S OVER.
COME ON. WHAT ABOUT THAT GUY WITH THE BURNS WHO WON "DANCING WITH THE STARS"?
YOU SUCK AT THIS, MATTIE. I AM NOT GOING OUT THERE.
BRANDON, THEY'RE MUTANTS. SOME OF THEM LOOK A LOT STRANGER THAN--
OH.
YOU KNOW I DIDN'T MEAN IT LIKE THAT.
DUDE. THOSE X-PUNKS ARE TALKING SMACK ALREADY.
LET'S GO SHUT 'EM UP.
ON MY WAY.
I WILL NEVER UNDERSTAND GUYS.

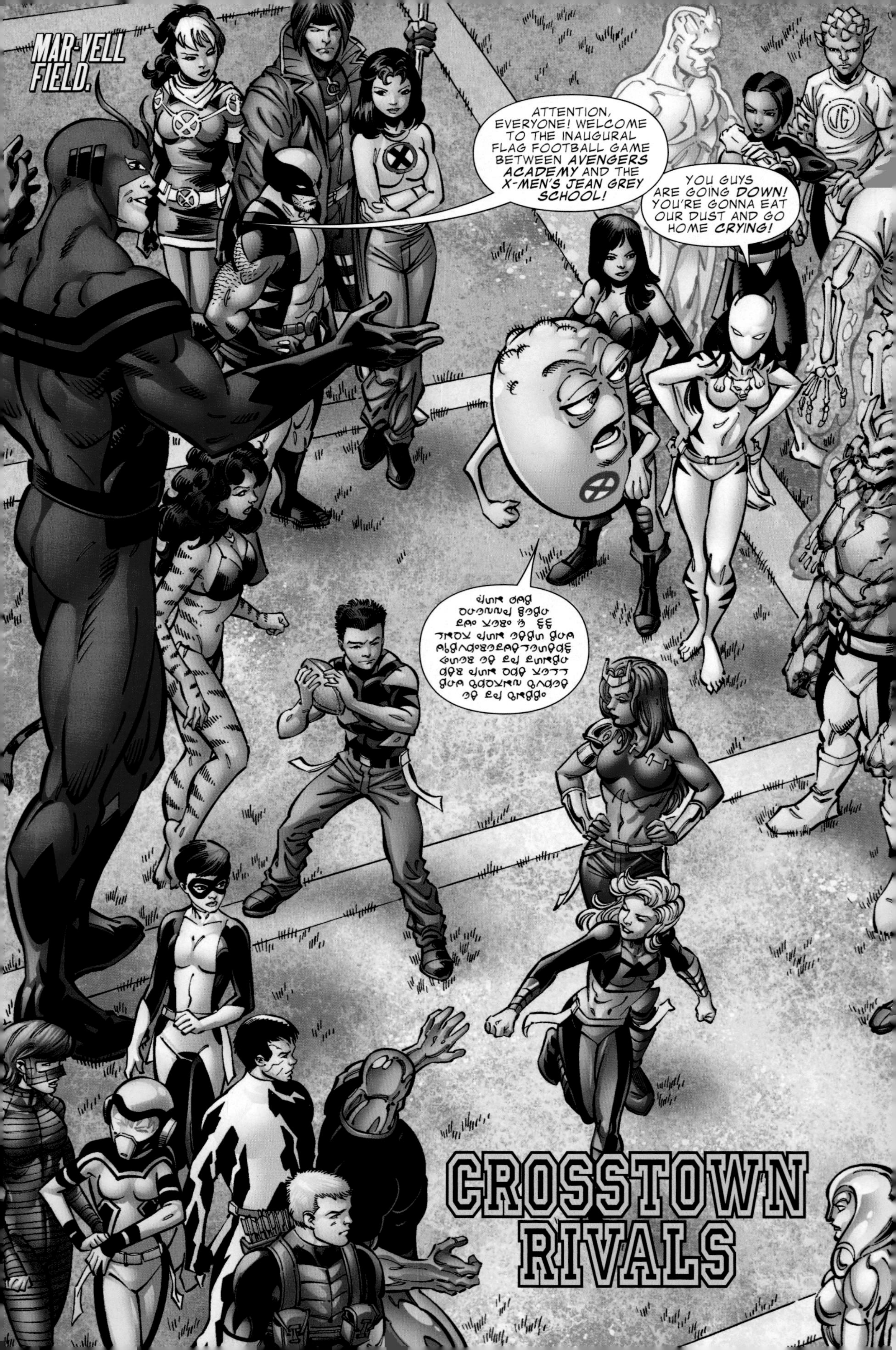
MAR-VELL FIELD.
ATTENTION, EVERYONE! WELCOME TO THE INAUGURAL FLAG FOOTBALL GAME BETWEEN AVENGERS ACADEMY AND THE X-MEN'S JEAN GREY SCHOOL!
YOU GUYS ARE GOING DOWN! YOU'RE GONNA EAT OUR DUST AND GO HOME CRYING!
CROSSTOWN RIVALS

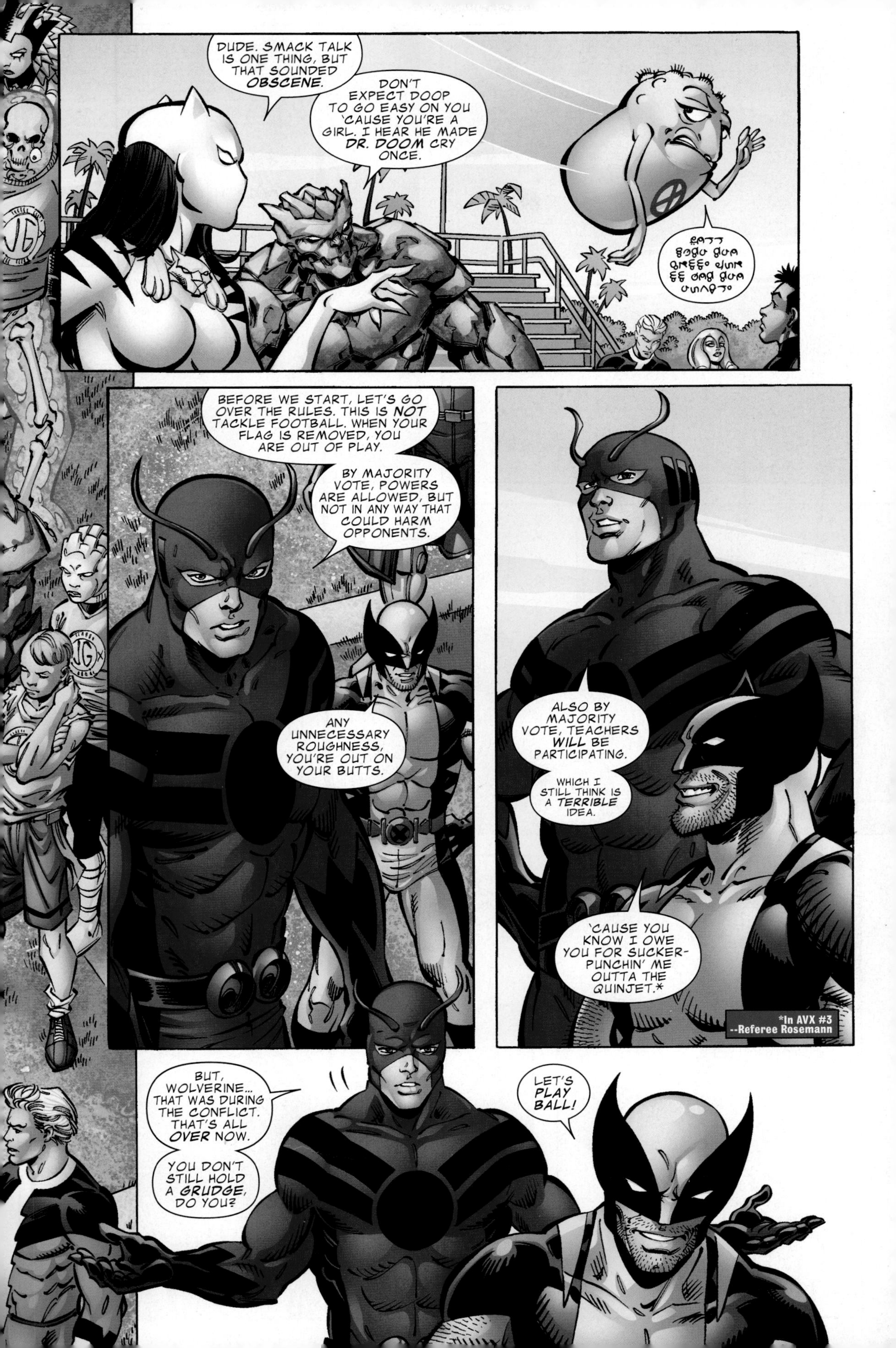
DUDE. SMACK TALK IS ONE THING, BUT THAT SOUNDED OBSCENE.
DON'T EXPECT DOOP TO GO EASY ON YOU 'CAUSE YOU'RE A GIRL. I HEAR HE MADE DR. DOOM CRY ONCE.
BEFORE WE START, LET'S GO OVER THE RULES. THIS IS NOT TACKLE FOOTBALL. WHEN YOUR FLAG IS REMOVED, YOU ARE OUT OF PLAY.
BY MAJORITY VOTE, POWERS ARE ALLOWED, BUT NOT IN ANY WAY THAT COULD HARM OPPONENTS.
ANY UNNECESSARY ROUGHNESS, YOU'RE OUT ON YOUR BUTTS.
ALSO BY MAJORITY VOTE, TEACHERS WILL BE PARTICIPATING.
WHICH I STILL THINK IS A TERRIBLE IDEA.
'CAUSE YOU KNOW I OWE YOU FOR SUCKER-PUNCHIN' ME OUTTA THE QUINJET.*
*In AVX #3 --Referee Rosemann
BUT, WOLVERINE... THAT WAS DURING THE CONFLICT. THAT'S ALL OVER NOW.
YOU DON'T STILL HOLD A GRUDGE, DO YOU?
LET'S PLAY BALL!

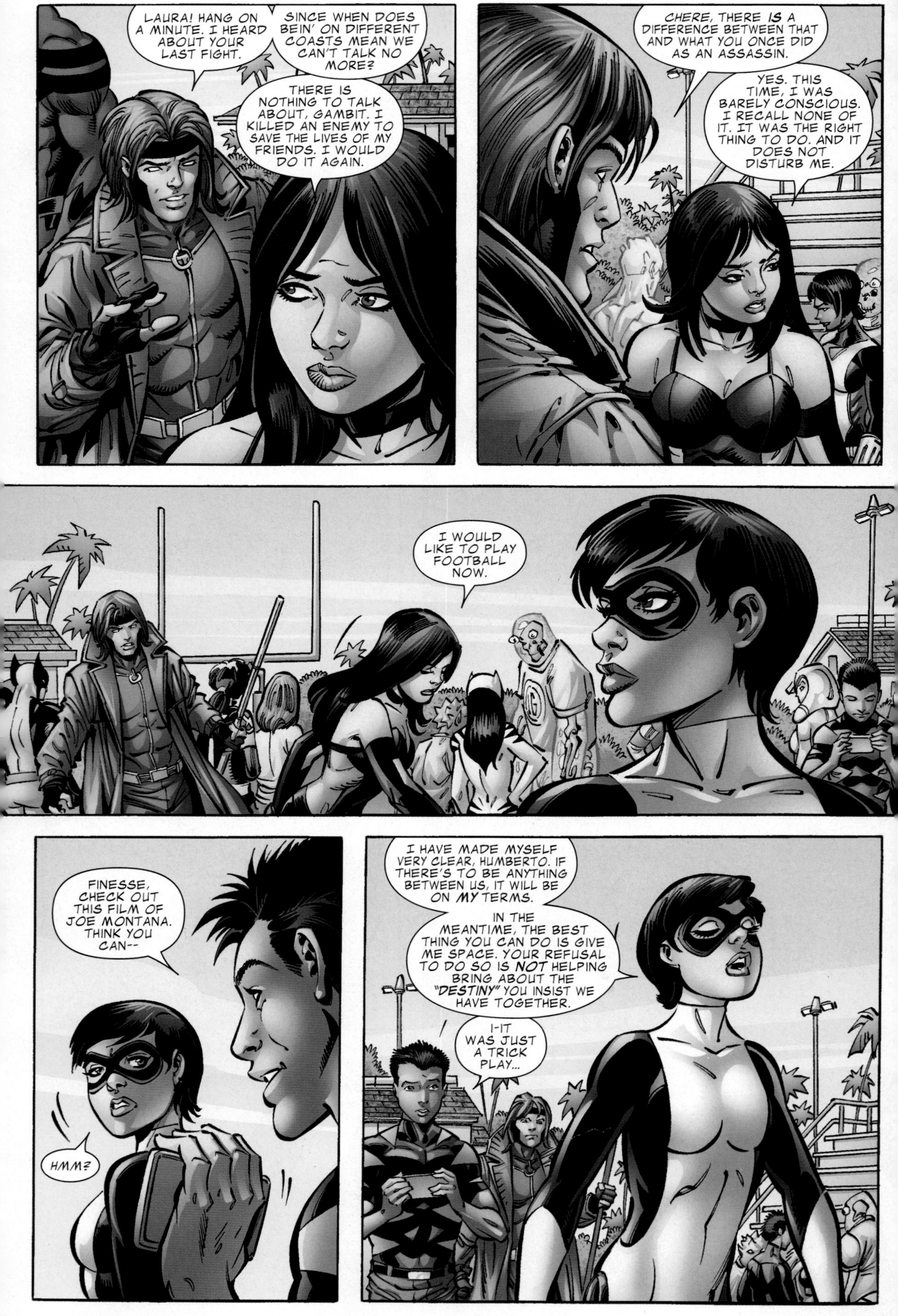
LAURA! HANG ON A MINUTE. I HEARD ABOUT YOUR LAST FIGHT.
SINCE WHEN DOES BEIN' ON DIFFERENT COASTS MEAN WE CAN'T TALK NO MORE?
THERE IS NOTHING TO TALK ABOUT, GAMBIT. I KILLED AN ENEMY TO SAVE THE LIVES OF MY FRIENDS. I WOULD DO IT AGAIN.
CHERE, THERE IS A DIFFERENCE BETWEEN THAT AND WHAT YOU ONCE DID AS AN ASSASSIN.
YES. THIS TIME, I WAS BARELY CONSCIOUS. I RECALL NONE OF IT. IT WAS THE RIGHT THING TO DO. AND IT DOES NOT DISTURB ME.
I WOULD LIKE TO PLAY FOOTBALL NOW.
FINESSE, CHECK OUT THIS FILM OF JOE MONTANA. THINK YOU CAN--
HMM?
I HAVE MADE MYSELF VERY CLEAR, HUMBERTO. IF THERE'S TO BE ANYTHING BETWEEN US, IT WILL BE ON MY TERMS.
IN THE MEANTIME, THE BEST THING YOU CAN DO IS GIVE ME SPACE. YOUR REFUSAL TO DO SO IS NOT HELPING BRING ABOUT THE "DESTINY" YOU INSIST WE HAVE TOGETHER.
I-IT WAS JUST A TRICK PLAY...

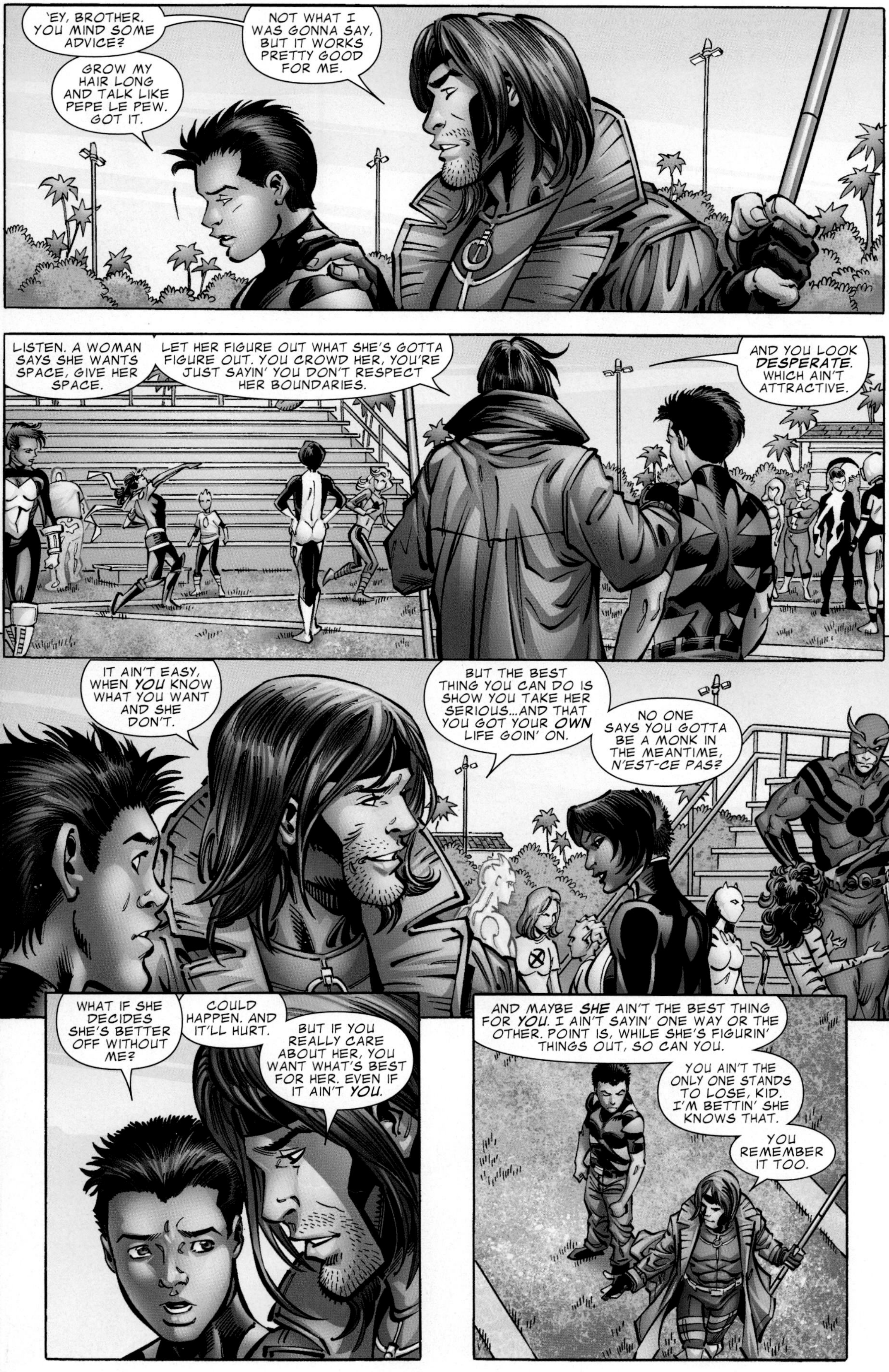
'EY, BROTHER. YOU MIND SOME ADVICE?
GROW MY HAIR LONG AND TALK LIKE PEPE LE PEW. GOT IT.
NOT WHAT I WAS GONNA SAY, BUT IT WORKS PRETTY GOOD FOR ME.
LISTEN. A WOMAN SAYS SHE WANTS SPACE, GIVE HER SPACE.
LET HER FIGURE OUT WHAT SHE'S GOTTA FIGURE OUT. YOU CROWD HER, YOU'RE JUST SAYIN' YOU DON'T RESPECT HER BOUNDARIES.
AND YOU LOOK DESPERATE. WHICH AIN'T ATTRACTIVE.
IT AIN'T EASY, WHEN YOU KNOW WHAT YOU WANT AND SHE DON'T.
BUT THE BEST THING YOU CAN DO IS SHOW YOU TAKE HER SERIOUS...AND THAT YOU GOT YOUR OWN LIFE GOIN' ON.
NO ONE SAYS YOU GOTTA BE A MONK IN THE MEANTIME, N'EST-CE PAS?
WHAT IF SHE DECIDES SHE'S BETTER OFF WITHOUT ME?
COULD HAPPEN. AND IT'LL HURT.
BUT IF YOU REALLY CARE ABOUT HER, YOU WANT WHAT'S BEST FOR HER. EVEN IF IT AIN'T YOU.
AND MAYBE SHE AIN'T THE BEST THING FOR YOU. I AIN'T SAYIN' ONE WAY OR THE OTHER. POINT IS, WHILE SHE'S FIGURIN' THINGS OUT, SO CAN YOU.
YOU AIN'T THE ONLY ONE STANDS TO LOSE, KID. I'M BETTIN' SHE KNOWS THAT.
YOU REMEMBER IT TOO.

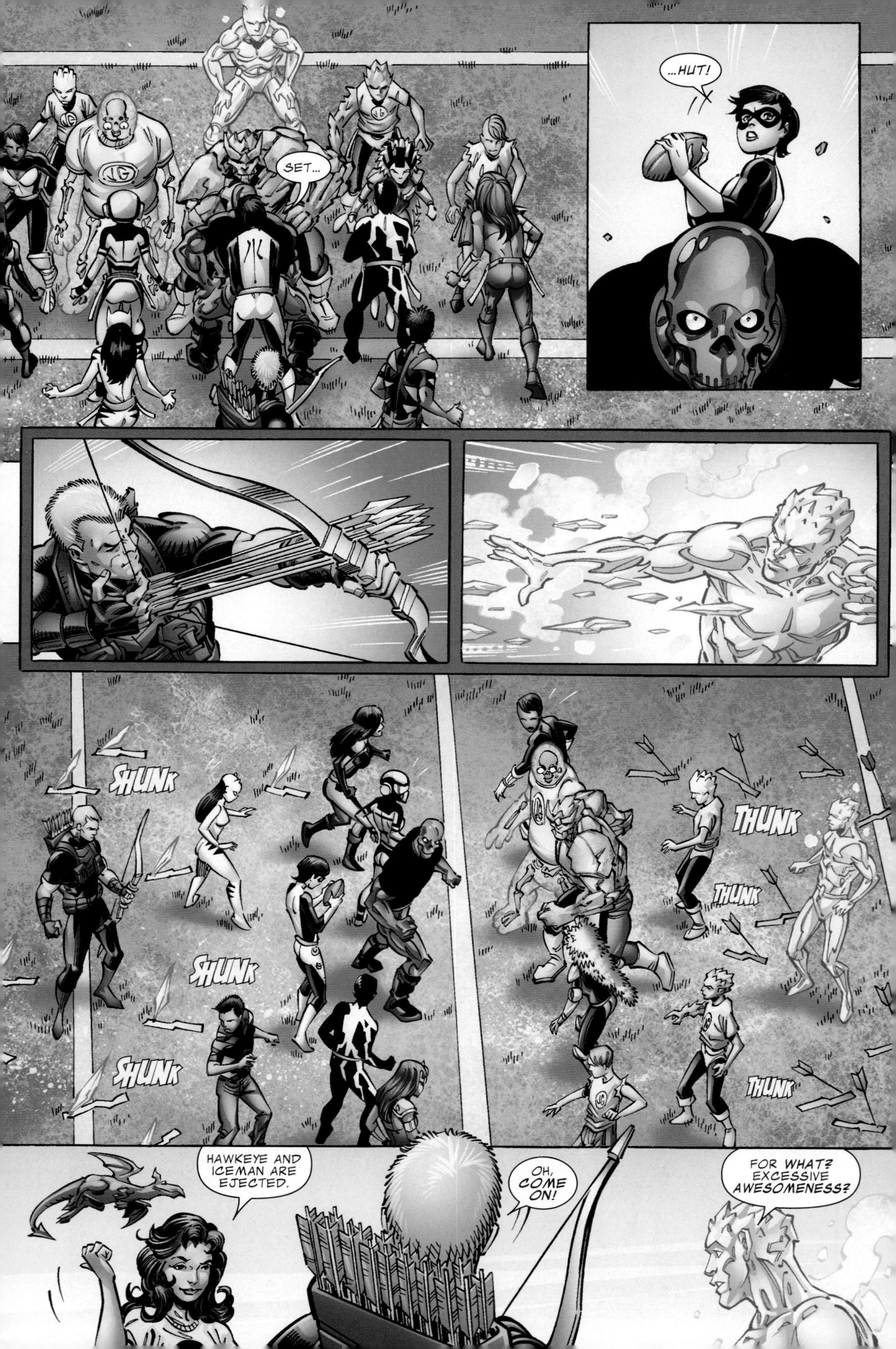
SET...
...HUT!
SHUNK
SHUNK
SHUNK
THUNK
THUNK
THUNK
HAWKEYE AND ICEMAN ARE EJECTED.
OH, COME ON!
FOR WHAT? EXCESSIVE AWESOMENESS?

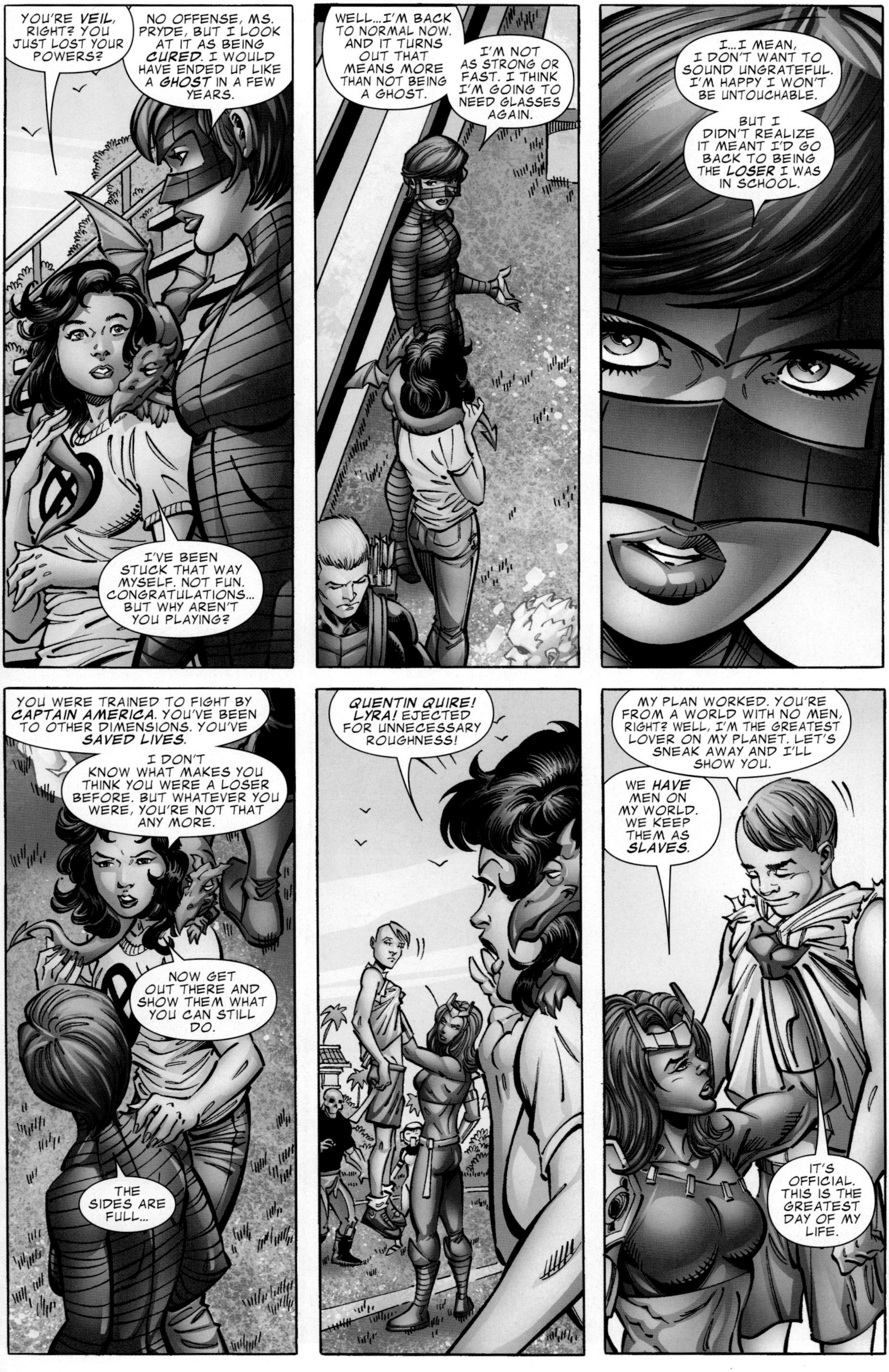
YOU'RE VEIL, RIGHT? YOU JUST LOST YOUR POWERS?
NO OFFENSE, MS. PRYDE, BUT I LOOK AT IT AS BEING CURED. I WOULD HAVE ENDED UP LIKE A GHOST IN A FEW YEARS.
I'VE BEEN STUCK THAT WAY MYSELF. NOT FUN. CONGRATULATIONS... BUT WHY AREN'T YOU PLAYING?
WELL...I'M BACK TO NORMAL NOW. AND IT TURNS OUT THAT MEANS MORE THAN NOT BEING A GHOST.
I'M NOT AS STRONG OR FAST. I THINK I'M GOING TO NEED GLASSES AGAIN.
I...I MEAN, I DON'T WANT TO SOUND UNGRATEFUL. I'M HAPPY I WON'T BE UNTOUCHABLE.
BUT I DIDN'T REALIZE IT MEANT I'D GO BACK TO BEING THE LOSER I WAS IN SCHOOL.
YOU WERE TRAINED TO FIGHT BY CAPTAIN AMERICA. YOU'VE BEEN TO OTHER DIMENSIONS. YOU'VE SAVED LIVES.
I DON'T KNOW WHAT MAKES YOU THINK YOU WERE A LOSER BEFORE. BUT WHATEVER YOU WERE, YOU'RE NOT THAT ANY MORE.
NOW GET OUT THERE AND SHOW THEM WHAT YOU CAN STILL DO.
THE SIDES ARE FULL...
QUENTIN QUIRE! LYRA! EJECTED FOR UNNECESSARY ROUGHNESS!
MY PLAN WORKED. YOU'RE FROM A WORLD WITH NO MEN, RIGHT? WELL, I'M THE GREATEST LOVER ON MY PLANET. LET'S SNEAK AWAY AND I'LL SHOW YOU.
WE HAVE MEN ON MY WORLD. WE KEEP THEM AS SLAVES.
IT'S OFFICIAL. THIS IS THE GREATEST DAY OF MY LIFE.

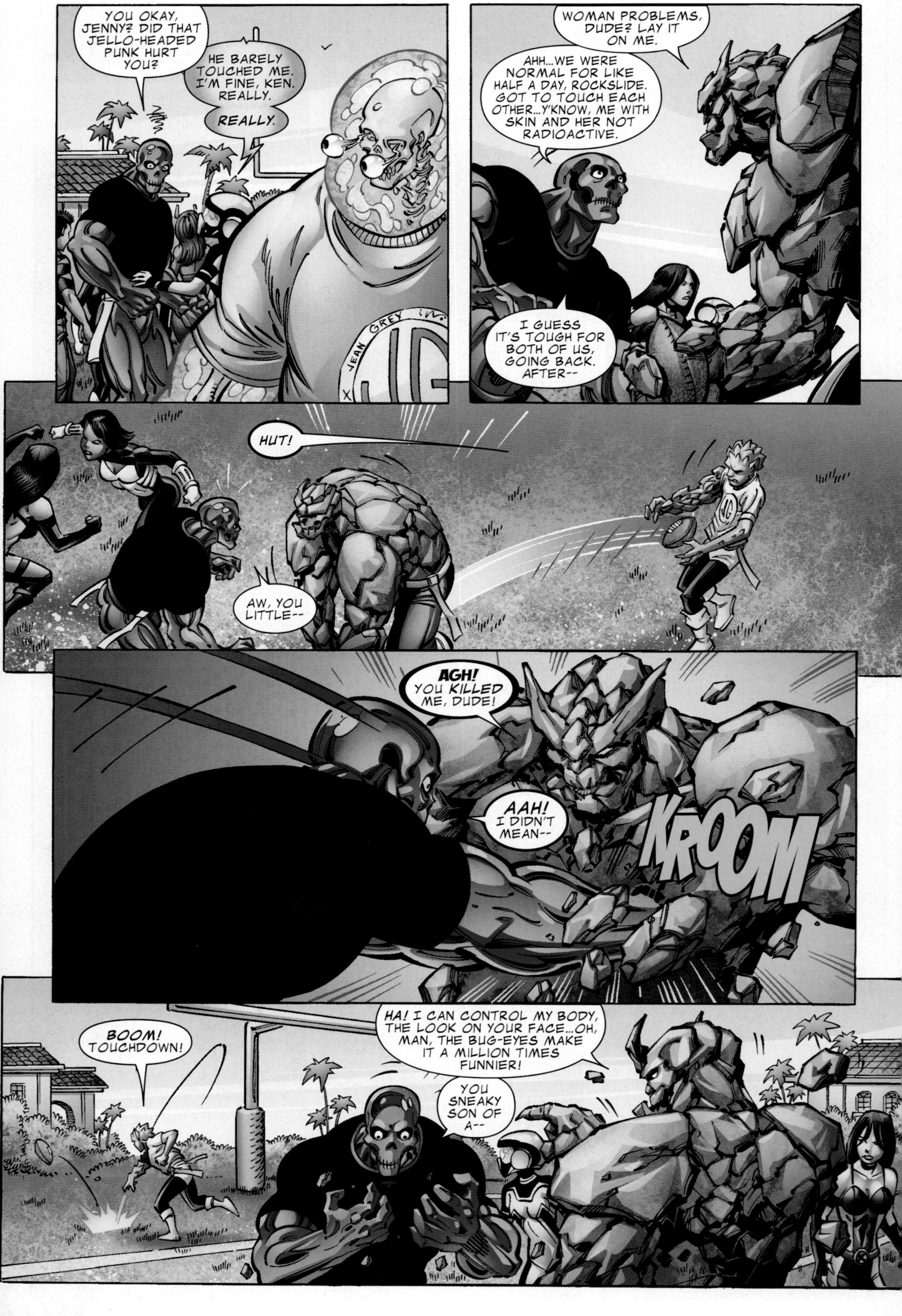
YOU OKAY, JENNY? DID THAT JELLO-HEADED PUNK HURT YOU?
HE BARELY TOUCHED ME. I'M FINE, KEN. REALLY.
REALLY.
JEAN GREY
WOMAN PROBLEMS, DUDE? LAY IT ON ME.
AHH...WE WERE NORMAL FOR LIKE HALF A DAY, ROCKSLIDE. GOT TO TOUCH EACH OTHER...Y'KNOW, ME WITH SKIN AND HER NOT RADIOACTIVE.
I GUESS IT'S TOUGH FOR BOTH OF US, GOING BACK. AFTER--
HUT!
AW, YOU LITTLE--
AGH! YOU KILLED ME, DUDE!
AAH! I DIDN'T MEAN--
KROOM
BOOM! TOUCHDOWN!
HA! I CAN CONTROL MY BODY, THE LOOK ON YOUR FACE...OH, MAN, THE BUG-EYES MAKE IT A MILLION TIMES FUNNIER!
YOU SNEAKY SON OF A--

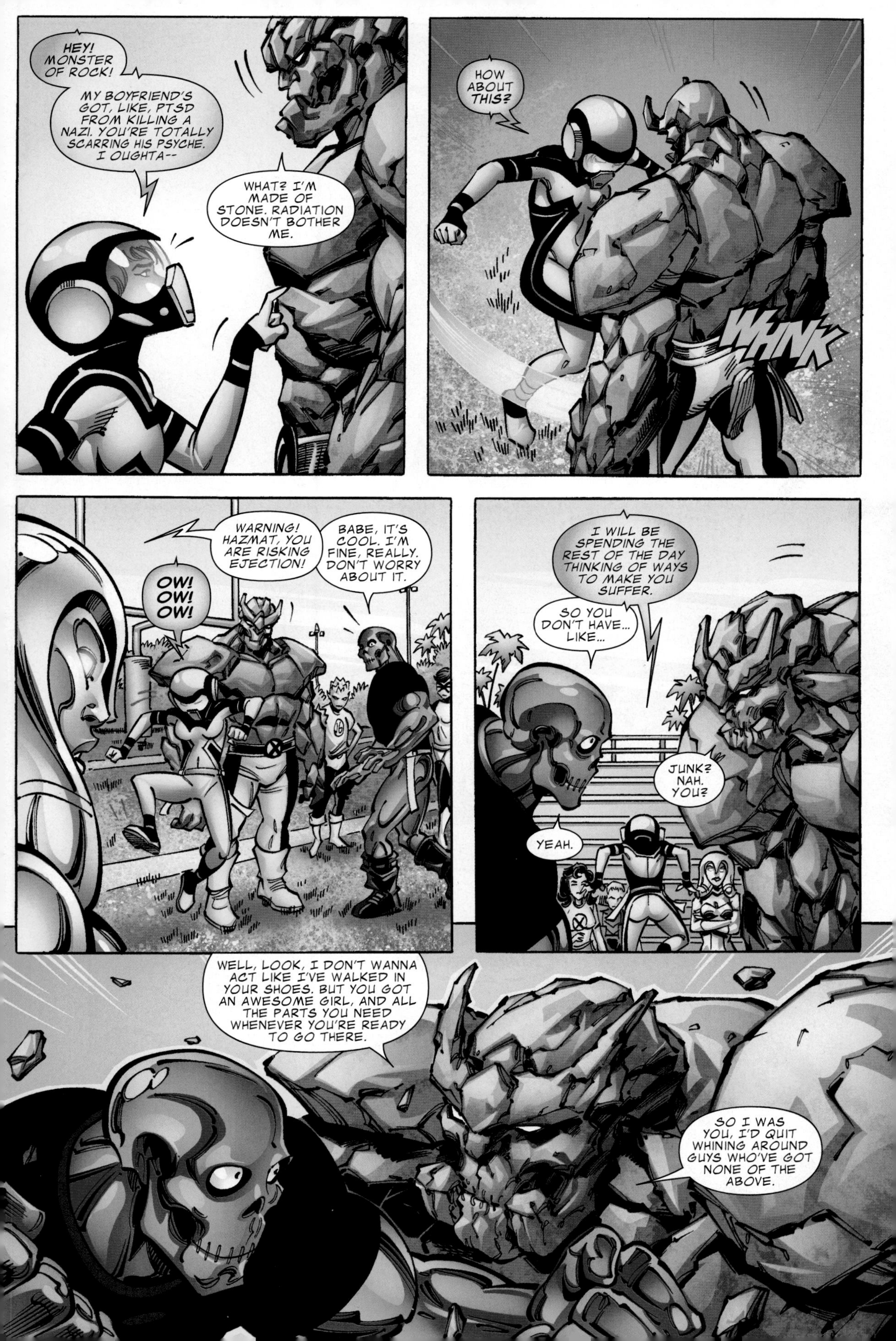
HEY! MONSTER OF ROCK!
MY BOYFRIEND'S GOT, LIKE, PTSD FROM KILLING A NAZI. YOU'RE TOTALLY SCARRING HIS PSYCHE. I OUGHTA--
WHAT? I'M MADE OF STONE. RADIATION DOESN'T BOTHER ME.
HOW ABOUT THIS?
WHNK
WARNING! HAZMAT, YOU ARE RISKING EJECTION!
OW! OW! OW!
BABE, IT'S COOL. I'M FINE, REALLY. DON'T WORRY ABOUT IT.
I WILL BE SPENDING THE REST OF THE DAY THINKING OF WAYS TO MAKE YOU SUFFER.
SO YOU DON'T HAVE... LIKE...
JUNK? NAH. YOU?
YEAH.
WELL, LOOK, I DON'T WANNA ACT LIKE I'VE WALKED IN YOUR SHOES. BUT YOU GOT AN AWESOME GIRL, AND ALL THE PARTS YOU NEED WHENEVER YOU'RE READY TO GO THERE.
SO I WAS YOU, I'D QUIT WHINING AROUND GUYS WHO'VE GOT NONE OF THE ABOVE.

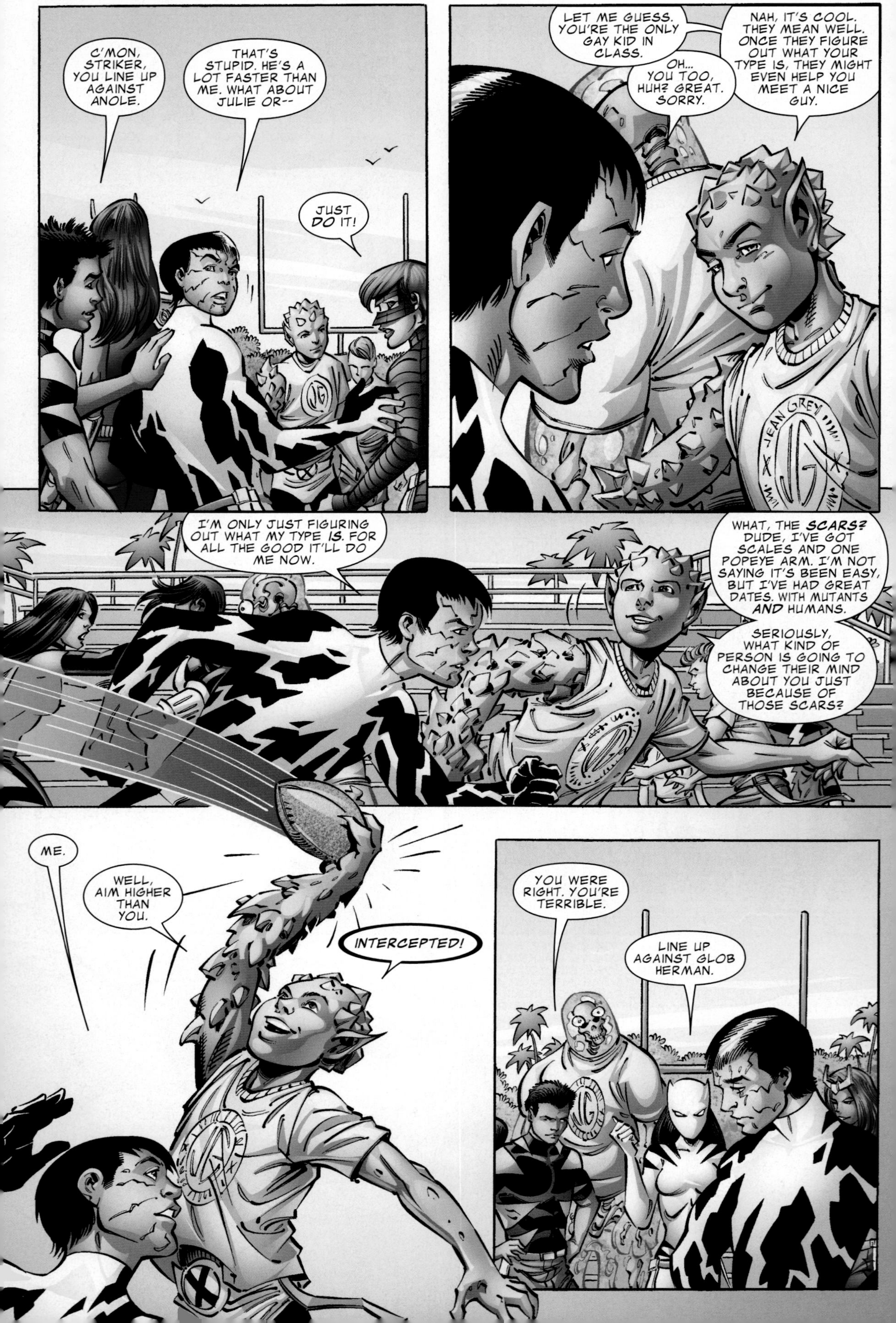
C'MON, STRIKER, YOU LINE UP AGAINST ANOLE.
THAT'S STUPID. HE'S A LOT FASTER THAN ME. WHAT ABOUT JULIE OR--
JUST DO IT!
LET ME GUESS. YOU'RE THE ONLY GAY KID IN CLASS.
OH... YOU TOO, HUH? GREAT. SORRY.
NAH, IT'S COOL. THEY MEAN WELL. ONCE THEY FIGURE OUT WHAT YOUR TYPE IS, THEY MIGHT EVEN HELP YOU MEET A NICE GUY.
I'M ONLY JUST FIGURING OUT WHAT MY TYPE IS. FOR ALL THE GOOD IT'LL DO ME NOW.
WHAT, THE SCARS? DUDE, I'VE GOT SCALES AND ONE POPEYE ARM. I'M NOT SAYING IT'S BEEN EASY, BUT I'VE HAD GREAT DATES. WITH MUTANTS AND HUMANS.
SERIOUSLY, WHAT KIND OF PERSON IS GOING TO CHANGE THEIR MIND ABOUT YOU JUST BECAUSE OF THOSE SCARS?
ME.
WELL, AIM HIGHER THAN YOU.
INTERCEPTED!
YOU WERE RIGHT. YOU'RE TERRIBLE.
LINE UP AGAINST GLOB HERMAN.

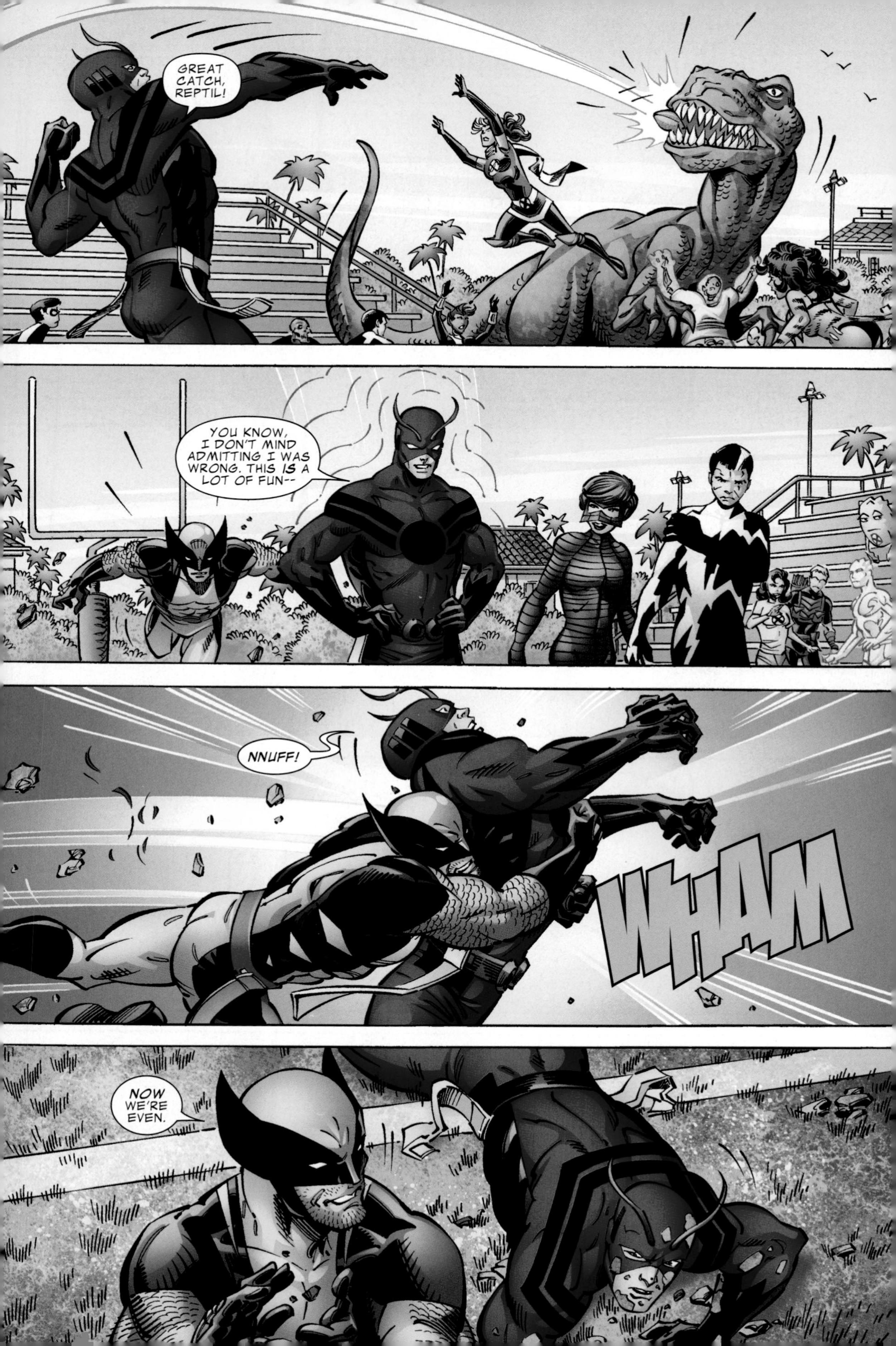
GREAT CATCH, REPTIL!
YOU KNOW, I DON'T MIND ADMITTING I WAS WRONG. THIS IS A LOT OF FUN--
NNUFF!
WHAM
NOW WE'RE EVEN.

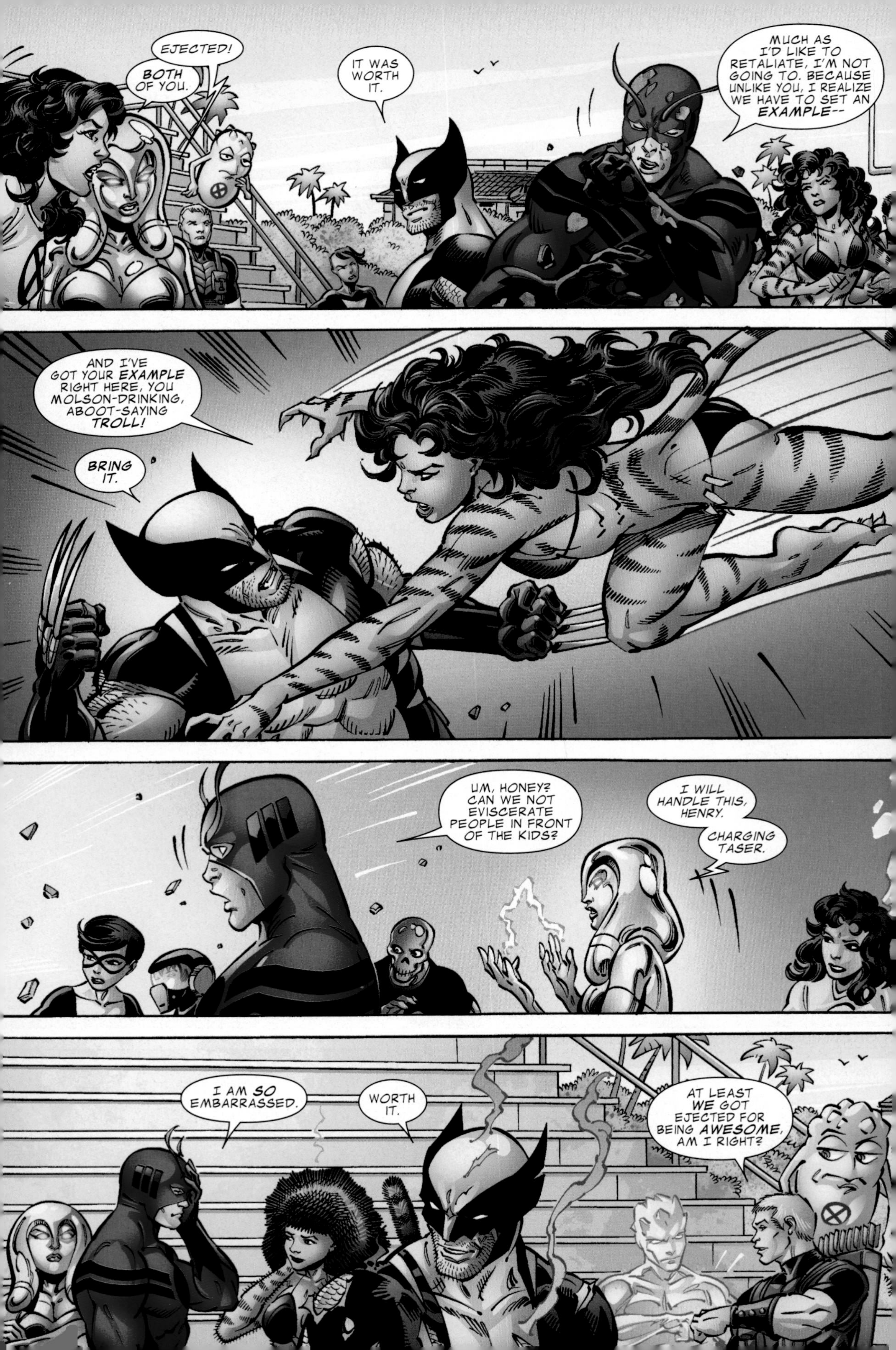
EJECTED!
BOTH OF YOU.
IT WAS WORTH IT.
MUCH AS I'D LIKE TO RETALIATE, I'M NOT GOING TO. BECAUSE UNLIKE YOU, I REALIZE WE HAVE TO SET AN EXAMPLE--
AND I'VE GOT YOUR EXAMPLE RIGHT HERE, YOU MOLSON-DRINKING, ABOOT-SAYING TROLL!
BRING IT.
UM, HONEY? CAN WE NOT EVISCERATE PEOPLE IN FRONT OF THE KIDS?
I WILL HANDLE THIS, HENRY.
CHARGING TASER.
I AM SO EMBARRASSED.
WORTH IT.
AT LEAST WE GOT EJECTED FOR BEING AWESOME, AM I RIGHT?

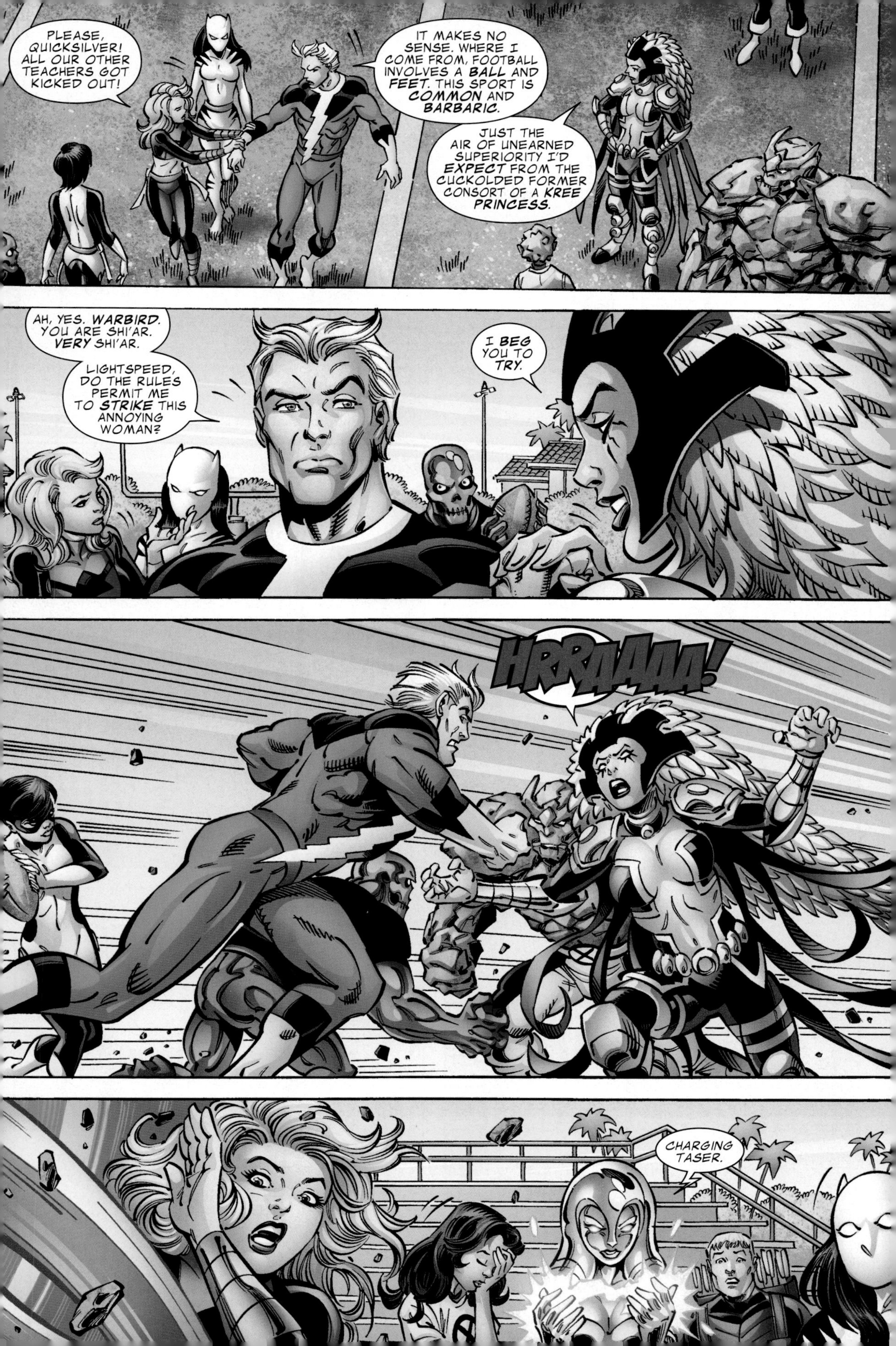
PLEASE, QUICKSILVER! ALL OUR OTHER TEACHERS GOT KICKED OUT!
IT MAKES NO SENSE. WHERE I COME FROM, FOOTBALL INVOLVES A BALL AND FEET. THIS SPORT IS COMMON AND BARBARIC.
JUST THE AIR OF UNEARNED SUPERIORITY I'D EXPECT FROM THE CUCKOLDED FORMER CONSORT OF A KREE PRINCESS.
AH, YES. WARBIRD. YOU ARE SHI'AR. VERY SHI'AR.
LIGHTSPEED, DO THE RULES PERMIT ME TO STRIKE THIS ANNOYING WOMAN?
I BEG YOU TO TRY.
HRRAAAAA!
CHARGING TASER.

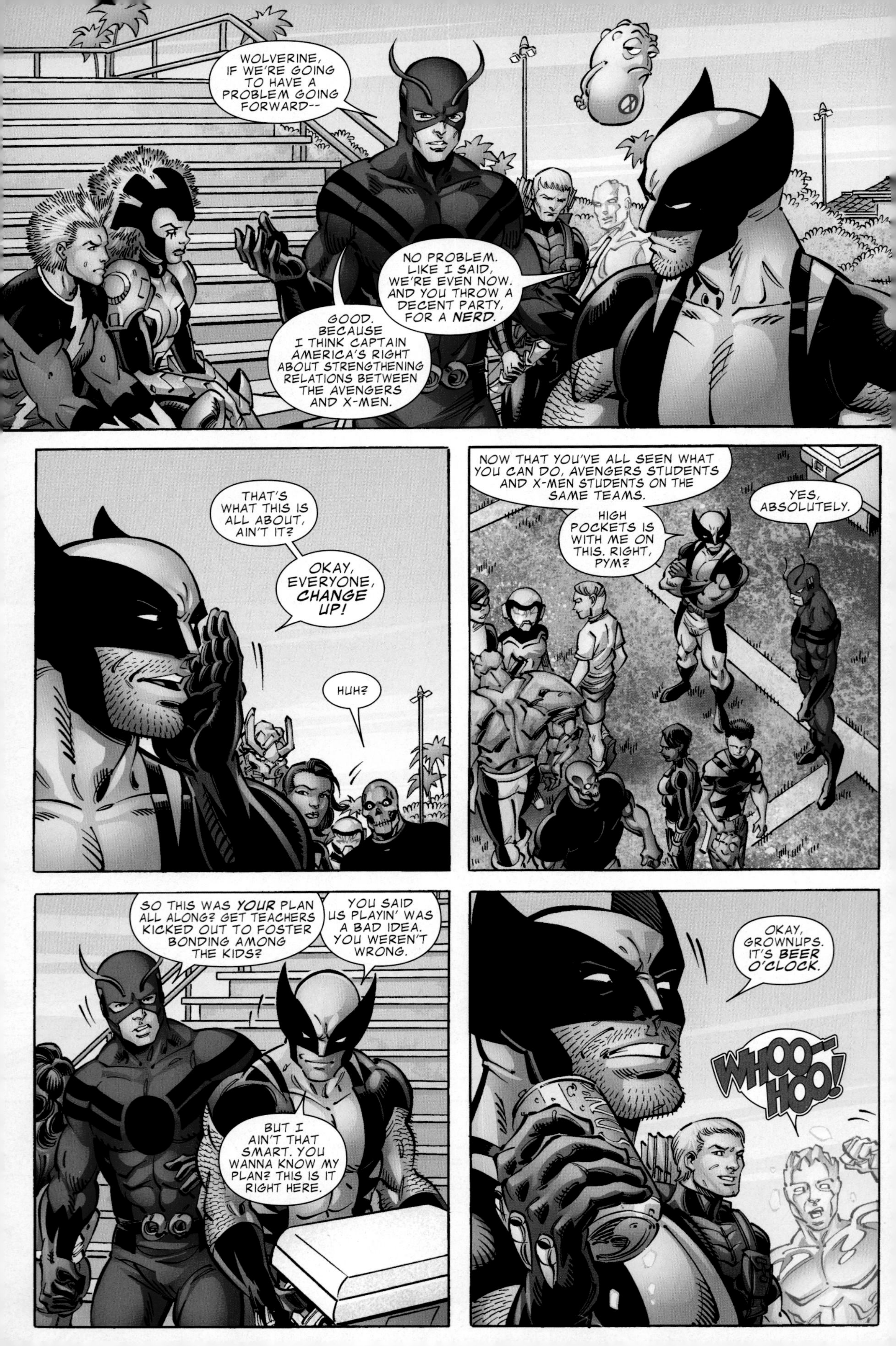
WOLVERINE, IF WE'RE GOING TO HAVE A PROBLEM GOING FORWARD--
NO PROBLEM. LIKE I SAID, WE'RE EVEN NOW. AND YOU THROW A DECENT PARTY, FOR A NERD.
GOOD. BECAUSE I THINK CAPTAIN AMERICA'S RIGHT ABOUT STRENGTHENING RELATIONS BETWEEN THE AVENGERS AND X-MEN.
THAT'S WHAT THIS IS ALL ABOUT, AIN'T IT?
OKAY, EVERYONE, CHANGE UP!
HUH?
NOW THAT YOU'VE ALL SEEN WHAT YOU CAN DO, AVENGERS STUDENTS AND X-MEN STUDENTS ON THE SAME TEAMS.
HIGH POCKETS IS WITH ME ON THIS. RIGHT, PYM?
YES, ABSOLUTELY.
SO THIS WAS YOUR PLAN ALL ALONG? GET TEACHERS KICKED OUT TO FOSTER BONDING AMONG THE KIDS?
YOU SAID US PLAYIN' WAS A BAD IDEA. YOU WEREN'T WRONG.
BUT I AIN'T THAT SMART. YOU WANNA KNOW MY PLAN? THIS IS IT RIGHT HERE.
OKAY, GROWNUPS. IT'S BEER O'CLOCK.
WHOO-HOO!

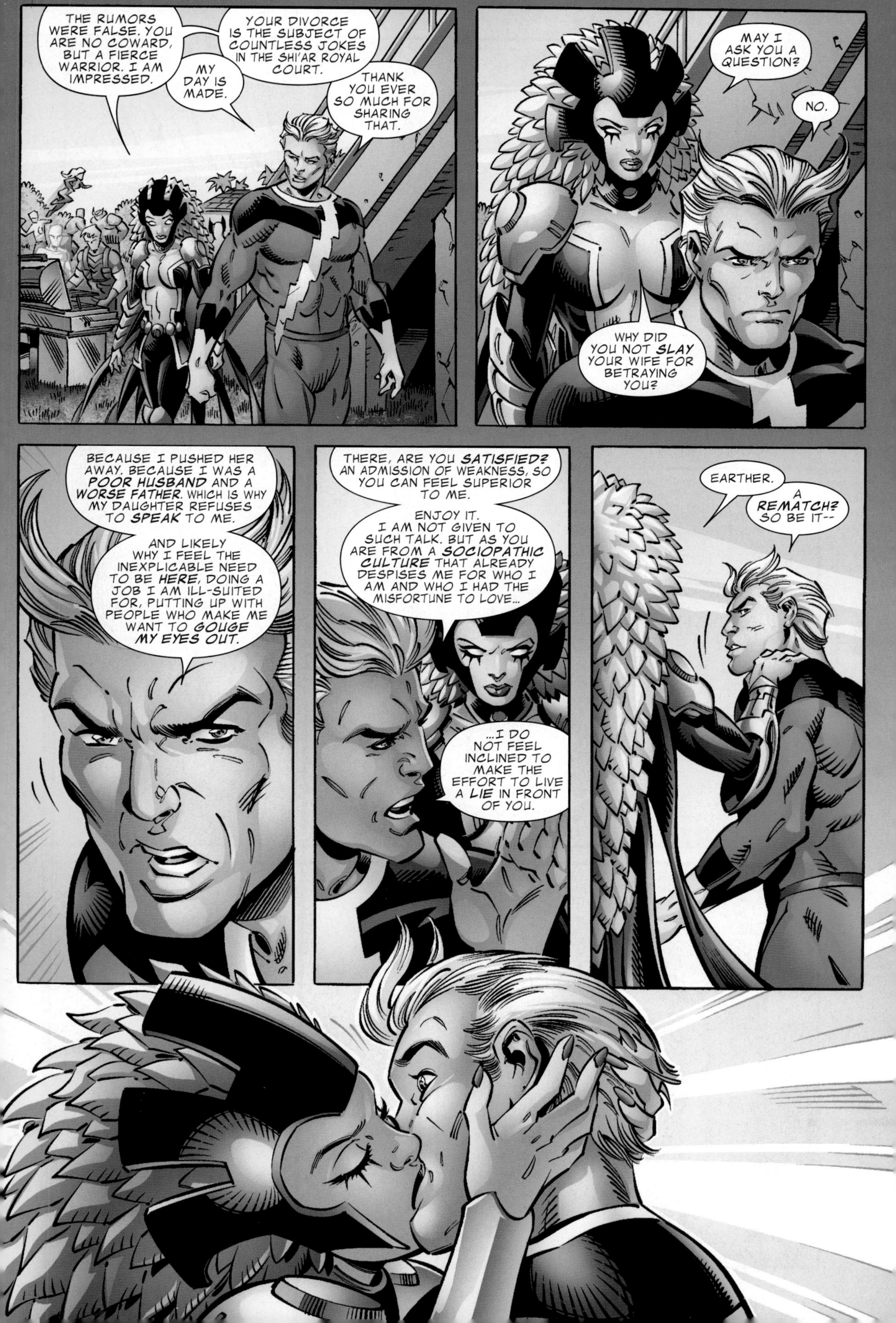
THE RUMORS WERE FALSE. YOU ARE NO COWARD, BUT A FIERCE WARRIOR. I AM IMPRESSED.
YOUR DIVORCE IS THE SUBJECT OF COUNTLESS JOKES IN THE SHI'AR ROYAL COURT.
MY DAY IS MADE.
THANK YOU EVER SO MUCH FOR SHARING THAT.
MAY I ASK YOU A QUESTION?
NO.
WHY DID YOU NOT SLAY YOUR WIFE FOR BETRAYING YOU?
BECAUSE I PUSHED HER AWAY. BECAUSE I WAS A POOR HUSBAND AND A WORSE FATHER. WHICH IS WHY MY DAUGHTER REFUSES TO SPEAK TO ME.
AND LIKELY WHY I FEEL THE INEXPLICABLE NEED TO BE HERE, DOING A JOB I AM ILL-SUITED FOR, PUTTING UP WITH PEOPLE WHO MAKE ME WANT TO GOUGE MY EYES OUT.
THERE, ARE YOU SATISFIED? AN ADMISSION OF WEAKNESS, SO YOU CAN FEEL SUPERIOR TO ME.
ENJOY IT. I AM NOT GIVEN TO SUCH TALK. BUT AS YOU ARE FROM A SOCIOPATHIC CULTURE THAT ALREADY DESPISES ME FOR WHO I AM AND WHO I HAD THE MISFORTUNE TO LOVE...
...I DO NOT FEEL INCLINED TO MAKE THE EFFORT TO LIVE A LIE IN FRONT OF YOU.
EARTHER.
A REMATCH? SO BE IT--

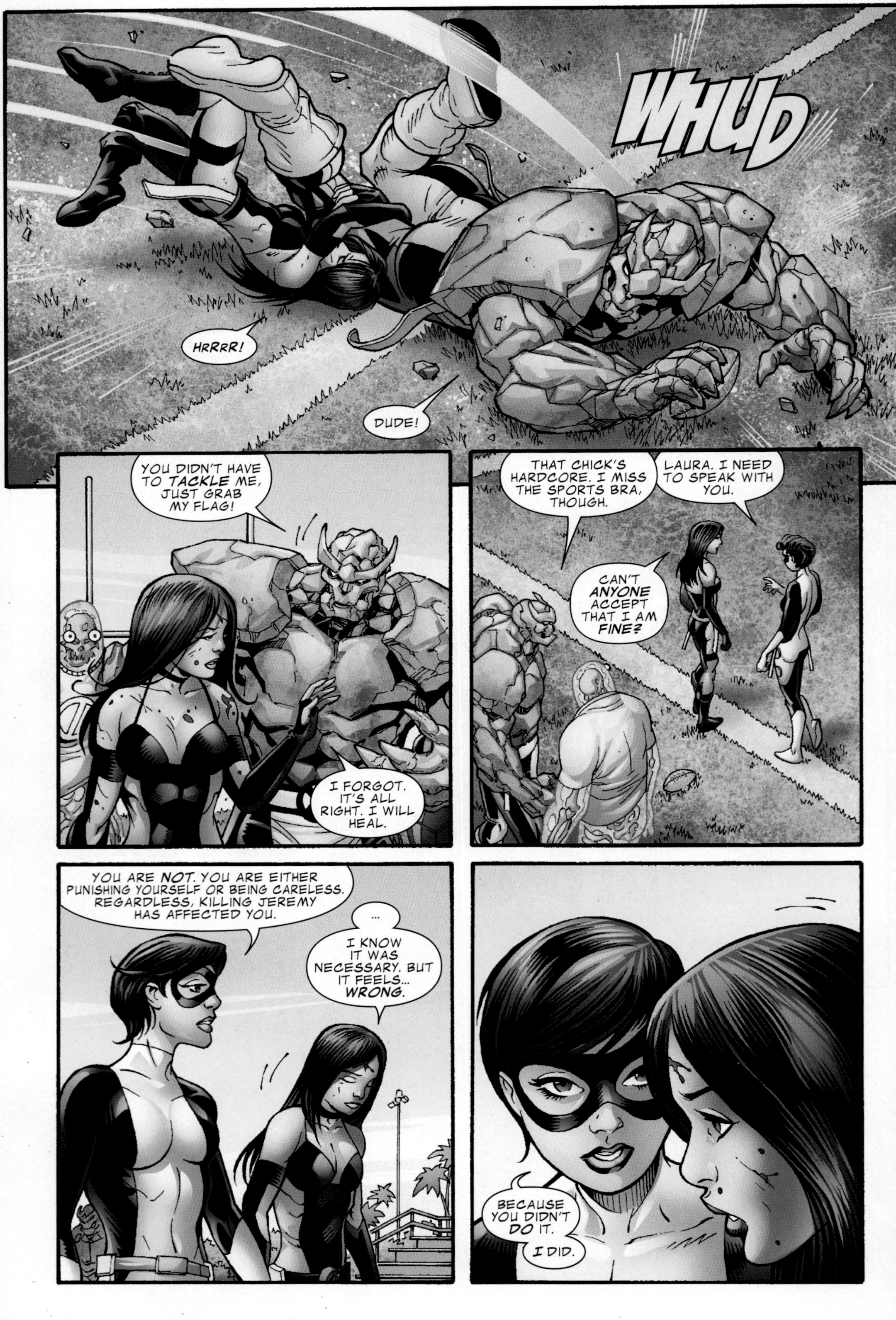
WHUD
HRRRR!
DUDE!
YOU DIDN'T HAVE TO TACKLE ME, JUST GRAB MY FLAG!
I FORGOT. IT'S ALL RIGHT. I WILL HEAL.
THAT CHICK'S HARDCORE. I MISS THE SPORTS BRA, THOUGH.
LAURA. I NEED TO SPEAK WITH YOU.
CAN'T ANYONE ACCEPT THAT I AM FINE?
YOU ARE NOT. YOU ARE EITHER PUNISHING YOURSELF OR BEING CARELESS. REGARDLESS, KILLING JEREMY HAS AFFECTED YOU.
...
I KNOW IT WAS NECESSARY. BUT IT FEELS... WRONG.
BECAUSE YOU DIDN'T DO IT.
I DID.

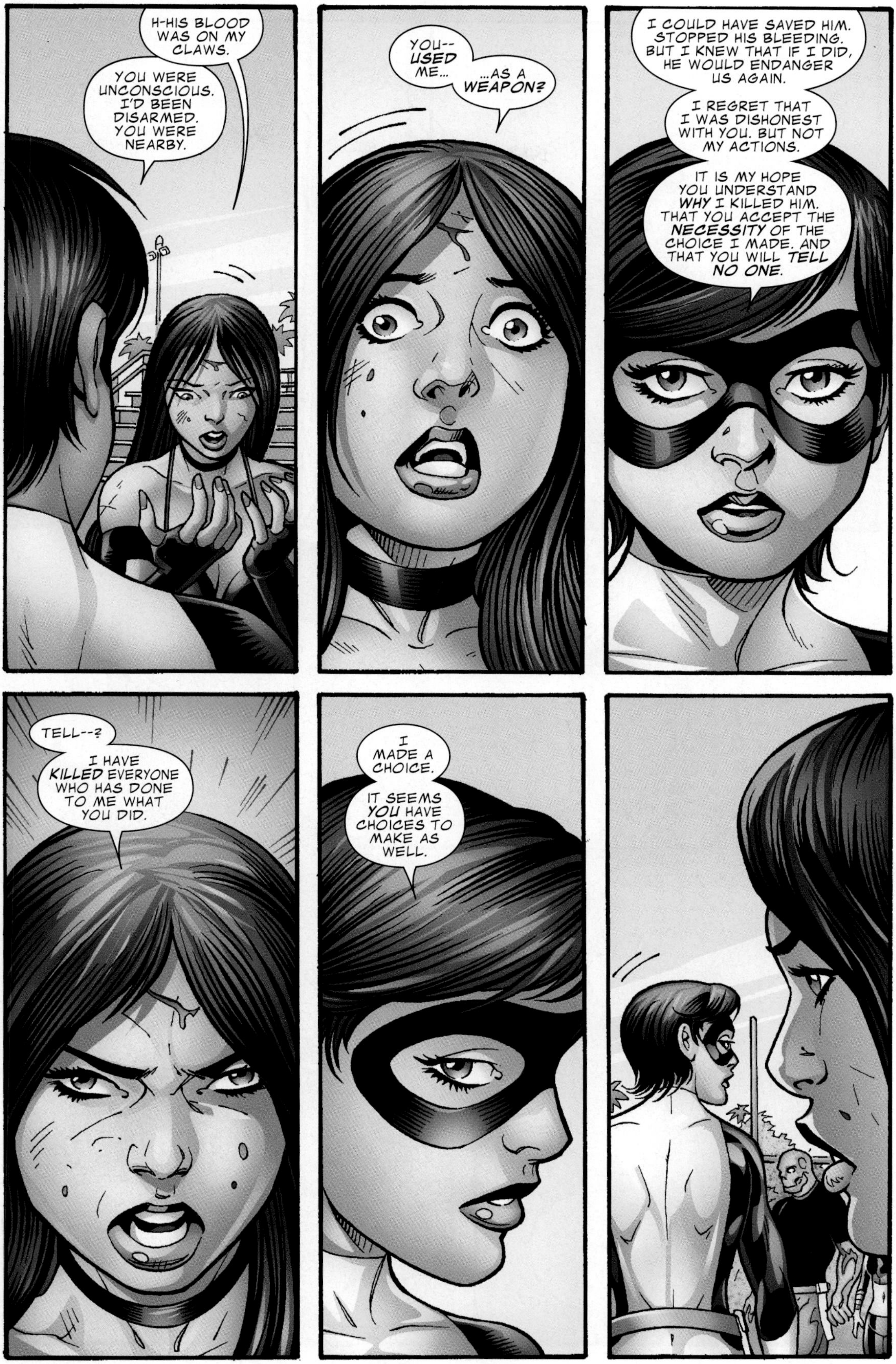
H-HIS BLOOD WAS ON MY CLAWS.
YOU WERE UNCONSCIOUS. I'D BEEN DISARMED. YOU WERE NEARBY.
YOU-- USED ME...
...AS A WEAPON?
I COULD HAVE SAVED HIM. STOPPED HIS BLEEDING. BUT I KNEW THAT IF I DID, HE WOULD ENDANGER US AGAIN.
I REGRET THAT I WAS DISHONEST WITH YOU. BUT NOT MY ACTIONS.
IT IS MY HOPE YOU UNDERSTAND WHY I KILLED HIM. THAT YOU ACCEPT THE NECESSITY OF THE CHOICE I MADE. AND THAT YOU WILL TELL NO ONE.
TELL--?
I HAVE KILLED EVERYONE WHO HAS DONE TO ME WHAT YOU DID.
I MADE A CHOICE.
IT SEEMS YOU HAVE CHOICES TO MAKE AS WELL.

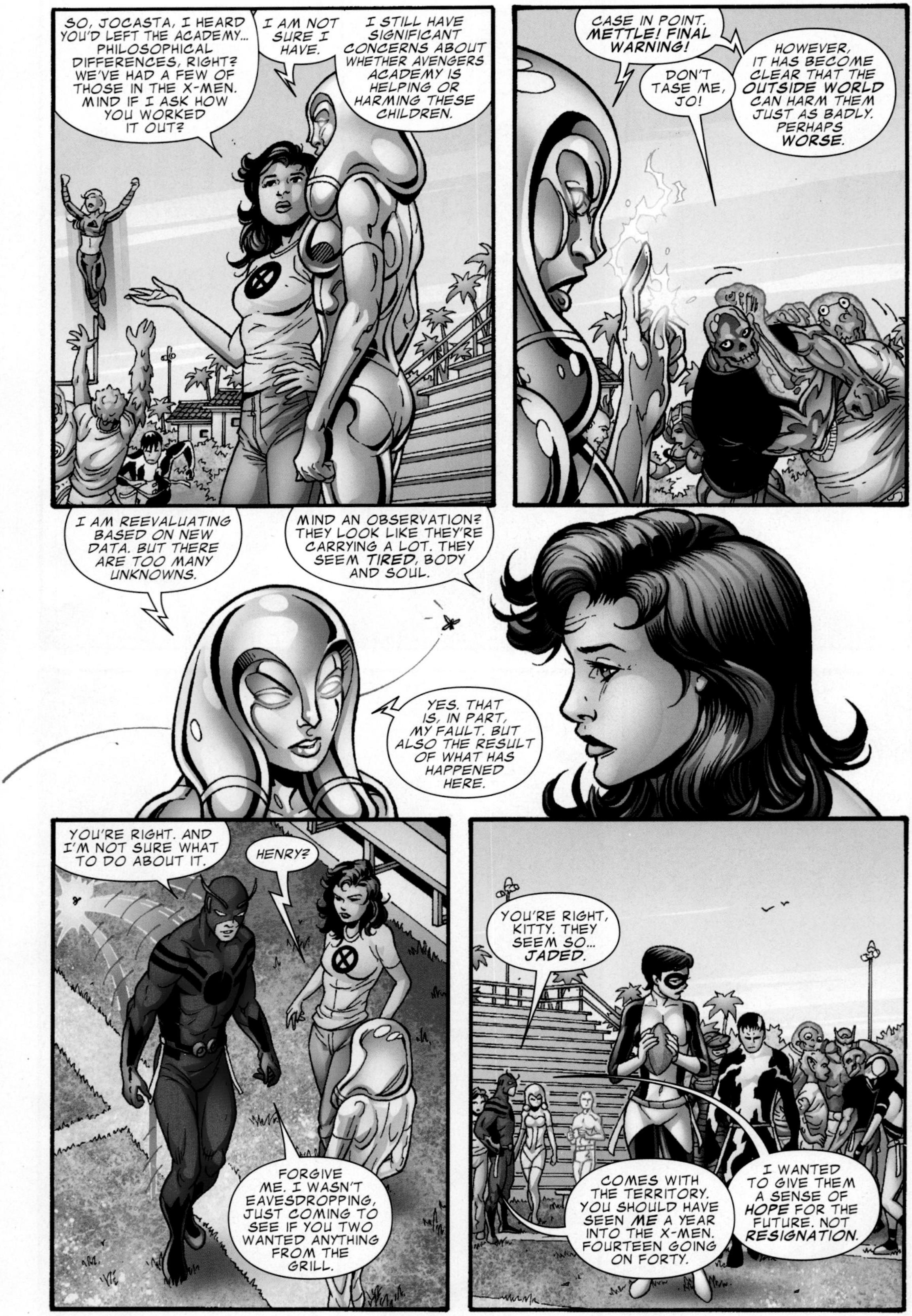
SO, JOCASTA, I HEARD YOU'D LEFT THE ACADEMY... PHILOSOPHICAL DIFFERENCES, RIGHT? WE'VE HAD A FEW OF THOSE IN THE X-MEN. MIND IF I ASK HOW YOU WORKED IT OUT?
I AM NOT SURE I HAVE.
I STILL HAVE SIGNIFICANT CONCERNS ABOUT WHETHER AVENGERS ACADEMY IS HELPING OR HARMING THESE CHILDREN.
CASE IN POINT. METTLE! FINAL WARNING!
DON'T TASE ME, JO!
HOWEVER, IT HAS BECOME CLEAR THAT THE OUTSIDE WORLD CAN HARM THEM JUST AS BADLY. PERHAPS WORSE.
I AM REEVALUATING BASED ON NEW DATA. BUT THERE ARE TOO MANY UNKNOWNS.
MIND AN OBSERVATION? THEY LOOK LIKE THEY'RE CARRYING A LOT. THEY SEEM TIRED, BODY AND SOUL.
YES. THAT IS, IN PART, MY FAULT. BUT ALSO THE RESULT OF WHAT HAS HAPPENED HERE.
YOU'RE RIGHT. AND I'M NOT SURE WHAT TO DO ABOUT IT.
HENRY?
FORGIVE ME. I WASN'T EAVESDROPPING, JUST COMING TO SEE IF YOU TWO WANTED ANYTHING FROM THE GRILL.
YOU'RE RIGHT, KITTY. THEY SEEM SO... JADED.
COMES WITH THE TERRITORY. YOU SHOULD HAVE SEEN ME A YEAR INTO THE X-MEN. FOURTEEN GOING ON FORTY.
I WANTED TO GIVE THEM A SENSE OF HOPE FOR THE FUTURE. NOT RESIGNATION.

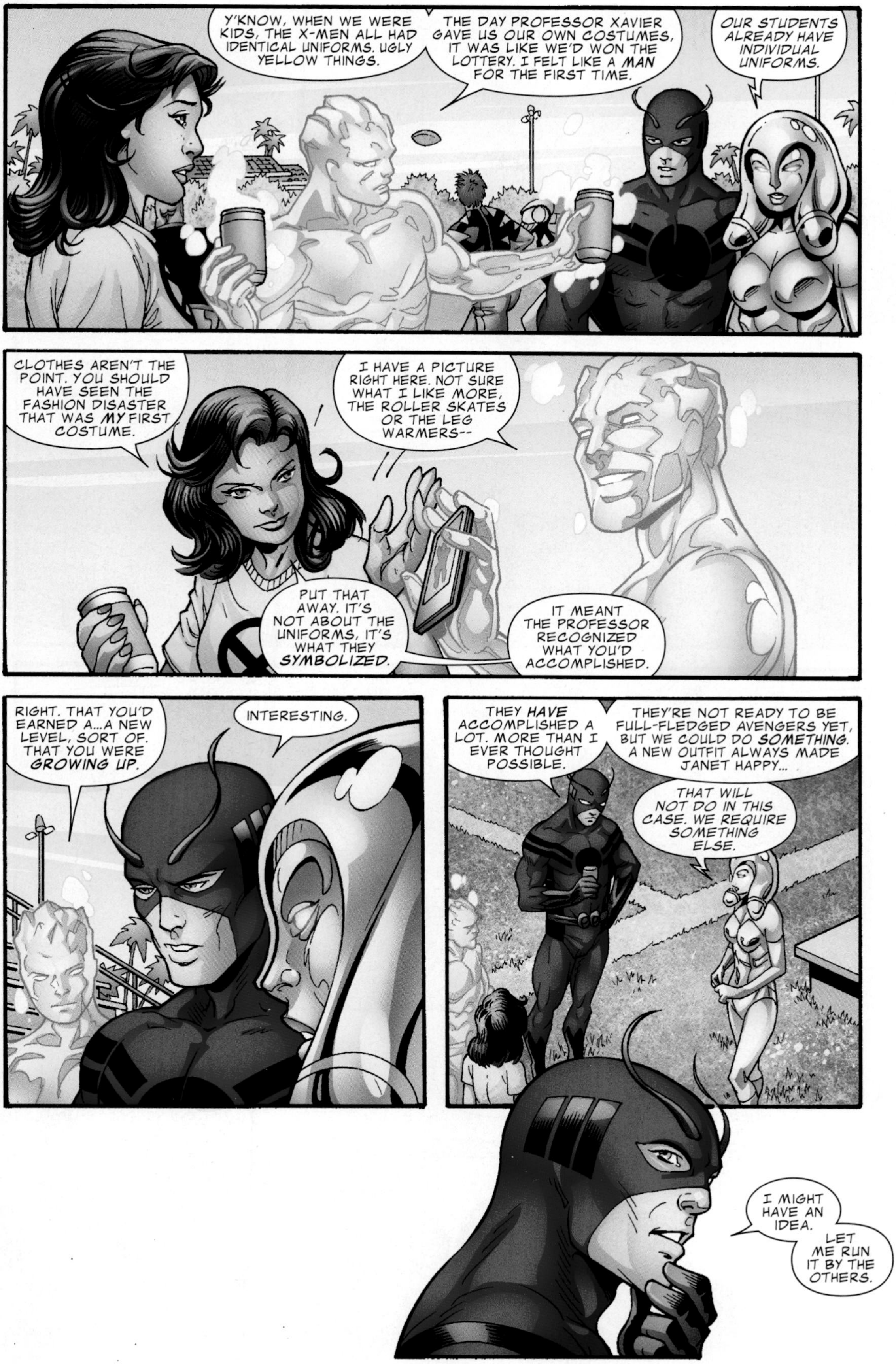
Y'KNOW, WHEN WE WERE KIDS, THE X-MEN ALL HAD IDENTICAL UNIFORMS. UGLY YELLOW THINGS.
THE DAY PROFESSOR XAVIER GAVE US OUR OWN COSTUMES, IT WAS LIKE WE'D WON THE LOTTERY. I FELT LIKE A MAN FOR THE FIRST TIME.
OUR STUDENTS ALREADY HAVE INDIVIDUAL UNIFORMS.
CLOTHES AREN'T THE POINT. YOU SHOULD HAVE SEEN THE FASHION DISASTER THAT WAS MY FIRST COSTUME.
I HAVE A PICTURE RIGHT HERE. NOT SURE WHAT I LIKE MORE, THE ROLLER SKATES OR THE LEG WARMERS--
PUT THAT AWAY. IT'S NOT ABOUT THE UNIFORMS, IT'S WHAT THEY SYMBOLIZED.
IT MEANT THE PROFESSOR RECOGNIZED WHAT YOU'D ACCOMPLISHED.
RIGHT. THAT YOU'D EARNED A...A NEW LEVEL, SORT OF. THAT YOU WERE GROWING UP.
INTERESTING.
THEY HAVE ACCOMPLISHED A LOT. MORE THAN I EVER THOUGHT POSSIBLE.
THEY'RE NOT READY TO BE FULL-FLEDGED AVENGERS YET, BUT WE COULD DO SOMETHING. A NEW OUTFIT ALWAYS MADE JANET HAPPY...
THAT WILL NOT DO IN THIS CASE. WE REQUIRE SOMETHING ELSE.
I MIGHT HAVE AN IDEA.
LET ME RUN IT BY THE OTHERS.

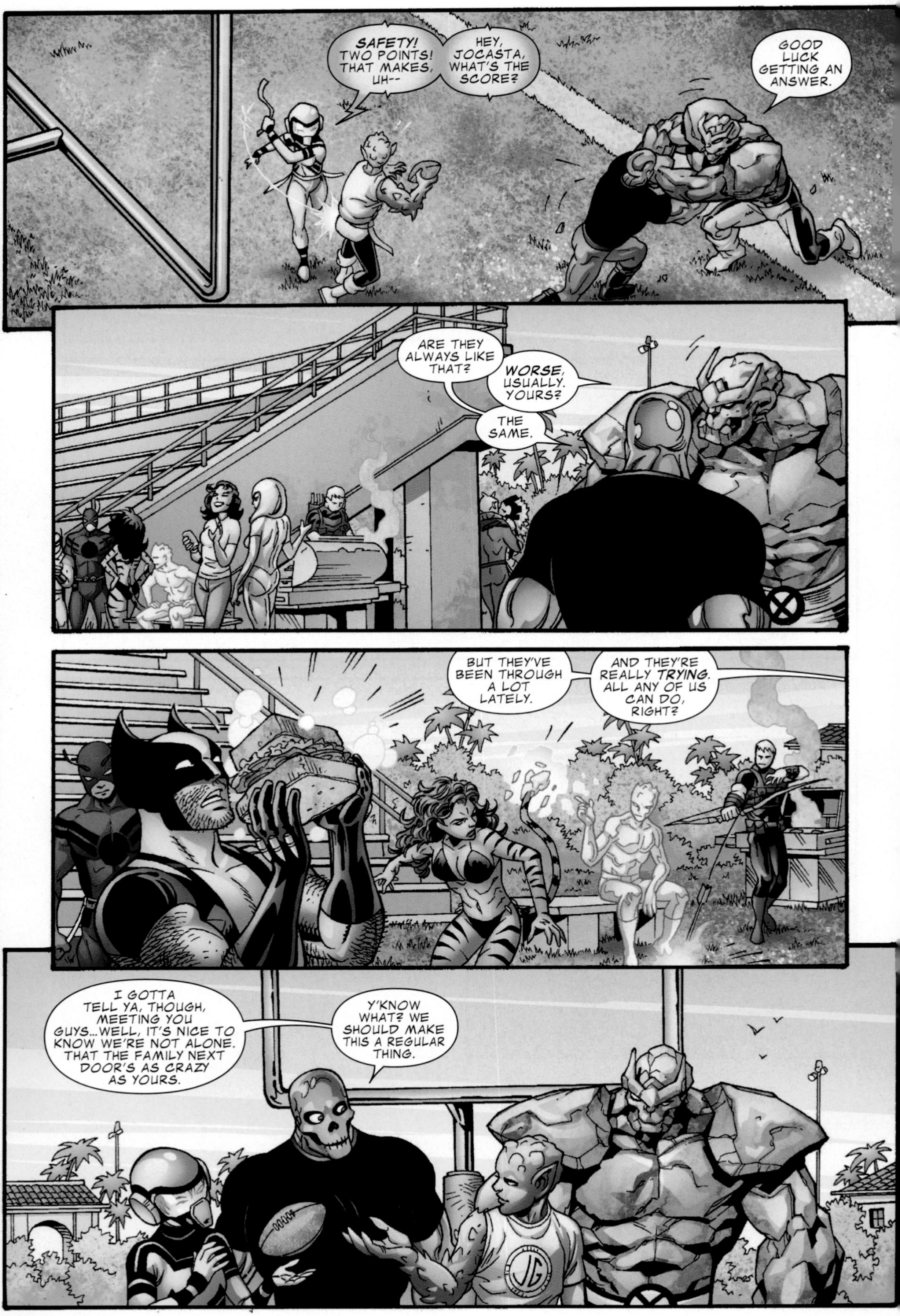
SAFETY! TWO POINTS! THAT MAKES, UH--
HEY, JOCASTA, WHAT'S THE SCORE?
GOOD LUCK GETTING AN ANSWER.
ARE THEY ALWAYS LIKE THAT?
WORSE, USUALLY. YOURS?
THE SAME.
BUT THEY'VE BEEN THROUGH A LOT LATELY.
AND THEY'RE REALLY TRYING. ALL ANY OF US CAN DO, RIGHT?
I GOTTA TELL YA, THOUGH, MEETING YOU GUYS...WELL, IT'S NICE TO KNOW WE'RE NOT ALONE. THAT THE FAMILY NEXT DOOR'S AS CRAZY AS YOURS.
Y'KNOW WHAT? WE SHOULD MAKE THIS A REGULAR THING.

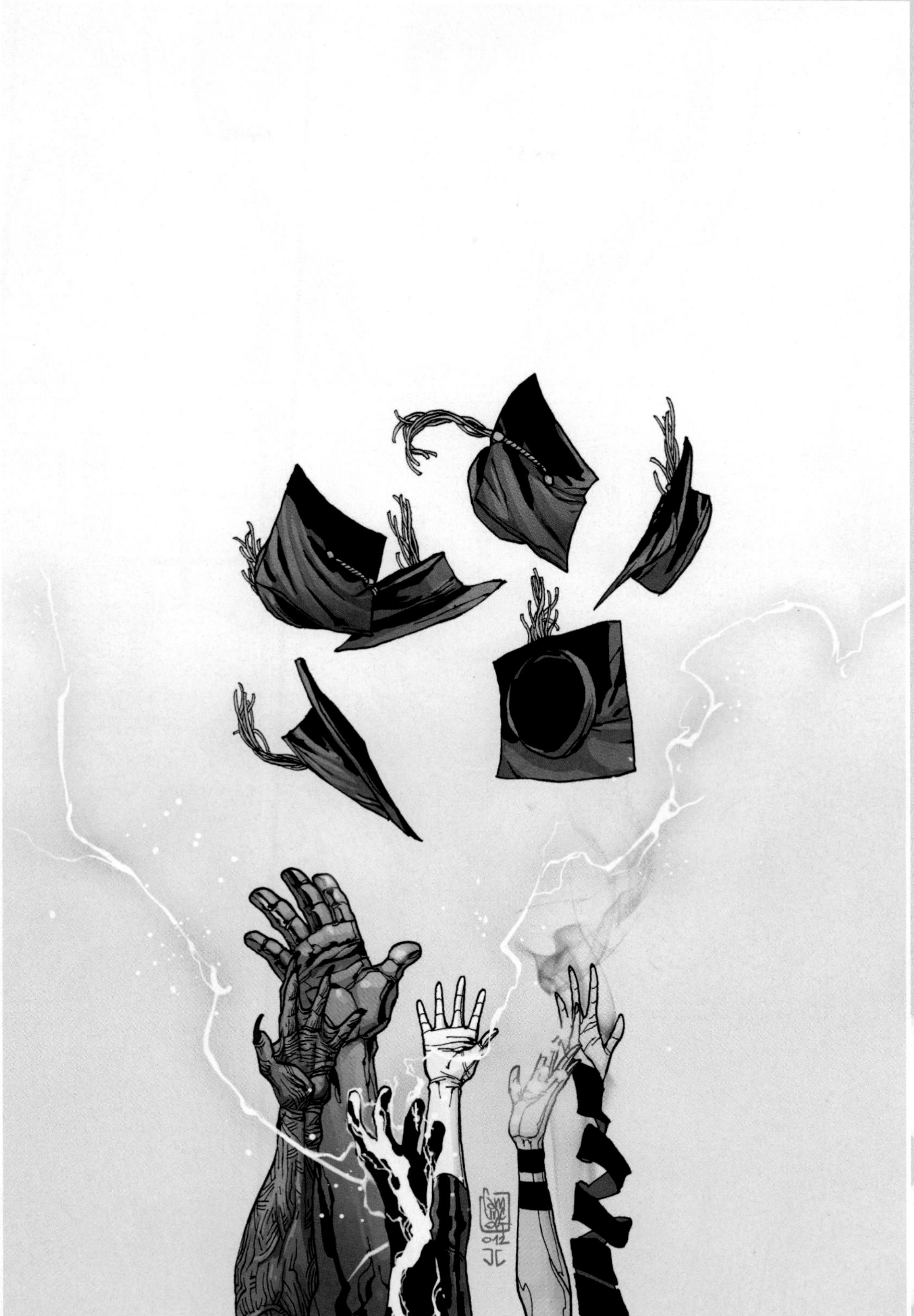

Avengers Academy #39

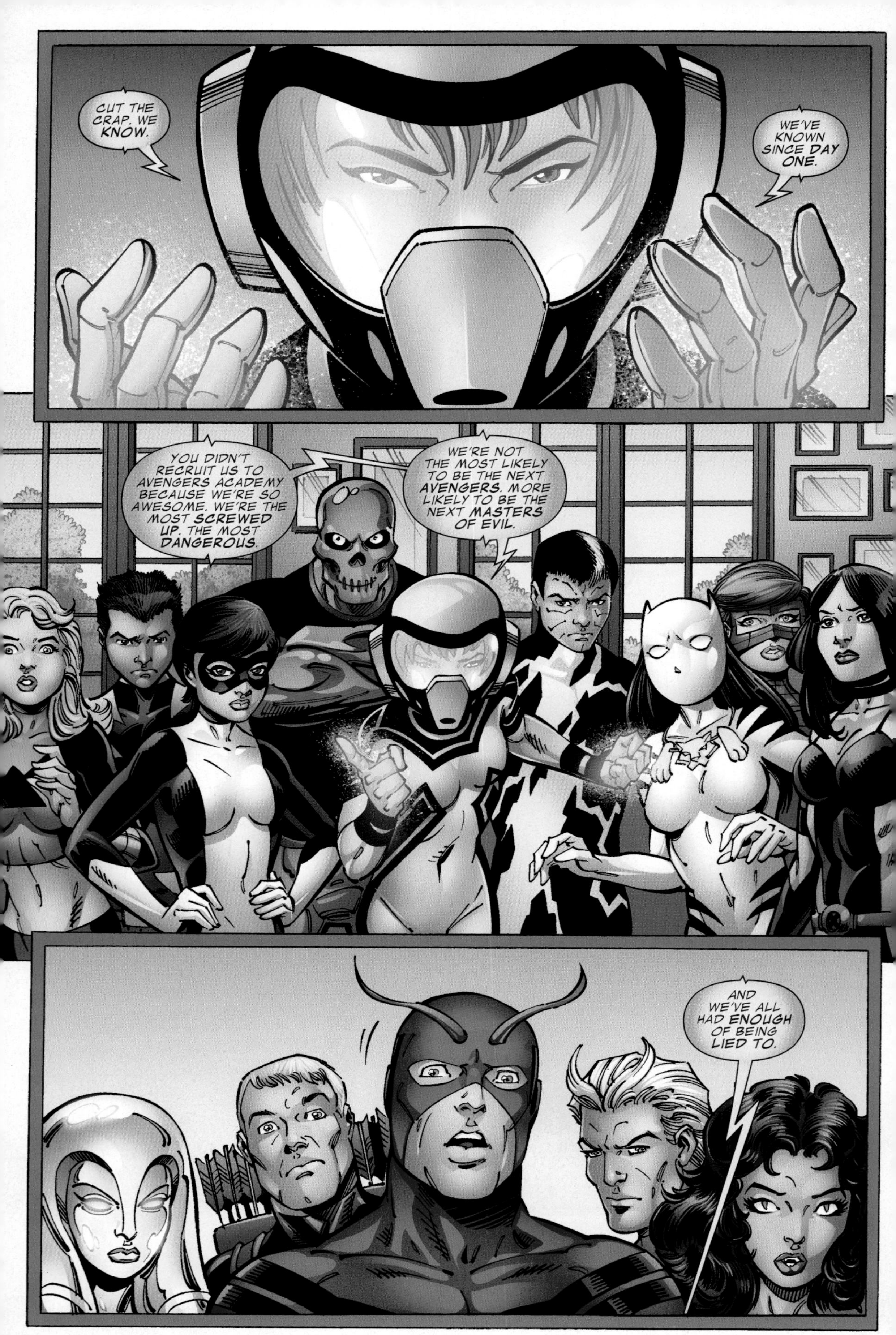
CUT THE CRAP. WE KNOW.
WE'VE KNOWN SINCE DAY ONE.
YOU DIDN'T RECRUIT US TO AVENGERS ACADEMY BECAUSE WE'RE SO AWESOME. WE'RE THE MOST SCREWED UP. THE MOST DANGEROUS.
WE'RE NOT THE MOST LIKELY TO BE THE NEXT AVENGERS. MORE LIKELY TO BE THE NEXT MASTERS OF EVIL.
AND WE'VE ALL HAD ENOUGH OF BEING LIED TO.

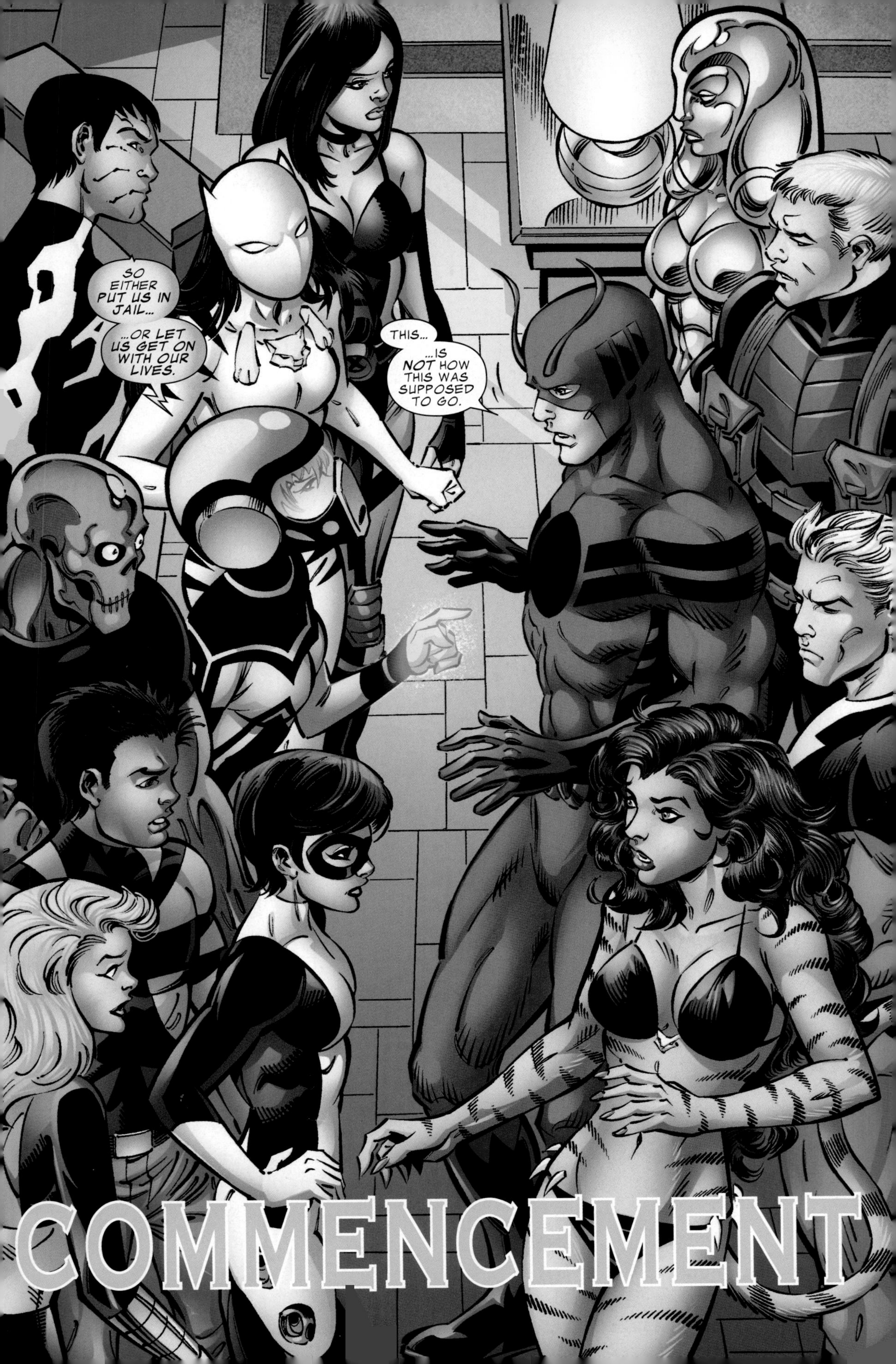
SO EITHER PUT US IN JAIL...
...OR LET US GET ON WITH OUR LIVES.
THIS...
...IS NOT HOW THIS WAS SUPPOSED TO GO.
COMMENCEMENT

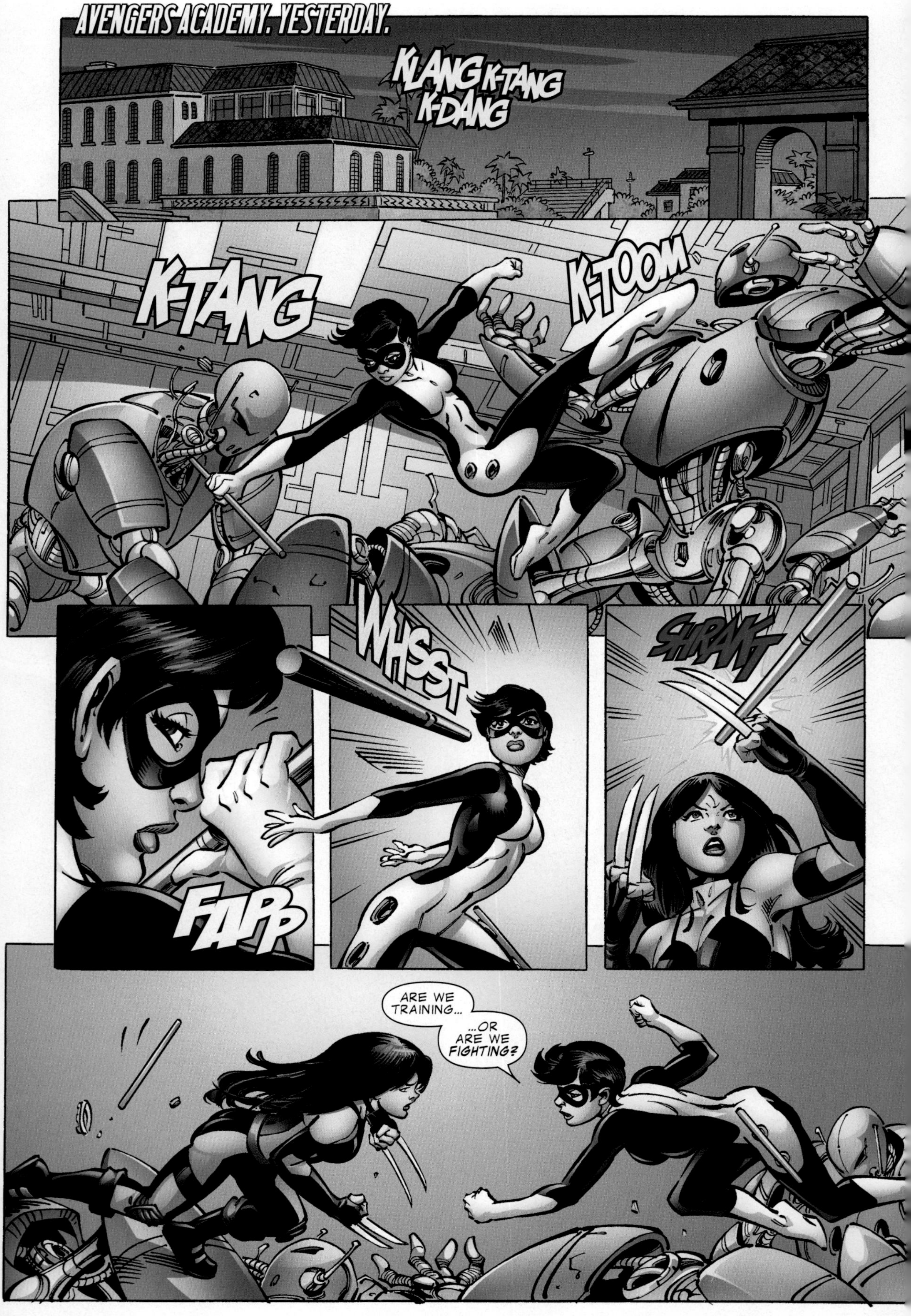
AVENGERS ACADEMY. YESTERDAY.
KLANG K-TANG K-DANG
K-TANG
K-TOOM
FAPP
WHSST
SHRAKT
ARE WE TRAINING...
...OR ARE WE FIGHTING?

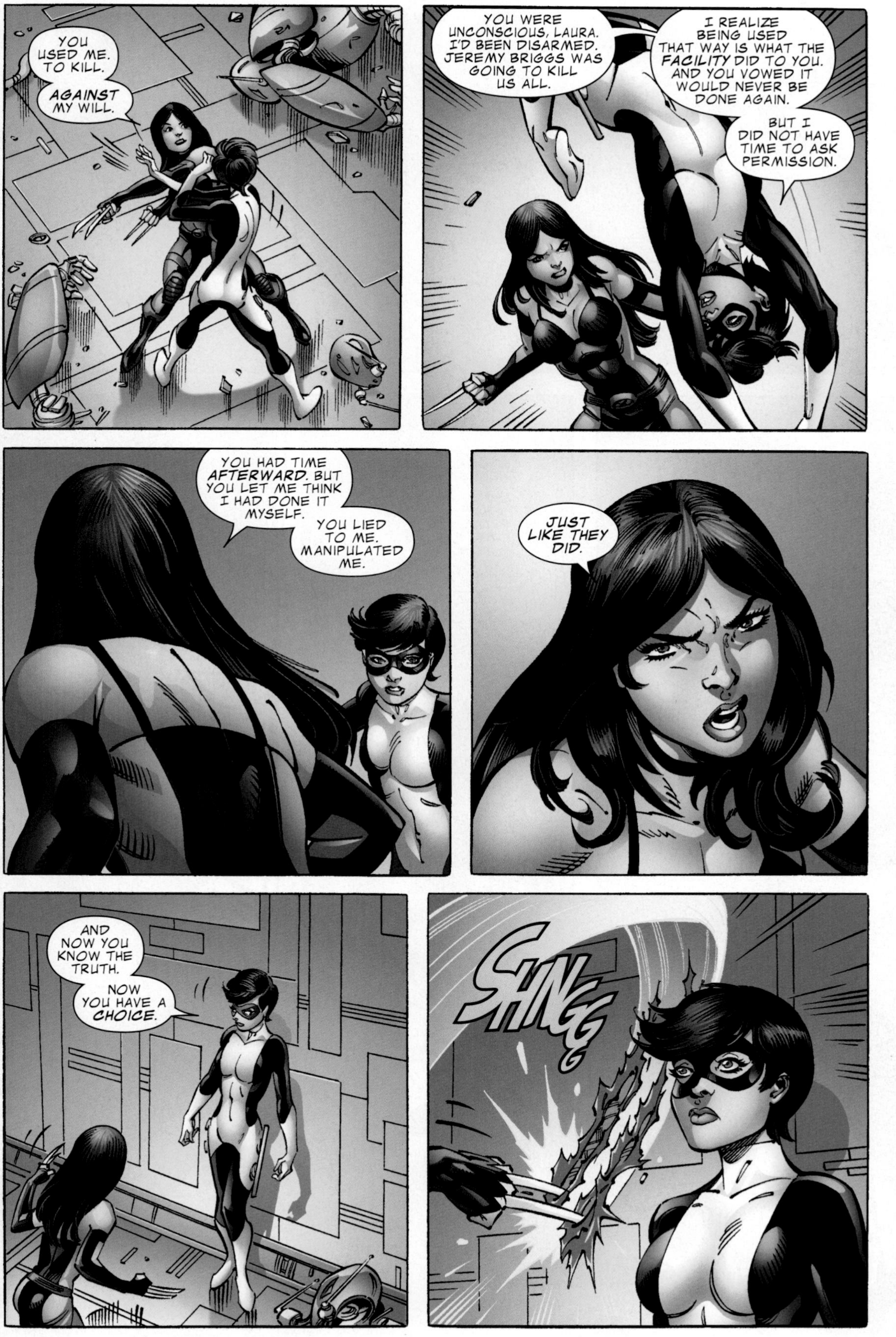
YOU USED ME. TO KILL.
AGAINST MY WILL.
YOU WERE UNCONSCIOUS, LAURA. I'D BEEN DISARMED. JEREMY BRIGGS WAS GOING TO KILL US ALL.
I REALIZE BEING USED THAT WAY IS WHAT THE FACILITY DID TO YOU. AND YOU VOWED IT WOULD NEVER BE DONE AGAIN.
BUT I DID NOT HAVE TIME TO ASK PERMISSION.
YOU HAD TIME AFTERWARD. BUT YOU LET ME THINK I HAD DONE IT MYSELF.
YOU LIED TO ME. MANIPULATED ME.
JUST LIKE THEY DID.
AND NOW YOU KNOW THE TRUTH.
NOW YOU HAVE A CHOICE.
SHNGG

IF I TOLD OUR TEACHERS WHAT YOU DID, THEY WOULD EXPEL YOU.

YES.

I WILL NOT.

BUT WE ARE NO LONGER FRIENDS.

STAY AWAY FROM ME.

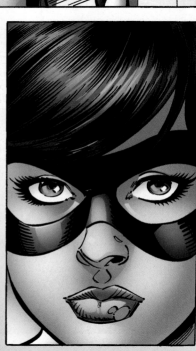

ONE MORE TIME, MADDIE. WHY AM I EVEN HERE?

BECAUSE THIS GUY WAS INSPIRED BY YOUR "IT GETS BETTER" VIDEO. BECAUSE HE'S THE ONLY GAY KID IN HIS CLASS AND HE ASKED YOU TO HIS PROM AND IF YOU STOOD HIM UP HE'D BE DEVASTATED.

AND ON BEHALF OF ALL THOSE WHO HAVE EVER BEEN STOOD UP, I WOULD KILL YOU SLOWLY AND PAINFULLY.

NEW YORK CITY.

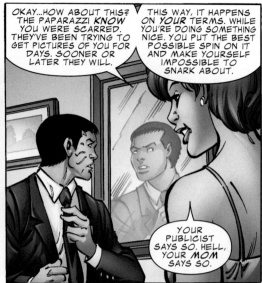

OKAY...HOW ABOUT THIS? THE PAPARAZZI *KNOW* YOU WERE SCARRED. THEY'VE BEEN TRYING TO GET PICTURES OF YOU FOR DAYS. SOONER OR LATER THEY WILL.

THIS WAY, IT HAPPENS ON *YOUR* TERMS. WHILE YOU'RE DOING SOMETHING NICE. YOU PUT THE BEST POSSIBLE SPIN ON IT AND MAKE YOURSELF IMPOSSIBLE TO SNARK ABOUT.

YOUR PUBLICIST SAYS SO. HELL, YOUR *MOM* SAYS SO.

AND THIS GUY, JONATHAN, WHO ASKED A *HOT, FAMOUS PERSON* TO HIS PROM...

...ENDS UP WITH ME.

TELL YOU WHAT, BRANDON, WE'LL ASK HIM. IF HE DOESN'T WANT TO GO THROUGH WITH IT, YOU'RE OFF THE HOOK.

FAIR ENOUGH?

JONATHAN? YOUR DATE'S READY.

OH...

...WOW. I STILL CAN'T BELIEVE THIS IS HAPPENING. YOU LOOK AMAZING.

YOU TOO.

LET'S DO THIS, HUH?

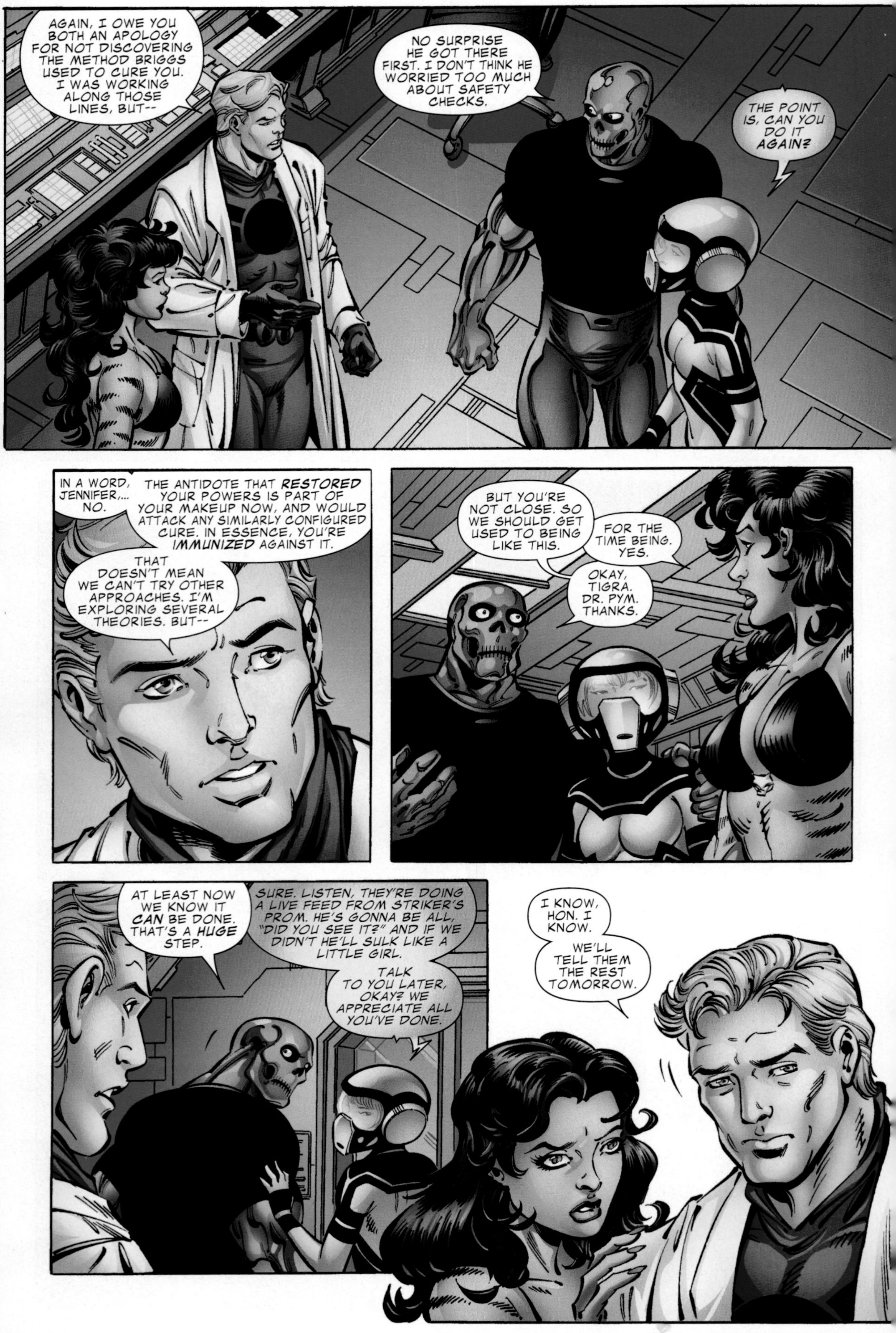
AGAIN, I OWE YOU BOTH AN APOLOGY FOR NOT DISCOVERING THE METHOD BRIGGS USED TO CURE YOU. I WAS WORKING ALONG THOSE LINES, BUT--
NO SURPRISE HE GOT THERE FIRST. I DON'T THINK HE WORRIED TOO MUCH ABOUT SAFETY CHECKS.
THE POINT IS, CAN YOU DO IT AGAIN?
IN A WORD, JENNIFER,... NO.
THE ANTIDOTE THAT RESTORED YOUR POWERS IS PART OF YOUR MAKEUP NOW, AND WOULD ATTACK ANY SIMILARLY CONFIGURED CURE. IN ESSENCE, YOU'RE IMMUNIZED AGAINST IT.
THAT DOESN'T MEAN WE CAN'T TRY OTHER APPROACHES. I'M EXPLORING SEVERAL THEORIES. BUT--
BUT YOU'RE NOT CLOSE. SO WE SHOULD GET USED TO BEING LIKE THIS.
FOR THE TIME BEING. YES.
OKAY, TIGRA. DR. PYM. THANKS.
AT LEAST NOW WE KNOW IT CAN BE DONE. THAT'S A HUGE STEP.
SURE. LISTEN, THEY'RE DOING A LIVE FEED FROM STRIKER'S PROM. HE'S GONNA BE ALL, "DID YOU SEE IT?" AND IF WE DIDN'T HE'LL SULK LIKE A LITTLE GIRL.
TALK TO YOU LATER, OKAY? WE APPRECIATE ALL YOU'VE DONE.
I KNOW, HON. I KNOW.
WE'LL TELL THEM THE REST TOMORROW.

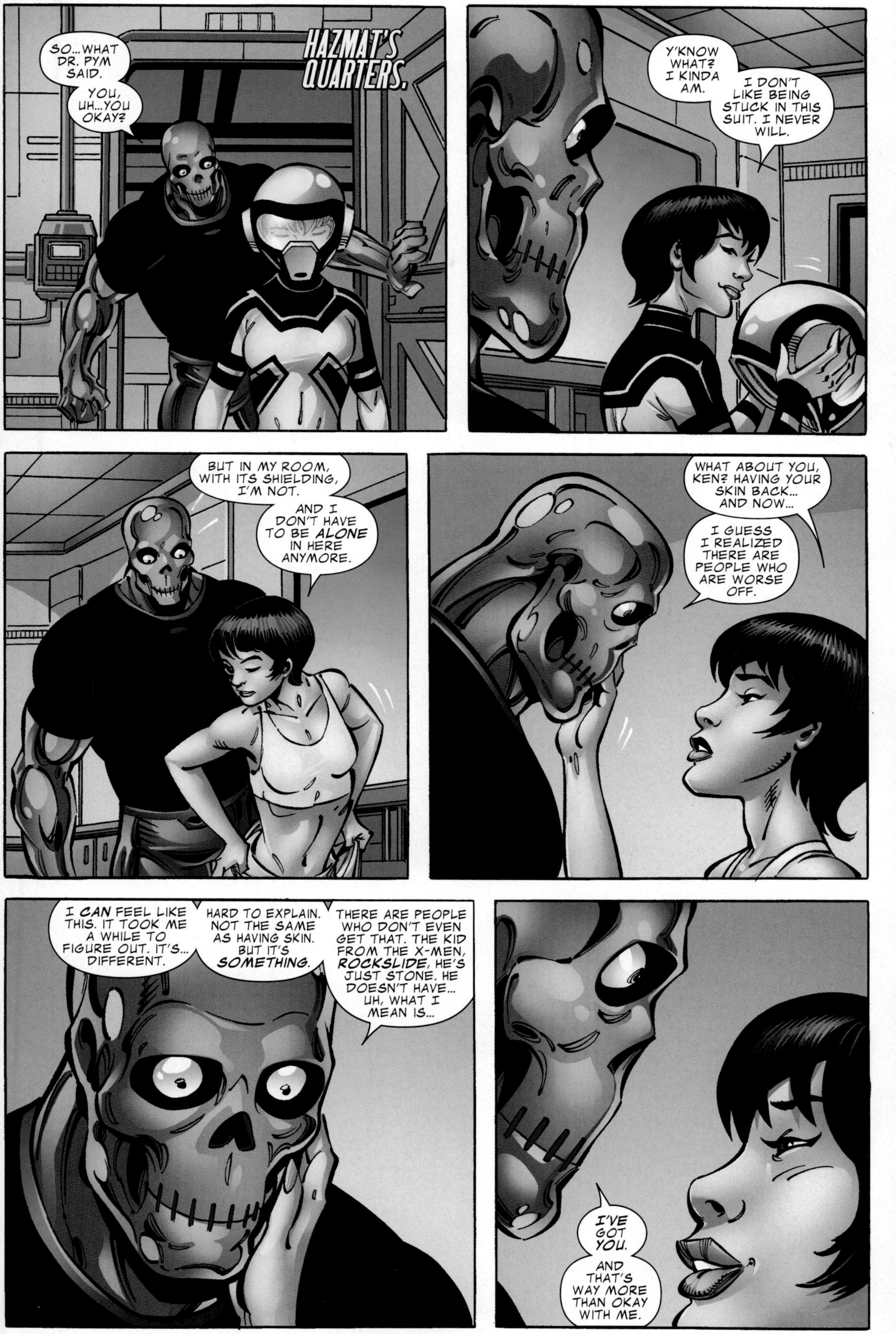
HAZMAT'S QUARTERS.
SO...WHAT DR. PYM SAID.
YOU, UH...YOU OKAY?
Y'KNOW WHAT? I KINDA AM.
I DON'T LIKE BEING STUCK IN THIS SUIT. I NEVER WILL.
BUT IN MY ROOM, WITH ITS SHIELDING, I'M NOT.
AND I DON'T HAVE TO BE ALONE IN HERE ANYMORE.
WHAT ABOUT YOU, KEN? HAVING YOUR SKIN BACK... AND NOW...
I GUESS I REALIZED THERE ARE PEOPLE WHO ARE WORSE OFF.
I CAN FEEL LIKE THIS. IT TOOK ME A WHILE TO FIGURE OUT. IT'S... DIFFERENT.
HARD TO EXPLAIN. NOT THE SAME AS HAVING SKIN. BUT IT'S SOMETHING.
THERE ARE PEOPLE WHO DON'T EVEN GET THAT. THE KID FROM THE X-MEN, ROCKSLIDE, HE'S JUST STONE. HE DOESN'T HAVE... UH, WHAT I MEAN IS...
I'VE GOT YOU.
AND THAT'S WAY MORE THAN OKAY WITH ME.

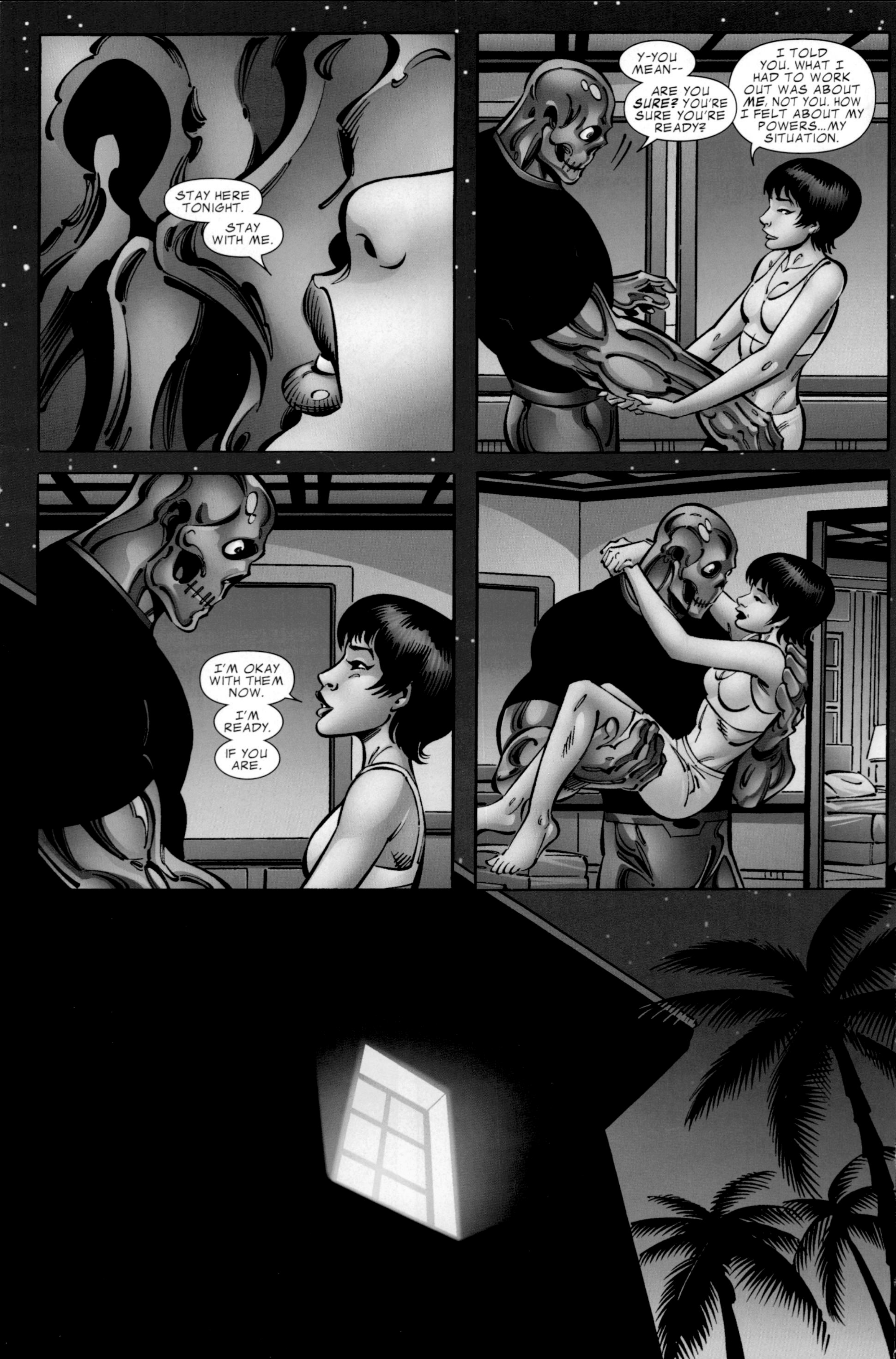
STAY HERE TONIGHT.
STAY WITH ME.
Y-YOU MEAN--
ARE YOU **SURE?** YOU'RE SURE YOU'RE READY?
I TOLD YOU. WHAT I HAD TO WORK OUT WAS ABOUT **ME**, NOT YOU. HOW I FELT ABOUT MY POWERS...MY SITUATION.
I'M OKAY WITH THEM NOW.
I'M READY.
IF YOU ARE.

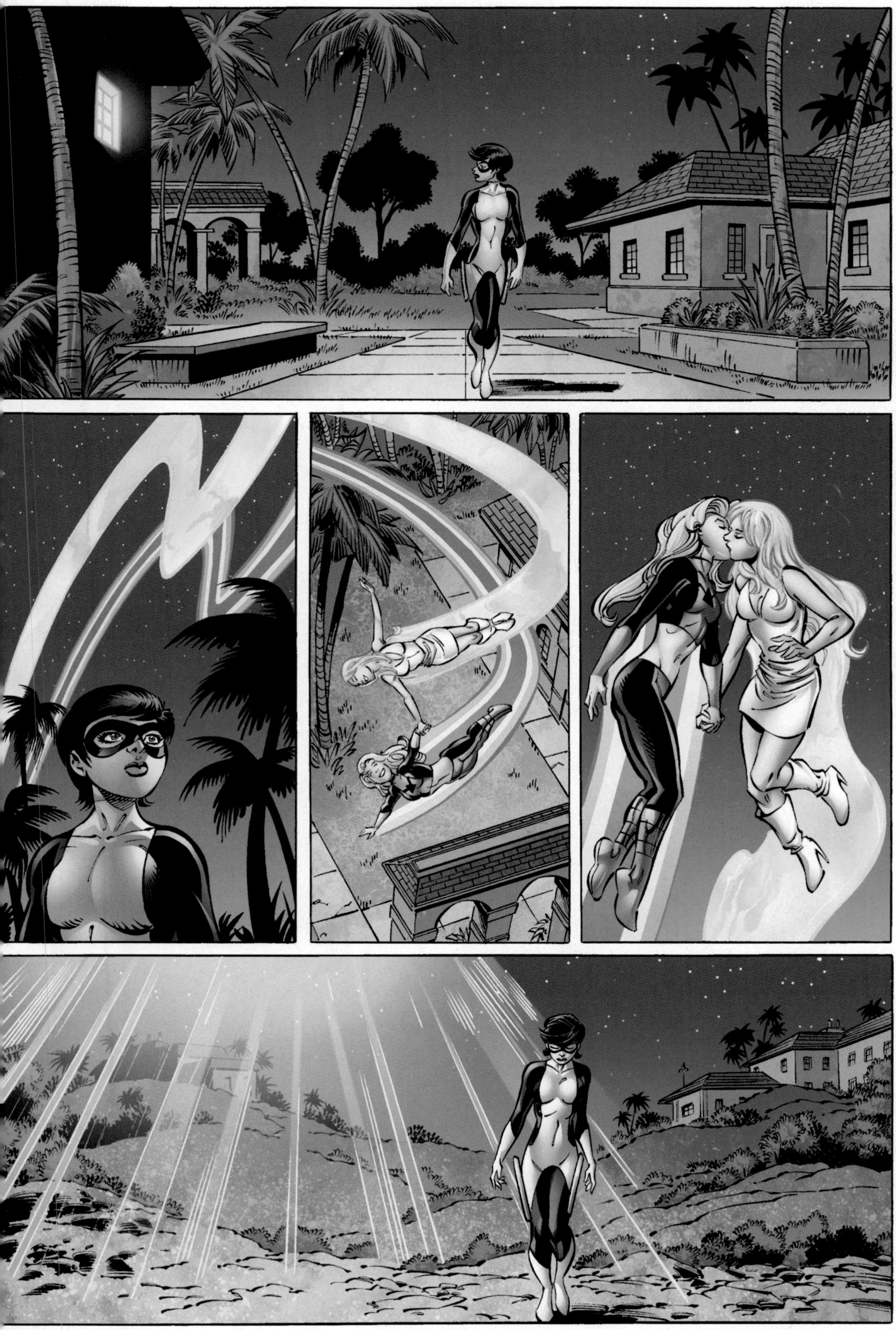

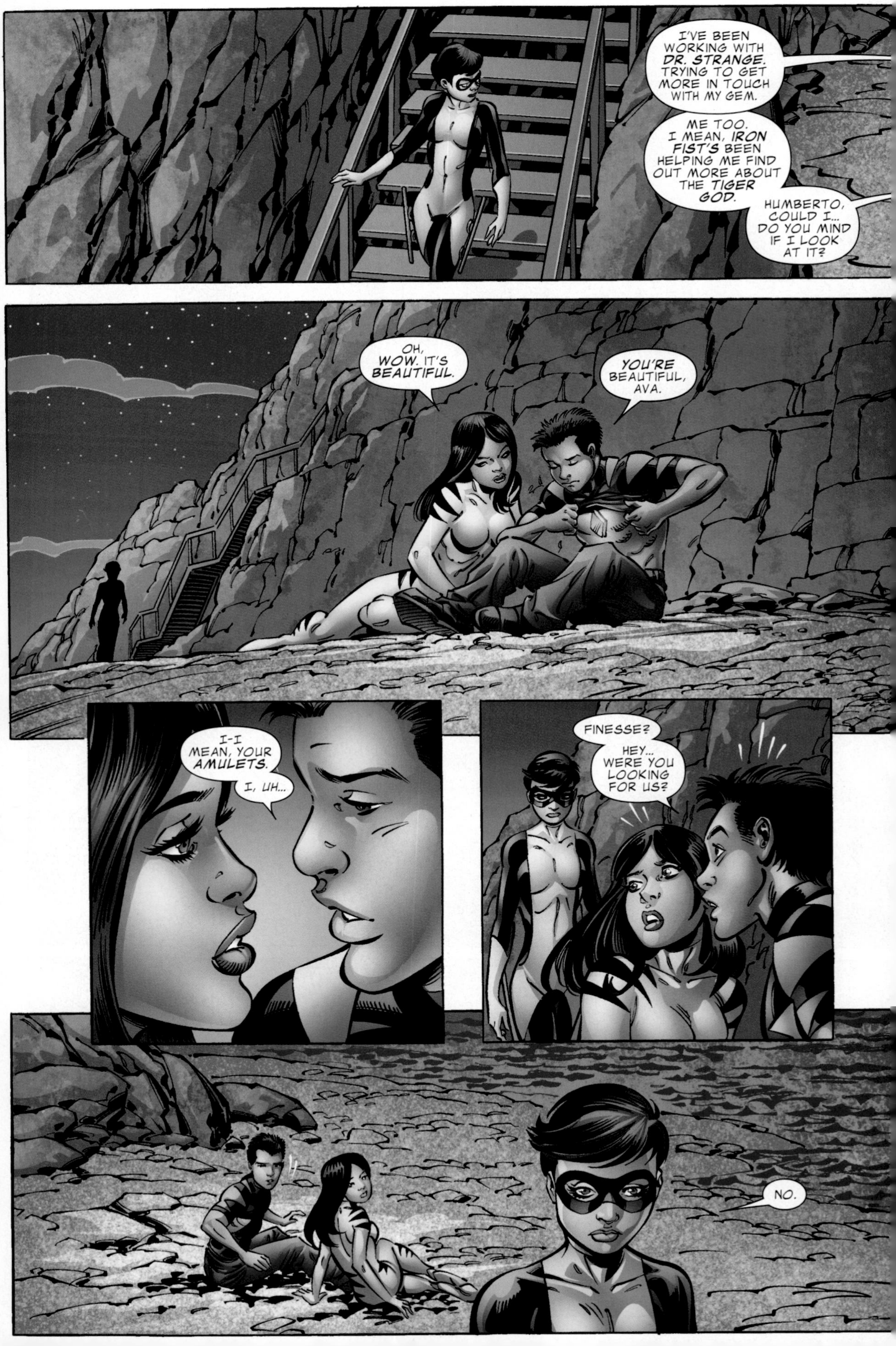
I'VE BEEN WORKING WITH DR. STRANGE. TRYING TO GET MORE IN TOUCH WITH MY GEM.
ME TOO. I MEAN, IRON FIST'S BEEN HELPING ME FIND OUT MORE ABOUT THE TIGER GOD.
HUMBERTO, COULD I... DO YOU MIND IF I LOOK AT IT?
OH, WOW. IT'S BEAUTIFUL.
YOU'RE BEAUTIFUL, AVA.
I-I MEAN, YOUR AMULETS.
I, UH...
FINESSE?
HEY... WERE YOU LOOKING FOR US?
NO.

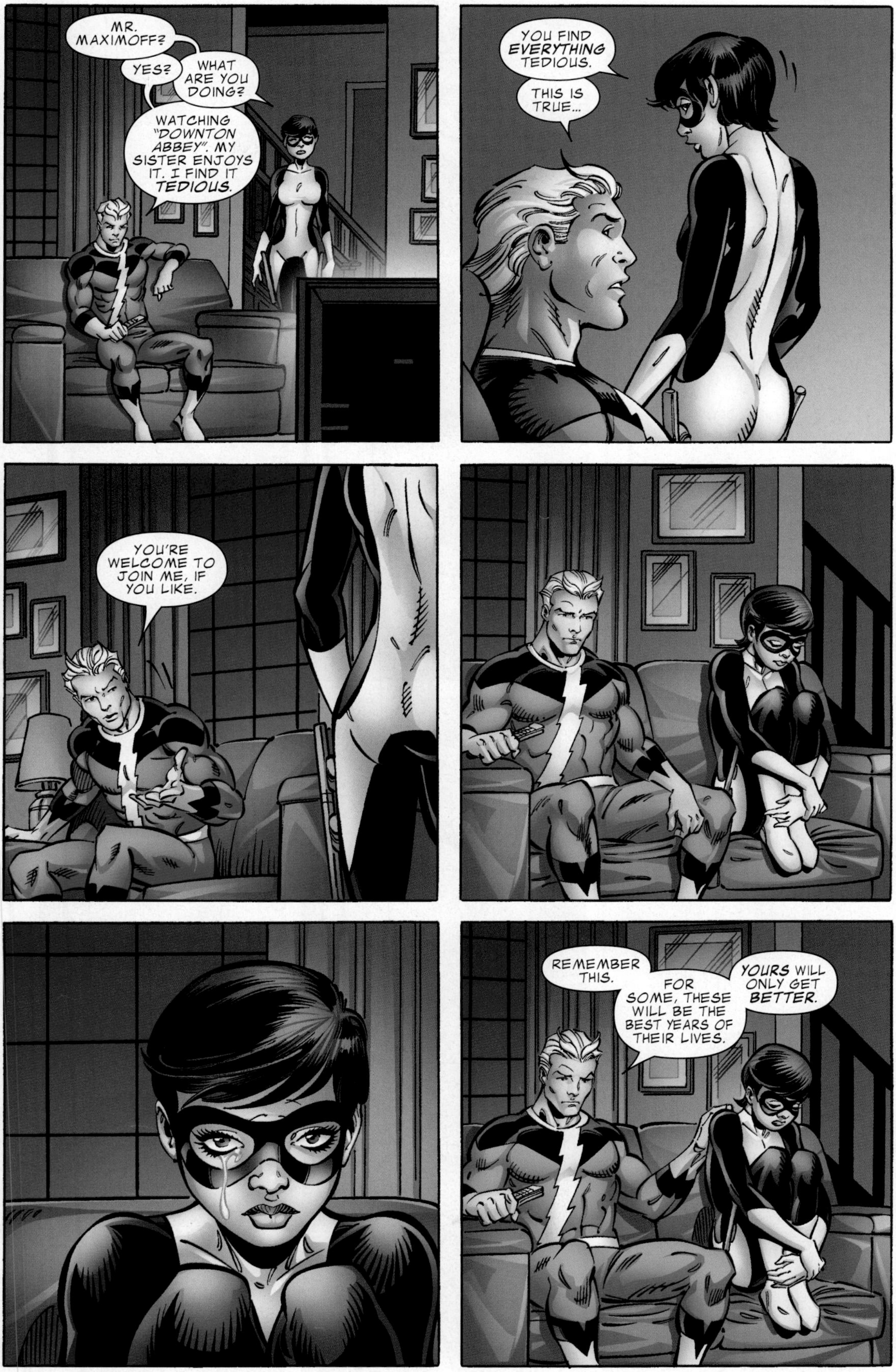
MR. MAXIMOFF?
YES?
WHAT ARE YOU DOING?
WATCHING "DOWNTON ABBEY". MY SISTER ENJOYS IT. I FIND IT TEDIOUS.
YOU FIND EVERYTHING TEDIOUS.
THIS IS TRUE...
YOU'RE WELCOME TO JOIN ME, IF YOU LIKE.
REMEMBER THIS.
FOR SOME, THESE WILL BE THE BEST YEARS OF THEIR LIVES.
YOURS WILL ONLY GET BETTER.

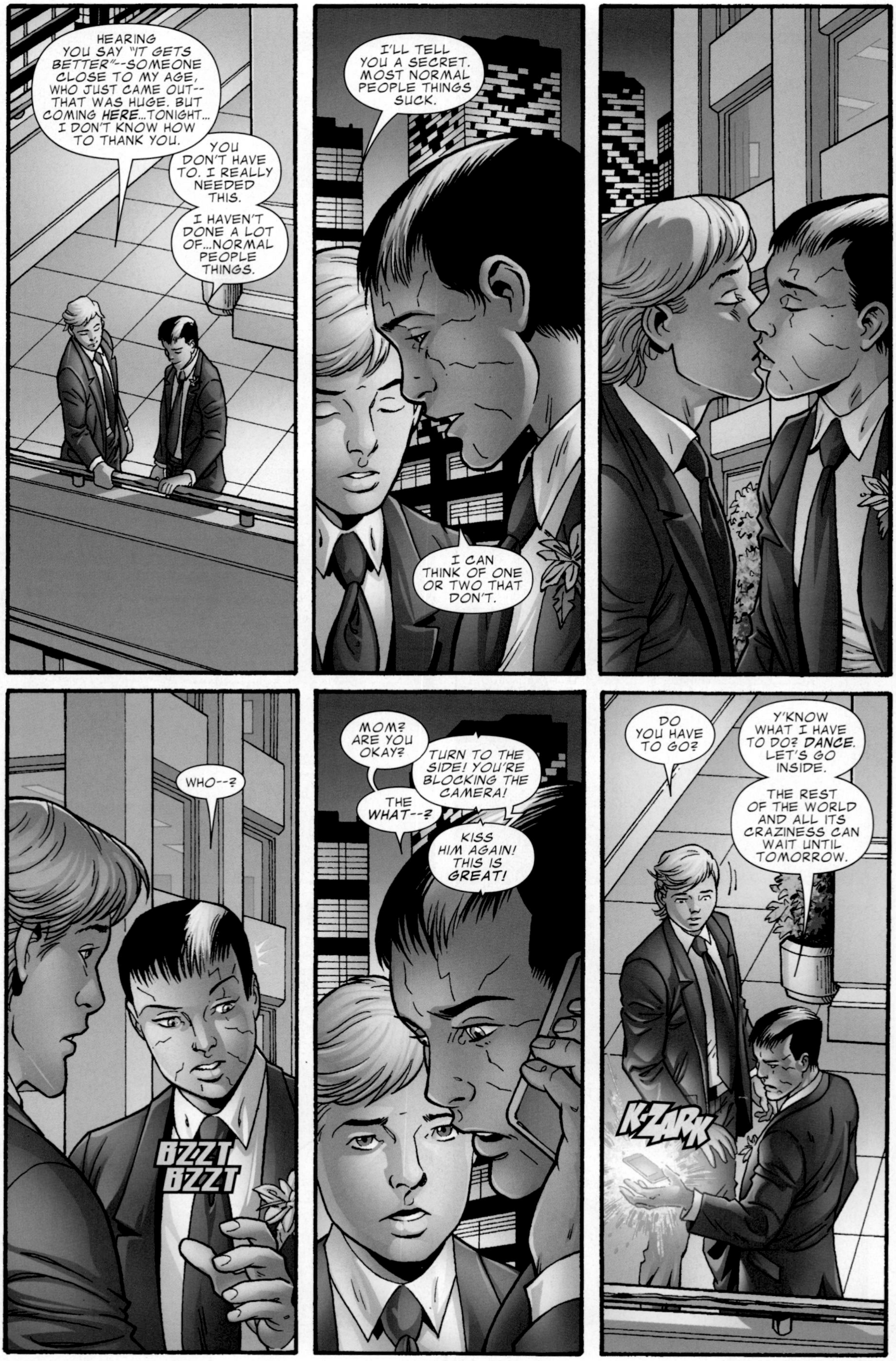
HEARING YOU SAY "IT GETS BETTER"--SOMEONE CLOSE TO MY AGE, WHO JUST CAME OUT--THAT WAS HUGE. BUT COMING HERE...TONIGHT... I DON'T KNOW HOW TO THANK YOU.
YOU DON'T HAVE TO. I REALLY NEEDED THIS.
I HAVEN'T DONE A LOT OF...NORMAL PEOPLE THINGS.
I'LL TELL YOU A SECRET. MOST NORMAL PEOPLE THINGS SUCK.
I CAN THINK OF ONE OR TWO THAT DON'T.
WHO--?
BZZT BZZT
MOM? ARE YOU OKAY?
TURN TO THE SIDE! YOU'RE BLOCKING THE CAMERA!
THE WHAT--?
KISS HIM AGAIN! THIS IS GREAT!
DO YOU HAVE TO GO?
Y'KNOW WHAT I HAVE TO DO? DANCE. LET'S GO INSIDE.
THE REST OF THE WORLD AND ALL ITS CRAZINESS CAN WAIT UNTIL TOMORROW.
K-ZARK

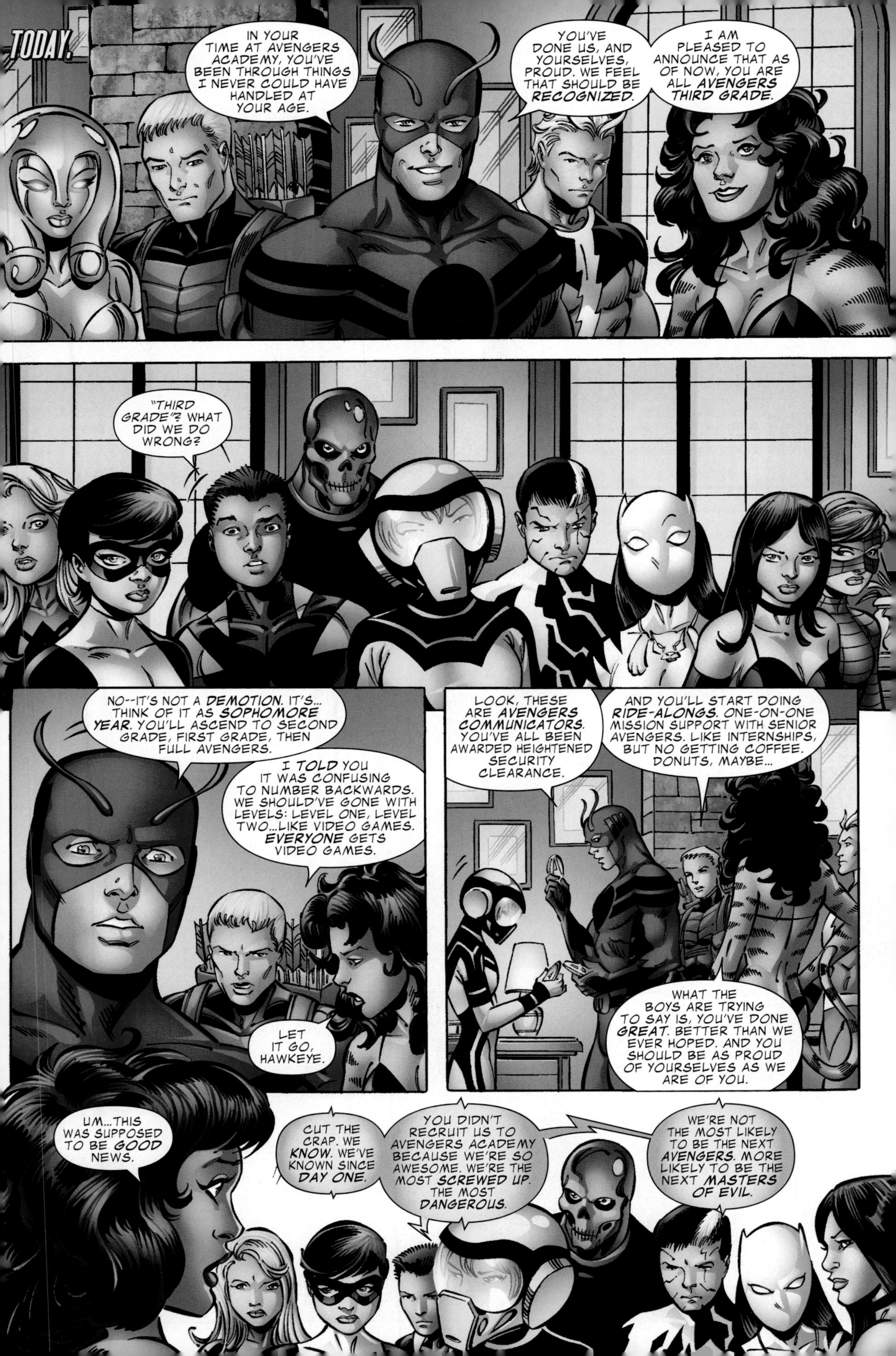
TODAY.
IN YOUR TIME AT AVENGERS ACADEMY, YOU'VE BEEN THROUGH THINGS I NEVER COULD HAVE HANDLED AT YOUR AGE.
YOU'VE DONE US, AND YOURSELVES, PROUD. WE FEEL THAT SHOULD BE RECOGNIZED.
I AM PLEASED TO ANNOUNCE THAT AS OF NOW, YOU ARE ALL AVENGERS THIRD GRADE.
"THIRD GRADE"? WHAT DID WE DO WRONG?
NO--IT'S NOT A DEMOTION. IT'S... THINK OF IT AS SOPHOMORE YEAR. YOU'LL ASCEND TO SECOND GRADE, FIRST GRADE, THEN FULL AVENGERS.
I TOLD YOU IT WAS CONFUSING TO NUMBER BACKWARDS. WE SHOULD'VE GONE WITH LEVELS: LEVEL ONE, LEVEL TWO...LIKE VIDEO GAMES. EVERYONE GETS VIDEO GAMES.
LET IT GO, HAWKEYE.
LOOK, THESE ARE AVENGERS COMMUNICATORS. YOU'VE ALL BEEN AWARDED HEIGHTENED SECURITY CLEARANCE.
AND YOU'LL START DOING RIDE-ALONGS. ONE-ON-ONE MISSION SUPPORT WITH SENIOR AVENGERS. LIKE INTERNSHIPS, BUT NO GETTING COFFEE. DONUTS, MAYBE...
WHAT THE BOYS ARE TRYING TO SAY IS, YOU'VE DONE GREAT. BETTER THAN WE EVER HOPED. AND YOU SHOULD BE AS PROUD OF YOURSELVES AS WE ARE OF YOU.
UM...THIS WAS SUPPOSED TO BE GOOD NEWS.
CUT THE CRAP. WE KNOW. WE'VE KNOWN SINCE DAY ONE.
YOU DIDN'T RECRUIT US TO AVENGERS ACADEMY BECAUSE WE'RE SO AWESOME. WE'RE THE MOST SCREWED UP. THE MOST DANGEROUS.
WE'RE NOT THE MOST LIKELY TO BE THE NEXT AVENGERS. MORE LIKELY TO BE THE NEXT MASTERS OF EVIL.

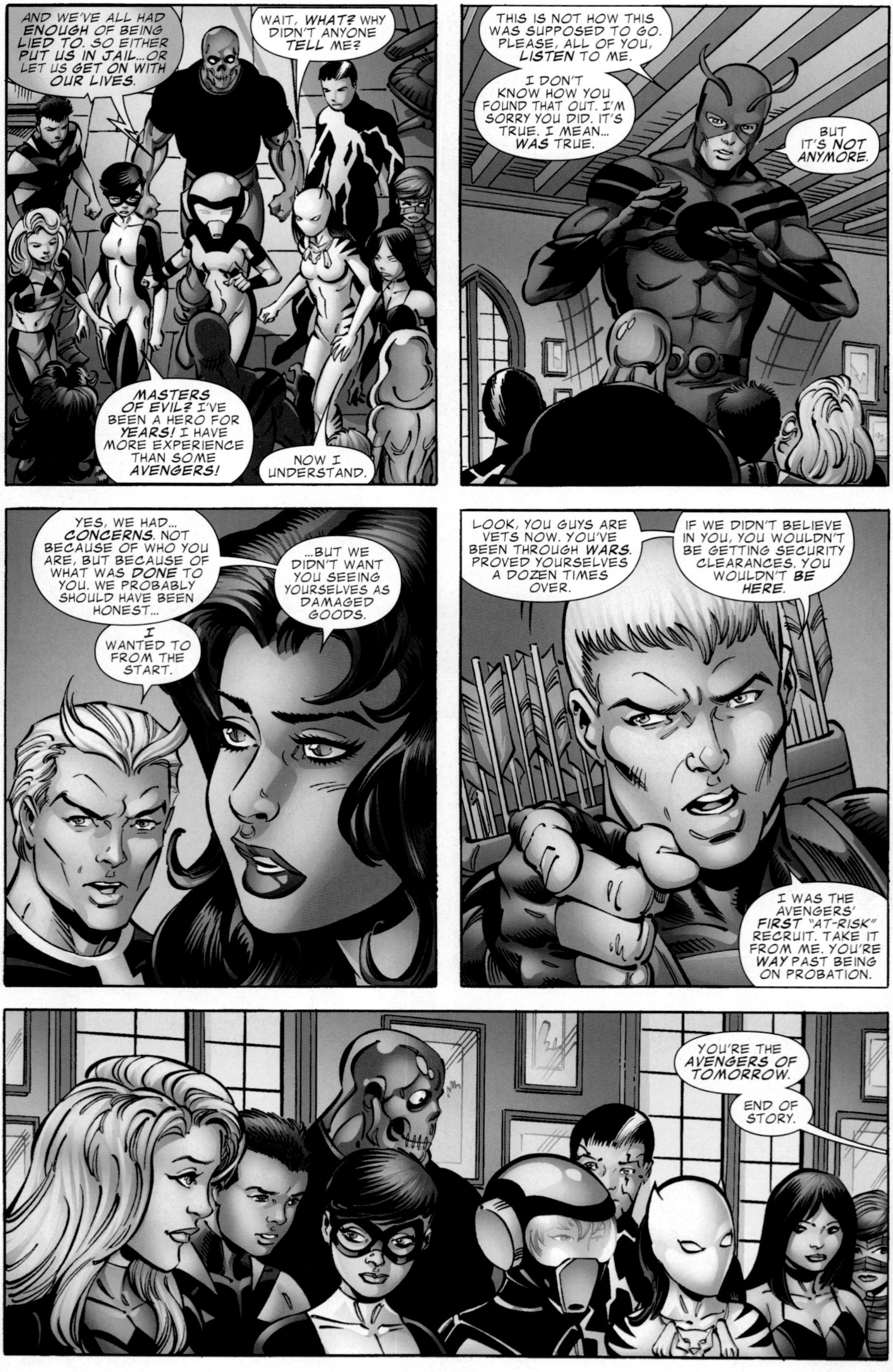

AND WE'VE ALL HAD ENOUGH OF BEING LIED TO. SO EITHER PUT US IN JAIL...OR LET US GET ON WITH OUR LIVES.
WAIT, WHAT? WHY DIDN'T ANYONE TELL ME?
MASTERS OF EVIL? I'VE BEEN A HERO FOR YEARS! I HAVE MORE EXPERIENCE THAN SOME AVENGERS!
NOW I UNDERSTAND.
THIS IS NOT HOW THIS WAS SUPPOSED TO GO. PLEASE, ALL OF YOU, LISTEN TO ME.
I DON'T KNOW HOW YOU FOUND THAT OUT. I'M SORRY YOU DID. IT'S TRUE. I MEAN... WAS TRUE.
BUT IT'S NOT ANYMORE.
YES, WE HAD... CONCERNS. NOT BECAUSE OF WHO YOU ARE, BUT BECAUSE OF WHAT WAS DONE TO YOU. WE PROBABLY SHOULD HAVE BEEN HONEST...
...BUT WE DIDN'T WANT YOU SEEING YOURSELVES AS DAMAGED GOODS.
I WANTED TO FROM THE START.
LOOK, YOU GUYS ARE VETS NOW. YOU'VE BEEN THROUGH WARS. PROVED YOURSELVES A DOZEN TIMES OVER.
IF WE DIDN'T BELIEVE IN YOU, YOU WOULDN'T BE GETTING SECURITY CLEARANCES. YOU WOULDN'T BE HERE.
I WAS THE AVENGERS' FIRST "AT-RISK" RECRUIT. TAKE IT FROM ME. YOU'RE WAY PAST BEING ON PROBATION.
YOU'RE THE AVENGERS OF TOMORROW.
END OF STORY.

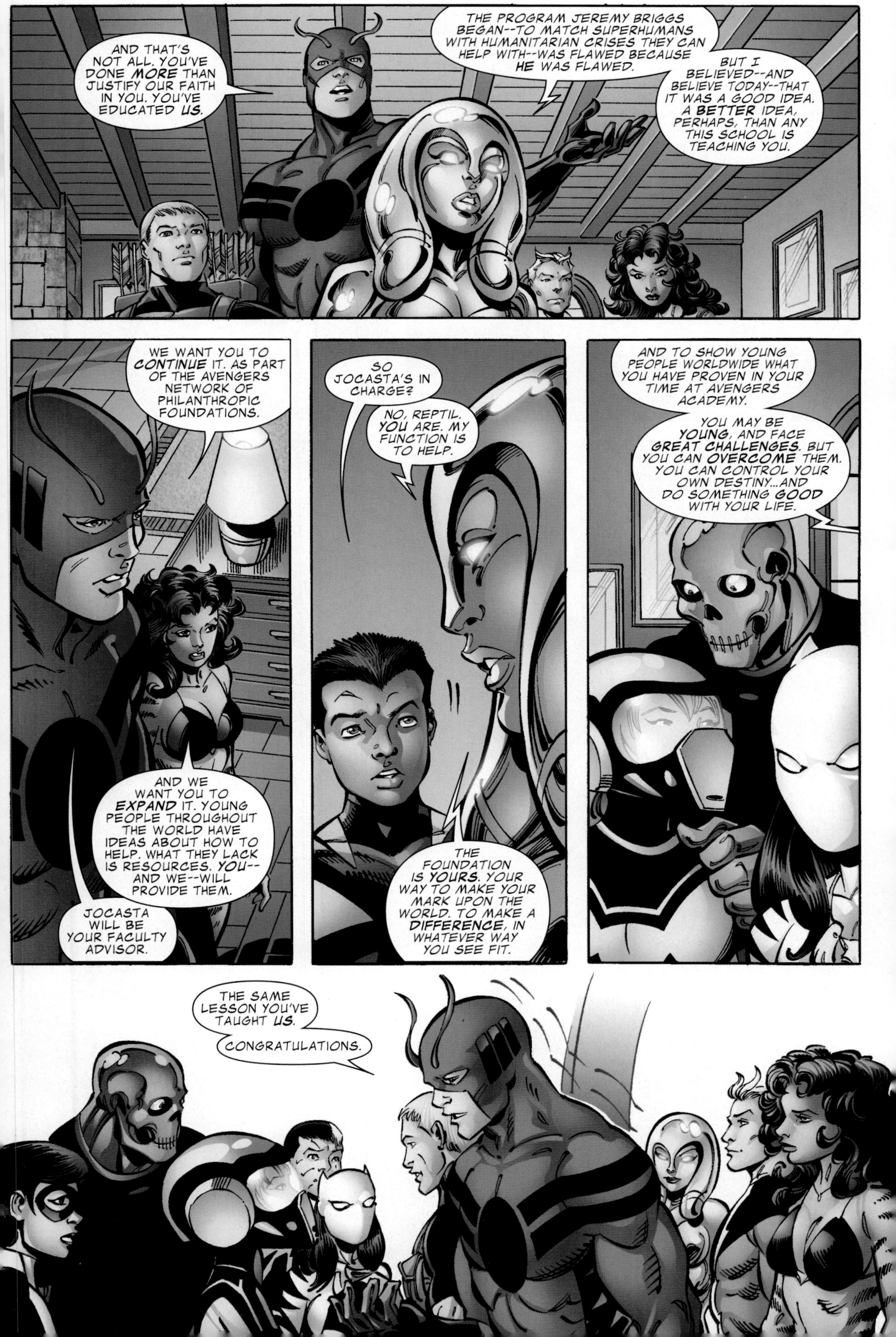
AND THAT'S NOT ALL. YOU'VE DONE MORE THAN JUSTIFY OUR FAITH IN YOU. YOU'VE EDUCATED US.
THE PROGRAM JEREMY BRIGGS BEGAN--TO MATCH SUPERHUMANS WITH HUMANITARIAN CRISES THEY CAN HELP WITH--WAS FLAWED BECAUSE HE WAS FLAWED.
BUT I BELIEVED--AND BELIEVE TODAY--THAT IT WAS A GOOD IDEA. A BETTER IDEA, PERHAPS, THAN ANY THIS SCHOOL IS TEACHING YOU.
WE WANT YOU TO CONTINUE IT. AS PART OF THE AVENGERS NETWORK OF PHILANTHROPIC FOUNDATIONS.
AND WE WANT YOU TO EXPAND IT. YOUNG PEOPLE THROUGHOUT THE WORLD HAVE IDEAS ABOUT HOW TO HELP. WHAT THEY LACK IS RESOURCES. YOU--AND WE--WILL PROVIDE THEM.
JOCASTA WILL BE YOUR FACULTY ADVISOR.
SO JOCASTA'S IN CHARGE?
NO, REPTIL. YOU ARE. MY FUNCTION IS TO HELP.
THE FOUNDATION IS YOURS. YOUR WAY TO MAKE YOUR MARK UPON THE WORLD. TO MAKE A DIFFERENCE, IN WHATEVER WAY YOU SEE FIT.
AND TO SHOW YOUNG PEOPLE WORLDWIDE WHAT YOU HAVE PROVEN IN YOUR TIME AT AVENGERS ACADEMY.
YOU MAY BE YOUNG, AND FACE GREAT CHALLENGES. BUT YOU CAN OVERCOME THEM. YOU CAN CONTROL YOUR OWN DESTINY...AND DO SOMETHING GOOD WITH YOUR LIFE.
THE SAME LESSON YOU'VE TAUGHT US.
CONGRATULATIONS.

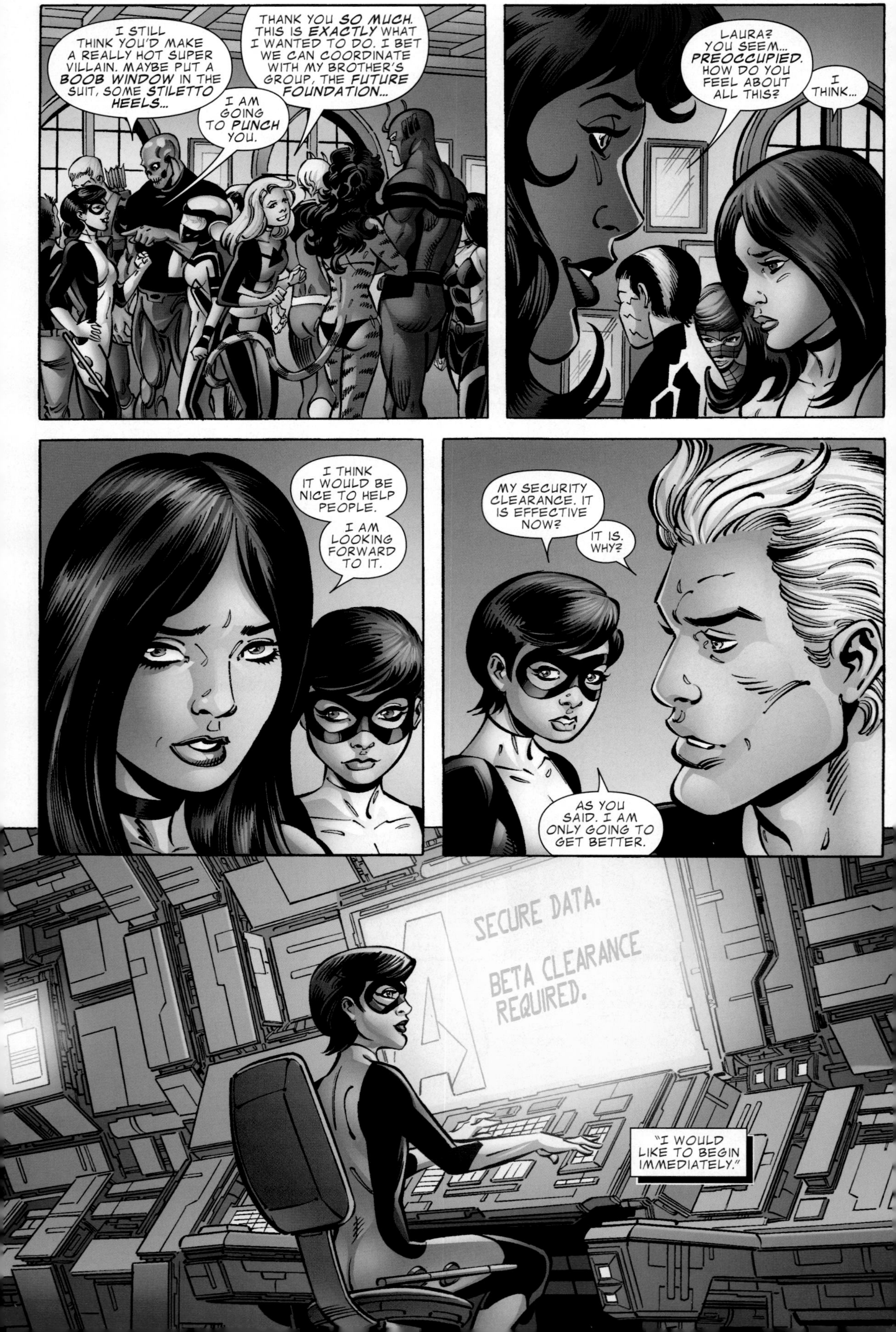
I STILL THINK YOU'D MAKE A REALLY HOT SUPER VILLAIN. MAYBE PUT A BOOB WINDOW IN THE SUIT, SOME STILETTO HEELS...
I AM GOING TO PUNCH YOU.
THANK YOU SO MUCH. THIS IS EXACTLY WHAT I WANTED TO DO. I BET WE CAN COORDINATE WITH MY BROTHER'S GROUP, THE FUTURE FOUNDATION...
LAURA? YOU SEEM... PREOCCUPIED. HOW DO YOU FEEL ABOUT ALL THIS?
I THINK...
I THINK IT WOULD BE NICE TO HELP PEOPLE.
I AM LOOKING FORWARD TO IT.
MY SECURITY CLEARANCE. IT IS EFFECTIVE NOW?
IT IS. WHY?
AS YOU SAID. I AM ONLY GOING TO GET BETTER.
SECURE DATA.
BETA CLEARANCE REQUIRED.
"I WOULD LIKE TO BEGIN IMMEDIATELY."

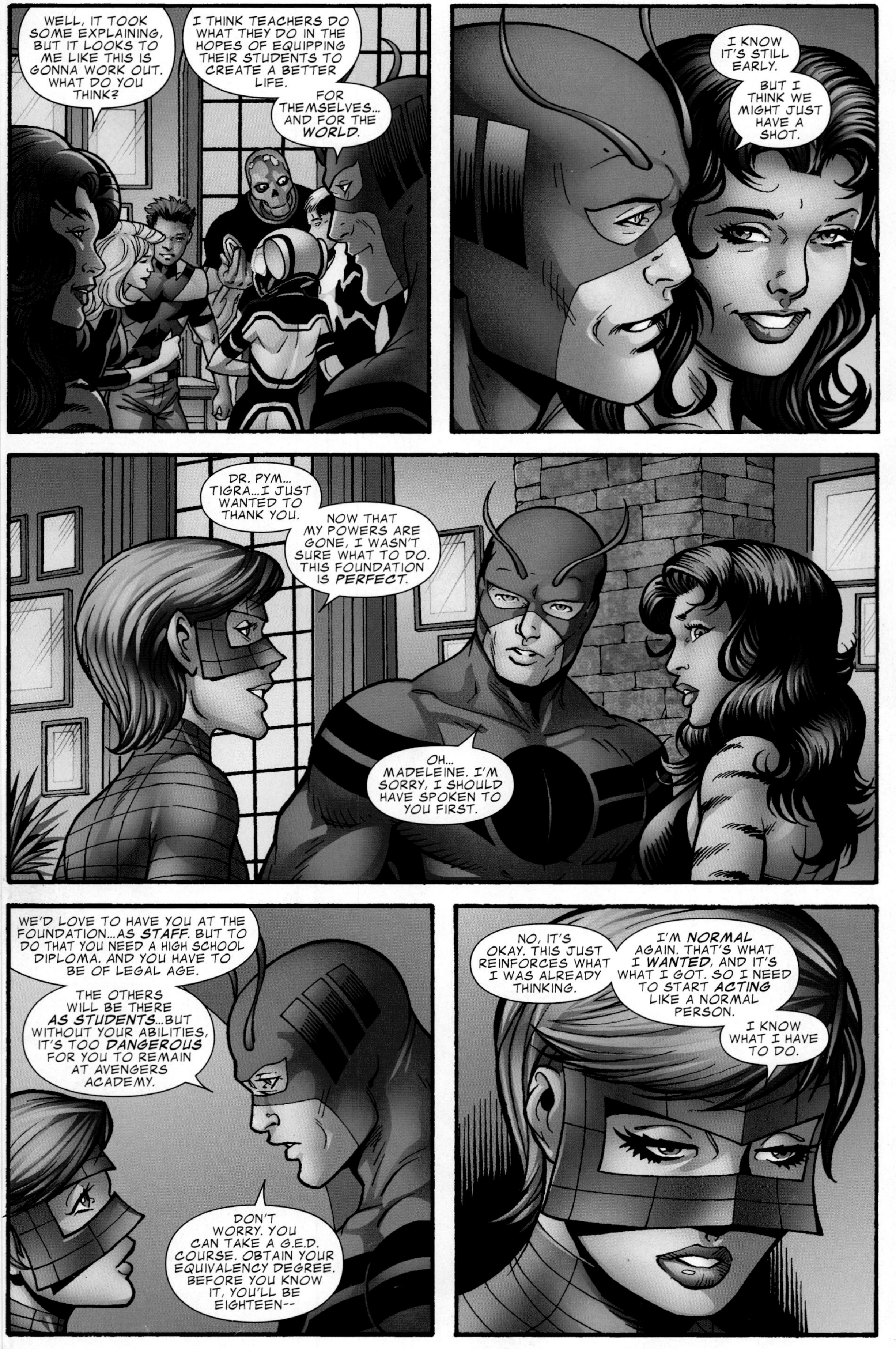

WELL, IT TOOK SOME EXPLAINING, BUT IT LOOKS TO ME LIKE THIS IS GONNA WORK OUT. WHAT DO YOU THINK?
I THINK TEACHERS DO WHAT THEY DO IN THE HOPES OF EQUIPPING THEIR STUDENTS TO CREATE A BETTER LIFE.
FOR THEMSELVES... AND FOR THE WORLD.
I KNOW IT'S STILL EARLY.
BUT I THINK WE MIGHT JUST HAVE A SHOT.
DR. PYM... TIGRA...I JUST WANTED TO THANK YOU.
NOW THAT MY POWERS ARE GONE, I WASN'T SURE WHAT TO DO. THIS FOUNDATION IS PERFECT.
OH... MADELEINE. I'M SORRY, I SHOULD HAVE SPOKEN TO YOU FIRST.
WE'D LOVE TO HAVE YOU AT THE FOUNDATION...AS STAFF. BUT TO DO THAT YOU NEED A HIGH SCHOOL DIPLOMA. AND YOU HAVE TO BE OF LEGAL AGE.
THE OTHERS WILL BE THERE AS STUDENTS...BUT WITHOUT YOUR ABILITIES, IT'S TOO DANGEROUS FOR YOU TO REMAIN AT AVENGERS ACADEMY.
DON'T WORRY. YOU CAN TAKE A G.E.D. COURSE. OBTAIN YOUR EQUIVALENCY DEGREE. BEFORE YOU KNOW IT, YOU'LL BE EIGHTEEN--
NO, IT'S OKAY. THIS JUST REINFORCES WHAT I WAS ALREADY THINKING.
I'M NORMAL AGAIN. THAT'S WHAT I WANTED, AND IT'S WHAT I GOT. SO I NEED TO START ACTING LIKE A NORMAL PERSON.
I KNOW WHAT I HAVE TO DO.

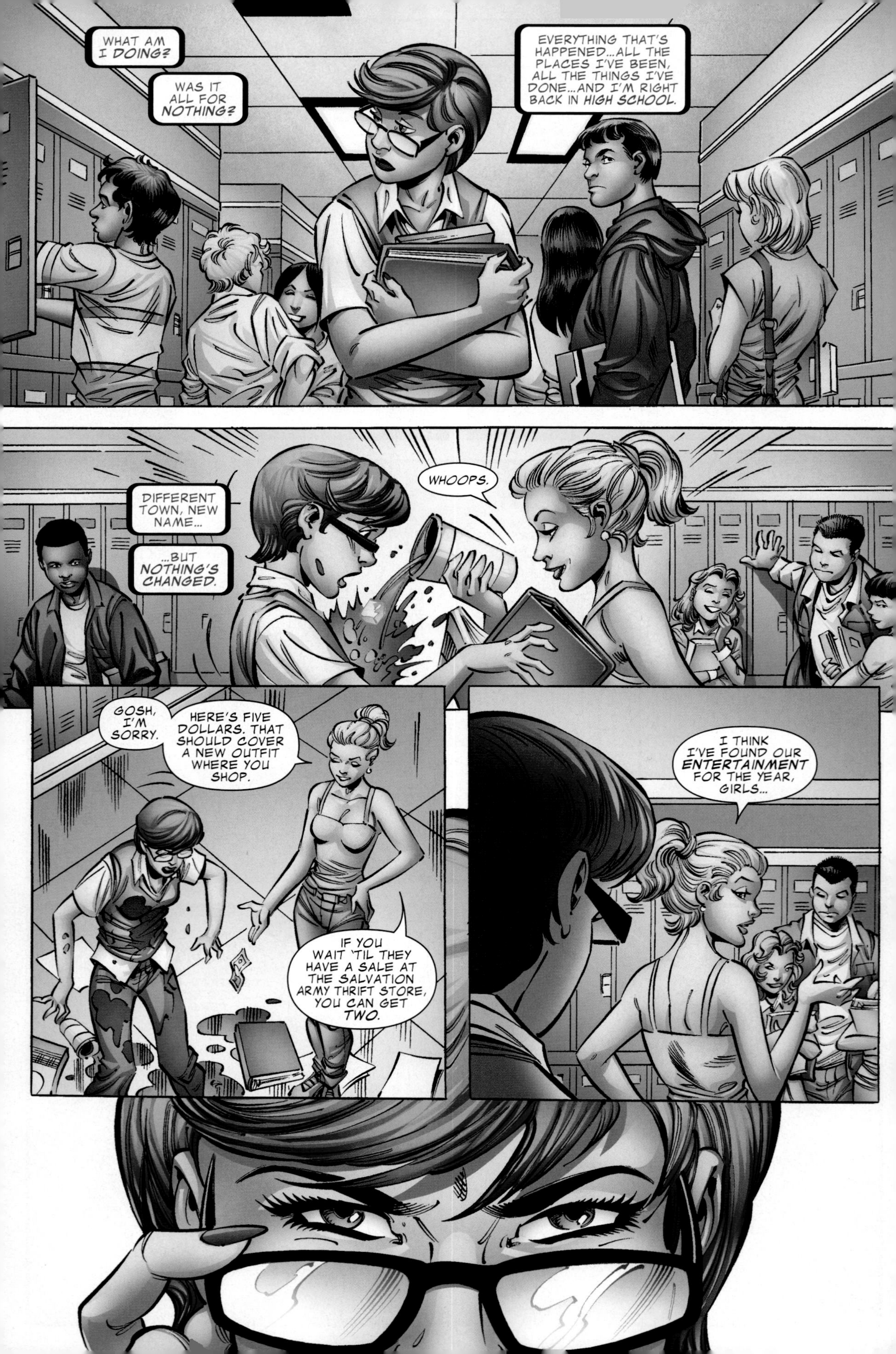
WHAT AM I DOING?
WAS IT ALL FOR NOTHING?
EVERYTHING THAT'S HAPPENED...ALL THE PLACES I'VE BEEN, ALL THE THINGS I'VE DONE...AND I'M RIGHT BACK IN HIGH SCHOOL.
DIFFERENT TOWN, NEW NAME...
...BUT NOTHING'S CHANGED.
WHOOPS.
GOSH, I'M SORRY.
HERE'S FIVE DOLLARS. THAT SHOULD COVER A NEW OUTFIT WHERE YOU SHOP.
IF YOU WAIT 'TIL THEY HAVE A SALE AT THE SALVATION ARMY THRIFT STORE, YOU CAN GET TWO.
I THINK I'VE FOUND OUR ENTERTAINMENT FOR THE YEAR, GIRLS...

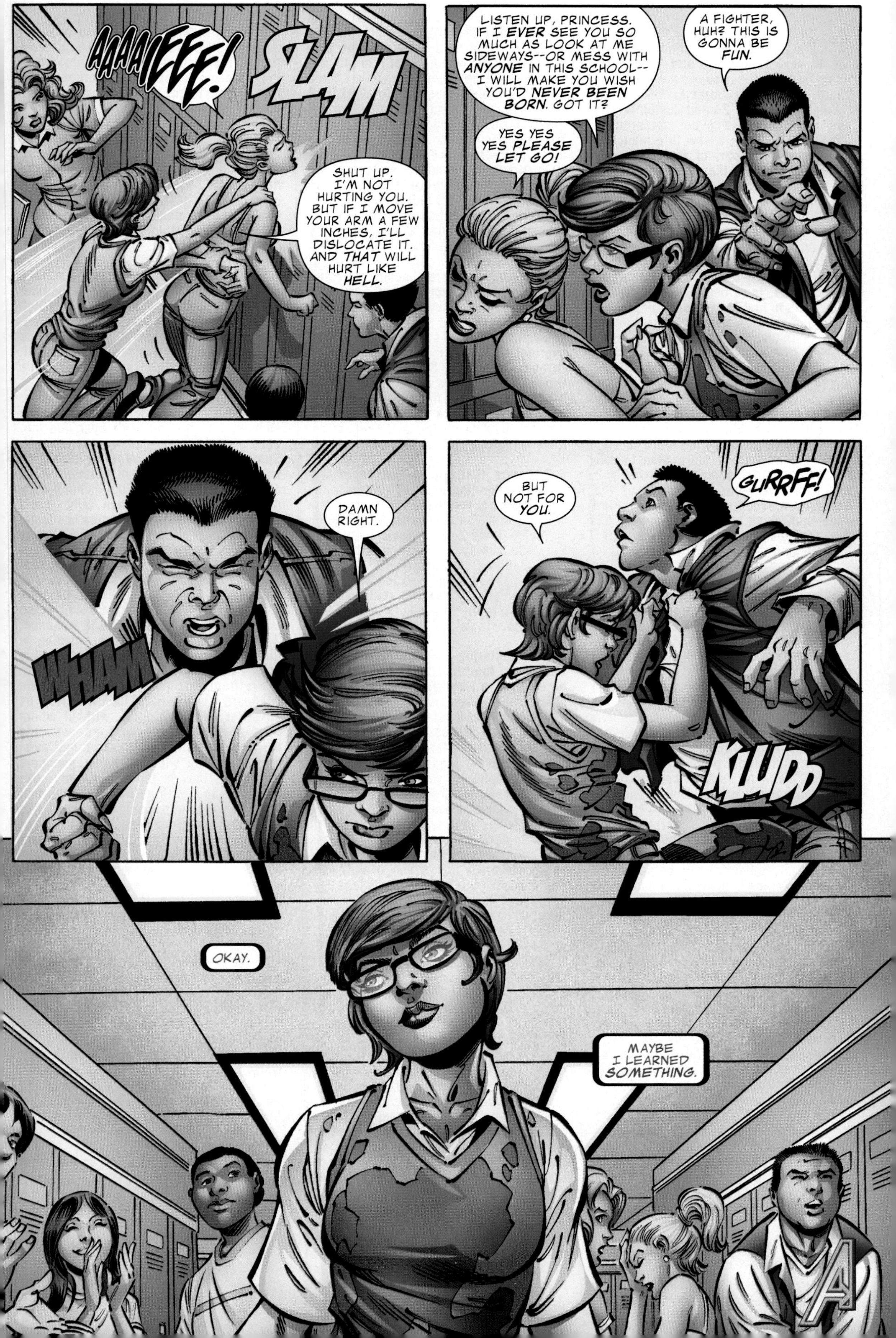
AAAAIEEE!
SLAM
SHUT UP. I'M NOT HURTING YOU. BUT IF I MOVE YOUR ARM A FEW INCHES, I'LL DISLOCATE IT. AND THAT WILL HURT LIKE HELL.
LISTEN UP, PRINCESS. IF I EVER SEE YOU SO MUCH AS LOOK AT ME SIDEWAYS--OR MESS WITH ANYONE IN THIS SCHOOL--I WILL MAKE YOU WISH YOU'D NEVER BEEN BORN. GOT IT?
YES YES YES PLEASE LET GO!
A FIGHTER, HUH? THIS IS GONNA BE FUN.
DAMN RIGHT.
WHAM
BUT NOT FOR YOU.
GURRFF!
KLUDD
OKAY.
MAYBE I LEARNED SOMETHING.

Well, here we are: the final chapter of AVENGERS ACADEMY. Hopefully you enjoyed it and found it a fitting end to the series. As you may have heard, some of our characters—like Reptil, Mettle, Hazmat, X-23 and Juston Seyfert and his Sentinel—will be appearing in AVENGERS ARENA, a new title launching in December as part of Marvel NOW! I hope you'll give it the same chance you gave our little book that could.

And that's really what I want to do with this last letters page: thank you for the opportunity you gave us to put out a comic book that is probably the most rewarding experience of my career. It's quite rare, in recent years, for a book focusing on new characters to last forty issues (39 plus our Point One edition). Heck, it's rare they last much more than six. Even with established characters it's a tough market. We can all think of great books we enjoyed that ended much too soon. (I'll never forget you, SHOGUN WARRIORS…sniff…) But thanks to shop owners recommending AVENGERS ACADEMY to their customers, and readers spreading the word to each other, we enjoyed a more than healthy run. We got to tell some stories that were fun, some that were sad, and some that hopefully moved you. And in this letters page—something else not common in this day and age—we formed a community I have come to love.

We had letters from folks who'd been reading since the beginning of the Marvel Age, as well as notes from people in their teens, or not quite. We had great discussions, about issues like characters' sexual orientation, how much skin X-23's costume showed, and what makes a hero. Best of all, it was always courteous, respectful and well thought out. I wouldn't have printed any abusive letters, but in a day when you hear and see a lot about the coarsening of our culture, we didn't get any. The letters page felt like a safe and fun place for fans of comics to get together, which is what I always hoped for.

And you were as great in person as you were on the page. I've met so many wonderful people at conventions and signings, I couldn't even begin to list them all. Suffice it to say that I appreciate every single one of you who has spoken to me, written in, or just bought and read the book. AVENGERS ACADEMY existed as long as it did because of you. I couldn't thank even a fraction of you in this space, but I'll single out one of you who I think is typical of the dedicated, intelligent and just generally awesome readers we have. Her name is Ashley, and I know her as @awyeahhash on Twitter. She runs a web site about AVENGERS ACADEMY whose name I can't repeat because there's a naughty word in it (used solely in exuberance and excitement, of course!) and when I did a signing in Portland, Oregon, she drove quite a ways to say hi and get some books signed. (She also loved the friendship between Finesse and X-23, so she's probably quite upset with me right now.) And she is just one example of the many, many terrific people I've met because of AVENGERS ACADEMY. Thanks, Ash – this book is for you…and all of you.

Of course, while your support made AVENGERS ACADEMY possible, it was the genius and hard work of some truly brilliant people who brought it to life, and I hope you'll bear with me while I thank them. I've been honored to work with some of the most outstanding talents in the art form, starting with my co-creator, Mike McKone, who both penciled and inked our early issues. He was followed by such amazing pencilers as Tom Raney, Sean Chen, Jorge Molina, Andrea Di Vito, Tom Grummett, Karl Moline and Timothy Green II, collaborating with inkers Scott Hanna, Cory Hamscher, Andrew Hennessy, Rick Ketcham, Cam Smith, Dave Meikis, Rebecca Buchman, Jim Fern and Jeff Huet. These guys were actors, directors and cinematographers all in one. They made it real, and they made it beautiful.

The contributions of colorists are too often overlooked, but the incredible skills of Jeromy Cox, Chris Sotomayor, Veronica Gandini and Andrew Crossley were such a huge part of this title. I hope you'll go back and take a look with an eye towards noticing how much the coloring adds to the story, and be as amazed as I was.

The covers that you talked about with eager anticipation online when each new solicit came out were the work of Mike and Jeromy; Billy Tan & Leonardo Olea; Rodin Esquejo; David Yardin; David Lafuente & Christina Strain; and Giuseppe Camuncoli & Jim Charalampidis (a fellow Greek whose eye-catching work on the FINAL EXAM storyline made me realize even I have been guilty of not fully appreciating what colorists do).

As for lettering, another skill whose fruits are too often under-appreciated, here we have been blessed as well. VC's Chris Eliopoulos (another Greek! It's a conspiracy!) and Clayton Cowles have graced a few issues, but for almost the entire run, our lettering's been done by VC's own living legend Joe Caramagna, who has lettered something like eight billion issues of AMAZING SPIDER-MAN, among other classics, and who is a heck of a writer as well, with some terrific all-ages Spider-Man books on the shelves. I've only met Joe once in person, but I consider him a true friend. He was the first audience we had for each issue, and more than once took the time out of his insanely busy schedule to compliment a story he'd enjoyed. Most touching of all, when I'd put a negative letter in this space, Joe—who puts it together—would invariably email me to say something to the effect of, "Don't listen to that! You're doing GREAT!" Thanks, Joe. Though I'm sure we'll work together in the future, I'm still gonna miss you.

Of course, there's stalwart editor Bill Rosemann, who has quarterbacked our team for every single issue. Without him, this book wouldn't have happened at all, or continued as long as it did. He's continuing on to AVENGERS ARENA as well, one of several reasons I'm not worried about our kids being in good hands—he loves them as much as I do. We've had great dedicated Assistant Editors, too: Rachel Pinnelas, John Denning, Jake Thomas and Jon Moisan. And without the support and guidance of Tom Brevoort, Axel Alonso, Joe Quesada, Dan Buckley and Alan Fine—and any number of people who didn't receive credit on the book but whose efforts were so important, from Arune Singh to Ben Morse to the designers in the Marvel Bullpen to the Marketing and Marvel.com teams to the living legend Flo Steinberg—none of us would be here.

These folks gave their all to really make these characters live and breathe. They're also people I'm massive fans of, and let me tell you, having people I admire so much tell me how special they think this book is, how much they enjoy working on it, and how much they'll miss it is as rewarding as hearing from all of you.

To them, and to you, thank you. A million times, thank you. I'll always remember and treasure this experience. Like high school friends, I hope we'll keep in touch, but we'll never again be together quite the same way. So I'm sad it had to end, but eternally grateful we had the time together we did.

Many of you have shared with me your sadness that the journey's over. Me too, but I'm even more glad we got to do it. Some have expressed anger or frustration with Marvel, or the new direction some of the characters are going in, but please don't feel that way. When Mike and I created the students of Avengers Academy, it wasn't to jealously hoard them. It was with the hope that they'd become part of the Marvel Universe. The only way that happens is if other creators use them, and AVENGERS ARENA has terrific creators doing just that. If it's not your cup of tea fair enough, but please give it a chance. As for Marvel, they've been amazing to me. They provided all the support for this book I could have wanted. For over five years (from the time I was invited to come on board AVENGERS: THE INITIATIVE as co-writer with Dan Slott, without whom none of this would have happened, and who my fuzzy memory thinks might even have come up with the name Avengers Academy), they've let me have my cake and eat it too, with an Avengers title that lets me write both iconic characters like Iron Man and Giant-Man as well as the fun and obscure denizens of the Marvel Universe, from Devil Dinosaur to Johnny Guitar, all mingling with brand new characters I got to co-create. It has been a dream come true. If you must be upset with someone, it should be me—I failed to deliver a book that sold enough copies to continue longer, and for that, I am sorry. Like you, I'm sad it's over, but I hope that, like me, you had fun while it lasted.

I realize this page has been pretty self-indulgent, but AVENGERS ACADEMY has meant so much to me I can't help it. So I hope you'll indulge me one final time while I say "I love you" to my wife Ruth, without whom I doubt I'd even be doing this, and my cats Josie and Francis, my furry muses, who have been by my side for the entirety of the run of this book, purring, yawning and looking at me sideways when my Internet breaks from writing last too long.

And I love you guys. All of you.

Thanks for everything.

-Christos Gage

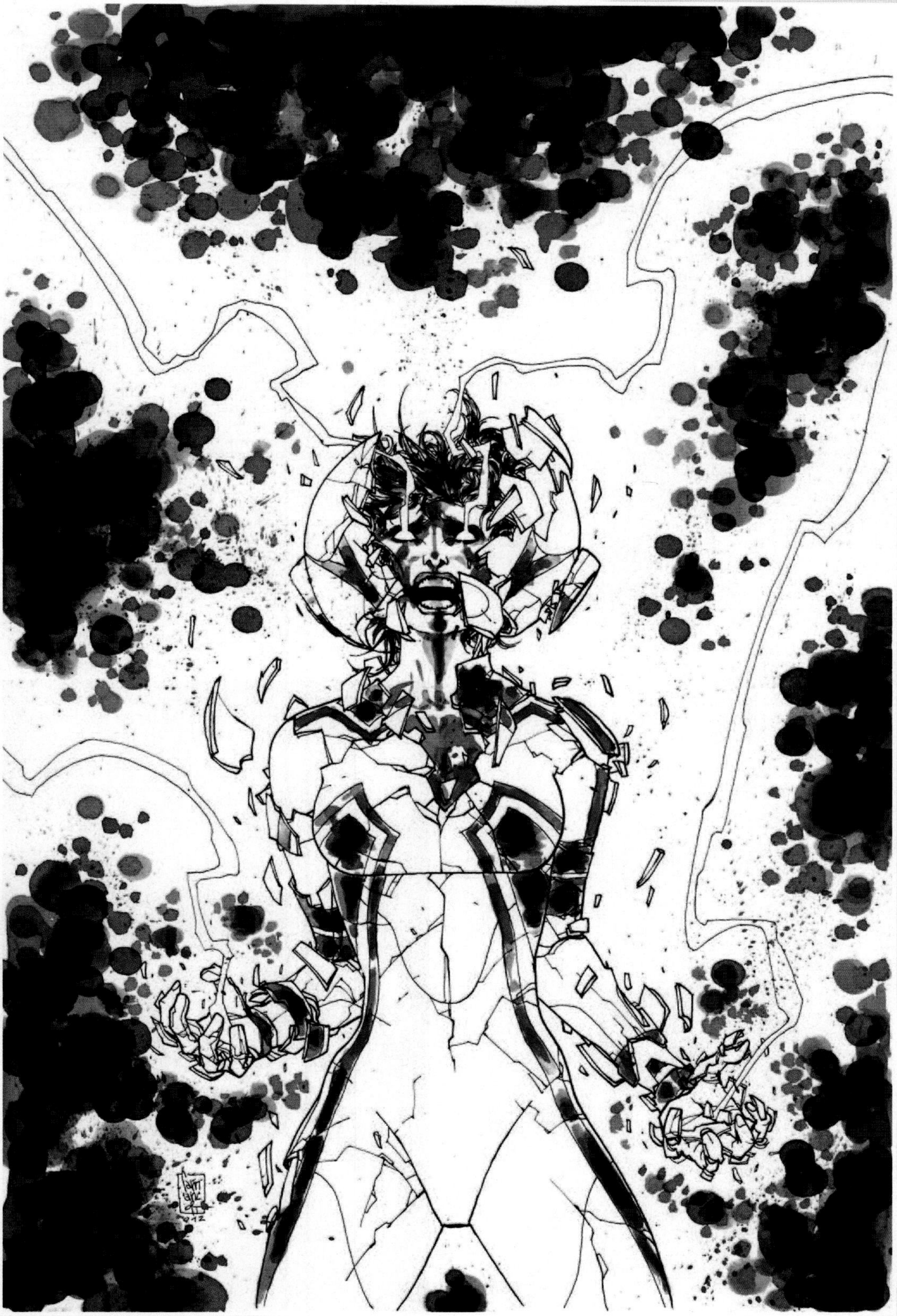

Avengers Academy #34 cover inks by Giuseppe Camuncoli

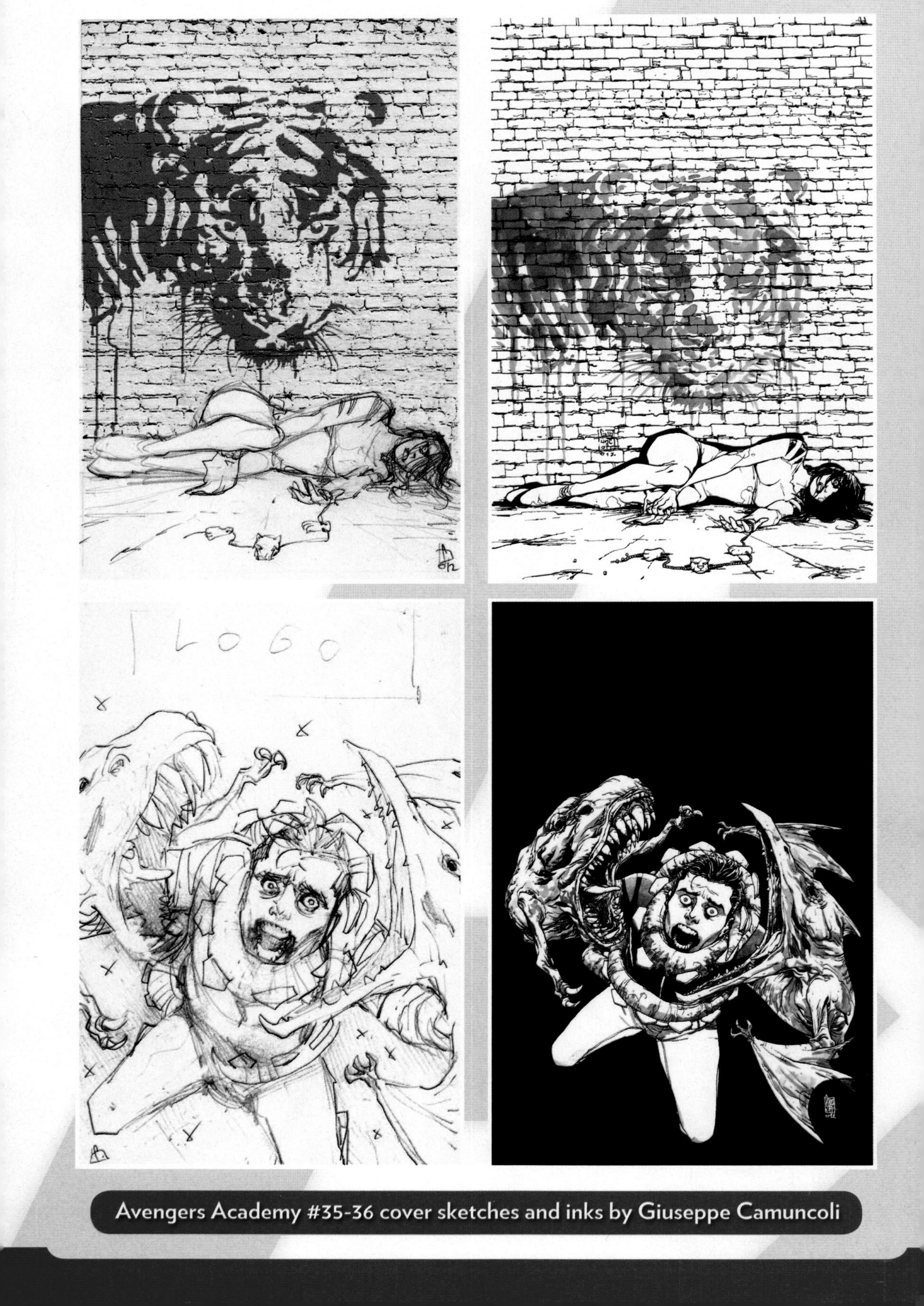
LOGO

Avengers Academy #35-36 cover sketches and inks by Giuseppe Camuncoli

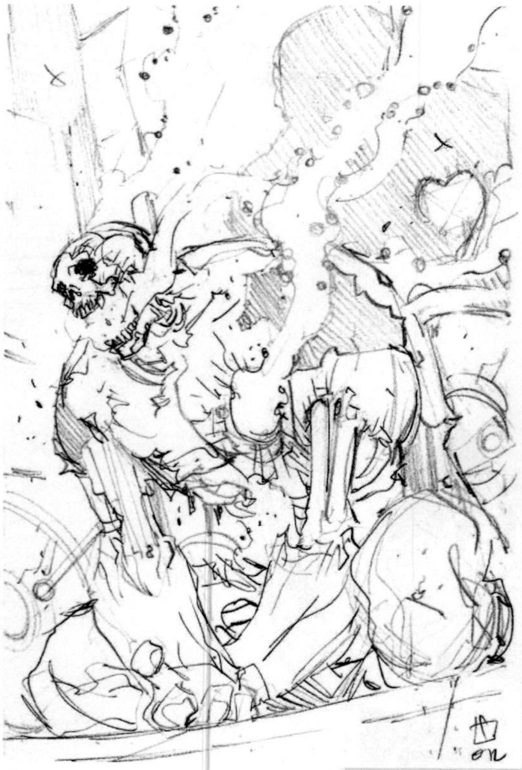
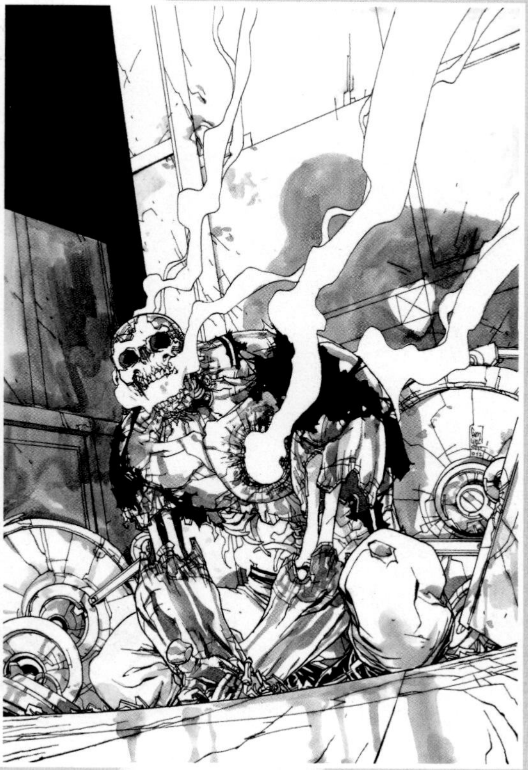
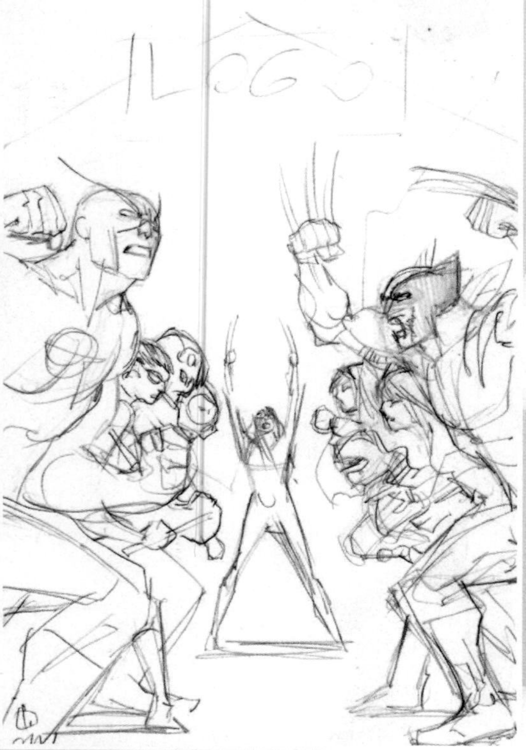
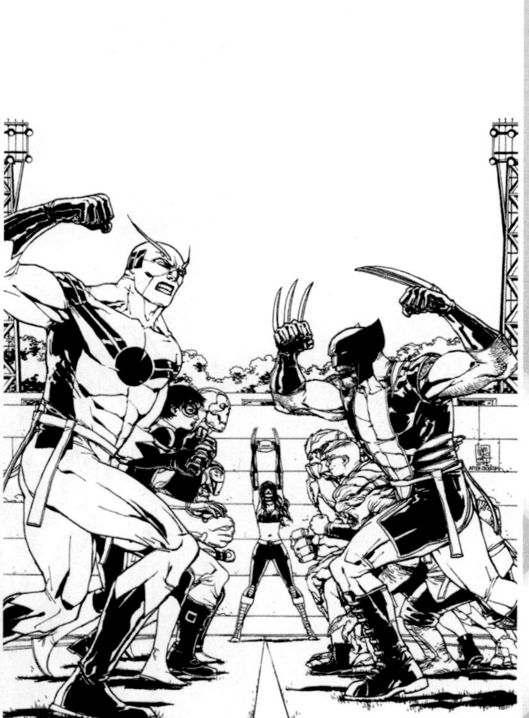

Avengers Academy #37-38 cover sketches and inks by Giuseppe Camuncoli